It's a riveting story expertly told of one of the darkest chapters in the history of the FBI as well as federal law enforcement. This startling saga of how organized crime infiltrated the FBI, using it for its own purposes and resulting in the savage deaths of many. The tragic irony that ultimate informants of so called FBI Top Echelon informant program of the FBI turned out to be the FBI itself. And not the mobsters.

> — **Jeffrey Denner,** prominent Boston trial attorney involved in both criminal and civil cases against the FBI and Irish Mob.

Domenic always had a big mouth, which got him in trouble with the Feds. Now, his big mouth is going to cause trouble for the G-Men.

> — **Oscar B. Goodman,** Mayor, City of Las Vegas

He Didn't Get It!
The FBI has 1.9 billion reasons not to want to find James "Whitey"Bulger. That's the dollar amount of the lawsuits currently pending against our government due to the greed and misdeeds of "Dishonest John" Connolly. The rogue agent left a blot on the FBI that the bureau may never live down. The name John Connolly has become synonymous with corrupt government law enforcement the way the name Al Capone has become synonymous with organized crime. And just like Dominic Spinale tells us, "He just didn't get it!"

> — **Allan May,** organized crime historian, AmericanMafia.com

G-Men and Gangsters: *A hard look into the realism of how the FBI lost control of their informants and more importantly their own agents. The death and*

destruction unleashed by both in grueling detail are shocking and no less than macabre, in this riveting book that every law enforcement officer in American should read.

— **Karl Kretser,** Homicide Detective
Lieutenant and author of *The Night Runner*

A shocking documentary of human weakness and disloyalty and yet another example of the power of organized crime to corrupt the law enforcers charged with their very elimination. Indeed a sad chapter in the history of our great FBI.

— **Rick Porrello** is a police lieutenant with a suburban Cleveland police department, and author of *The Rise and Fall of the Cleveland Mafia* and *To Kill the Irishman*.

G-MEN and GANGSTERS

A chilling true narration of the FBI's marriage
with Boston's Irish gangsters

G-MEN and GANGSTERS

PARTNERS IN CRIME

Dominic Spinale

SEVEN LOCKS PRESS

Santa Ana, California

Seven Locks Press
P.O. Box 25689
Santa Ana, CA 92799
(800) 354-5348

Individual Sales. This book is available through most bookstores or can be ordered directly from Seven Locks Press at the address above.

Quantity Sales. Special discounts are available on quantity purchases by corporations, associations, and others. For details, contact the "Special Sales Department" at the publisher's address above.

Printed in the United States of America

Library of Congress Cataloging-in-Publication Data
is available from the publisher
ISBN 1-931643-40-7

Cover and Interior Design by Heather Buchman

CONTENTS

PROLOGUE

On April 15, 1920, a daring robbery at the Slater Mirill Shoe Company in Braintree, Massachusetts, resulted in the slaying of two employees. Witnesses reported that the murderers were Italians. Nicolo Sacco and Bartolomeo Vanzetti were charged with the murders. Both men were associated with Boston Mafia leaders Frank and Joseph Morelli.

The Mafia, then known as *La Mano Nera*, the Black Hand, had control of the bootlegging and gambling in the ethnic North End section of Boston. The trial of Sacco and Vanzetti would garner national attention. Neither man had any criminal record, nor was there any evidence of their having had any of the money.

In July 1921, despite little evidence tying the two men to the crime, they were found guilty and sentenced to death. The conduct of the trial by Judge Webster Thayer was particularly criticized. Later, much of the evidence against them was discredited.

History would prove the two men had been falsely accused and convicted.

Protest meetings were held and appeals were made to Governor Alvin Fuller. All would fail.

On August 22, 1927, Sacco and Vanzetti were executed despite worldwide demonstrations. The local police, comprised mostly of Irish-Americans, were thought to be behind the frame-up.

A vendetta between the Italians and Irish-dominated law enforcement had taken root, and would continue for decades.

INTRODUCTION

This book was inspired by revelations exposing the macabre side of the FBI, which condoned crimes of drug dealing, extortion, and murder to protect their star informants. Most troubling was the hypocrisy directed by the government to persons I have known personally.

Before Robert Kennedy became Attorney General, it was next to impossible to get the FBI to enter into the investigation of the Mafia. J. Edgar Hoover was under the delusion that there was no such thing as a national crime organization. However, when Joseph Valachi came forward with testimony exposing the existence of a secret society, it confirmed reports developed by the FBI.

Facing mounting pressure from the Kennedys, Hoover and his fair-haired boys were now ready to focus their attention on the Italian mob.

Spearheaded by the FBI's zeal to understand and identify the Italian-American Mafia, the Bureau entered into a marriage with mobsters throughout the nation. The newly formed Top Echelon Informant Program would become a high priority for the Bureau. FBI agents would begin developing informants, in particular those designated as Top Echelon Informants.

Operating in stealth, Top Echelon Informants would infiltrate the Mafia without the knowledge of others. Their identities were never revealed to anyone outside the Bureau. Code names would be used to communicate with their FBI handlers. Informants were authorized to commit minor crimes in order to maintain a favorable reputation in the underworld. Guidelines were established to provide assurances that informants would not run amok.

Agents Paul Rico and John Connolly eagerly embraced the FBI's new concerted action against the Mafia. Neither agent resembled the typical stereotype. Wearing hand-tailored suits, both were considered *dappers*. Chewing on an expensive cigar, with his Mediterranean looks, Rico could easily be mistaken for a true Sicilian Mafioso. However, Rico was not of Italian descent, but rather part Irish, some Spanish. Stephen "The Rifleman" Flemmi was receptive to the alliance with the FBI that Rico proposed. Being an informant offered Flemmi an opportunity to use the FBI to disable his enemies and enhance his safety, and make his own criminal activities more profitable. He would have carte blanche throughout the city. It was a quid pro quo.

Rico was well aware that Flemmi had participated in a score of murders. However, those suspicions did not discourage him from forming an alliance with the ruthless gangster, or making him a Top Echelon Informant. Rico had selfish reasons. The recruitment of a Top Echelon Informant carried with it the opportunity for advancements in the Bureau, along with financial rewards.

John Connolly and Whitey Bulger had grown up in the Irish-American community of South Boston, where people look out for one another, no matter what. Connolly had worshipped the cocksure gangster while growing up in the same South Boston housing project. His bold plan was to use Whitey as a Top Echelon Informant in the Bureau's war against the Italian Mafia. With his expensively-styled hair, the arrogant Connolly was the-man-about town, the Prince of the City.

Irish G-Men would form an alliance with Irish gangsters in a crusade against the Italian Mafia in predominantly Irish Boston. The extremes to which the FBI handlers would go to protect Bulger and Flemmi from prosecution are chilling. Standard FBI guidelines on the use of informants were disregarded. It was a scandal that would last for decades. The G-Men and the gangsters would not just socialize, but meet for dinners and exchange gifts.

Bulger and Flemmi would supply the Boston Bureau with information needed to take down La Cosa Nostra. They would identify new Mafia-made men and report on murders committed by their rival gangsters. The two informants would assist the Boston FBI in its efforts to install microphones at the headquarters of key Mafia leaders in Boston's North End. Soon, the Boston Bureau began putting together a number of devastating cases against the FBI's top priority, the Anguilo gambling syndicate. Scores of La Cosa Nostra members were sent off to prison, including mob bosses Raymond Patriarca and Larry Zannino. Through the efforts of Bulger and Flemmi, John Connolly was able to give the FBI its biggest prize yet, the opportunity to record an actual Mafia induction ceremony.

A Mafia induction ceremony had never been captured on tape before. The notion of men pricking their fingers and burning holy cards in cupped hands while swearing an oath to "This Thing of Ours" was a fairy tale. Proving the existence of a Mafia with such overwhelming evidence was the sort of thing agents dreamed about.

Connolly and a handful of corrupt agents would file inaccurate reports in an effort to mask the evils committed by their prized informants. As those reports kept piling up, so would the corpses. Agents would engage in illegal conduct in order to protect Bulger and Flemmi.

Soon, information began flowing the wrong way, and the gangsters would put it to deadly use. The Boston FBI, led by John Connolly, began providing Bulger and Flemmi with information on where wiretaps had been installed, and the identities of those willing to testify against them. It was Bulger and Flemmi who had infiltrated the FBI.

The alliance between the G-Men and the gangsters would cause the two informants to become drunk with their sense of belonging and their power. Bulger and Flemmi were running their own show. They committed crimes of extortion, drug dealing, and were key suspects in a string of murders, while Connolly and a handful of rogue agents looked the other way.

The local cops, State Police, and the DEA all wanted Bulger and Flemmi behind bars. A number of aggressive and time-consuming investigations directed at Bulger and Flemmi by other law enforcement agencies would all fail, thanks to John Connolly and his merry men. The FBI's institutional arrogance would cause long-lasting anger between the Bureau and local law enforcement.

One of the most shocking events exposed by a Justice Department probe of FBI corruption in Boston would reveal that the Bureau knew the wrong men were convicted of a 1965 gangland murder. Not only did agents know the identities of the real killers, but they were told about the plot two days before the slaying, and did nothing to prevent it.

The alliance between the Boston Bureau and murderous gangsters would expose the very macabre side of the FBI. The nation's most powerful crime-fighting agency was co-opted by its own ambitious war against the Italian Mafia.

The Boston FBI office would become the most heavily investigated in the Bureau's history. The scandals, and their repercussions, are still being felt today.

Chapter 1

THE BOSTON MAFIA

Concealed between the modern downtown high-rises, sits the Italian-American community of Boston, the North End. The city's oldest section is caught in a web of serpentine streets and passageways that mark the design of early settlements.

Here in the North End, you can find the oldest bakery in the country. The early residents, Paul Revere, John Hancock, and Ben Franklin, could often be seen purchasing bread there. You can visit this landmark of historic events, the scene of the Boston Massacre, the Boston Tea Party, and the home of Paul Revere. Situated in the heart of the North End is the Old North Church, where the lanterns were hung, warning that the British were coming. It was here that Paul Revere's midnight ride began, and the American Revolution was born.

Irish immigrants were the first to settle in the North End district. Decades earlier the Great Potato Famine had caused thousands to migrate from Ireland to Boston; Joe Kennedy had been one of the early residents.

Soon, a flood of Italian immigrants would settle in the North End as well. They would begin to fill a vacuum created by the Irish, who had gone on to a newly-developed area called South Boston. The North End would now become overwhelmingly populated by the Italians, fiercely loyal and protective of one another. The North End would become one of the safest areas in the country in which to live. Residents of the community would take care of their own, without going to any outsiders. They had their own form of justice, retaining many customs of their native Italy. The mob leaders would ensure that the area remained mostly Italian. Drugs were kept out; the mob would deal harshly with anyone suspected of dealing drugs.

As in most Sicilian villages, the Mafia's presence loomed large over the North End. Residents learned early on to mind their own business. You didn't hear anything, and you most certainly didn't see anything. Everyone knew everyone in the ethnic community. New residents were often looked upon with suspicion. Compared to other parts of the country, those who lived in the North End never experienced concerns about street crime. The Mafia kept the neighborhood safe.

When walking along narrow streets, you have the scent of the nearby Atlantic Ocean mingling with aromas from bakeries, fresh mozzarella shops, and never-ending rows of restaurants. The web of winding streets features old, well-kept tenement buildings along with local shops, some displaying freshly killed rabbits hanging in their windows. Many of the streets lead to hidden courtyards where you can hear the voices of elderly women speaking their native dialect.

It is here in the North End that the Boston Mafia exercises its control. From the beginning, there were the Morelli brothers, Frank and Joseph, who set in motion the crimes of bootlegging, loan sharking, gambling, and extortion. They, along with their followers, engaged in armed robberies as well. One such robbery was the Slater Mirill Shoe Company on April 15, 1920. During the course of the hold-up, two employees were slain. Nicolo Sacco and Bartolomeo Vanzetti would be charged in the murders, found guilty, and hanged. The local police, comprised mostly of Irish-Americans, were thought to be behind the frame-up. A distinct hatred between the Mafia and Irish-dominated law enforcement had taken root, and would continue to escalate for decades. The then-Italians were known as *La Mano Nera* (the Black Hand).

Following the Morellis was Phil Buccola, who had been appointed by the newly-formed commission. The Mafia chief and his crew controlled all the bootlegging along the New England coastline. Buccola and others were reaping huge profits smuggling liquor all throughout New England.

Frankie Wallace, leader of Boston's strongest Irish gang, the Gustins, decided he wanted a piece of the action. Wallace, along with Barney Walsh and Timothy Coffey, was ready to make his move. However, in order to do so, the Irish gangsters had to, first, contend with Italian mobsters who had no intention of giving up control of the waterfront to them.

On December 22, 1931, Frankie Wallace, Barney Walsh, and Timothy Coffey were called to a sit-down in the Italian North End. They were going to dictate their terms for control of the waterfront to the *wops*. As the three men entered an old abandoned warehouse, a hidden Frank "The Cheeseman" Cucchiara stepped out from behind a pillar with two guns blazing, killing Frankie Wallace and Barney Walsh. Timothy Coffey was only wounded. Cucchiara, along with Joseph Lombardo and Salvatore Congemi, was arrested for the murders, but Timothy Coffey refused to testify. The Mafia had survived, and the Irish would stay in South Boston, but now a much weaker gang. As far as the Italians were concerned, the Mafia was the final word, and no outsiders would challenge their authority again.

In 1950, Senate probes led by Senator Kefauver would travel to Boston for hearings on mob activities. Joe Lombardo, then boss of the Boston Mafia, decided it would be a good idea to shut down gambling in Boston. Lombardo, also known as "J.L.," decided to frustrate the probe by having as few targets as possible and pulled his men out of the numbers racket. His plan worked, and J.L. came out unscathed. However, he decided the heat would continue and remained out of the numbers game.

Phil Buccola would succeed Lombardo. However, heat from the investigation was relentless. Buccola would give up the numbers racket as well. He yearned for a return to his native Sicily. He, along with his wife, would return to the old country.

A vacuum that had been created in the numbers game was quickly filled by Gennaro "Jerry" Anguilo. Jerry, however, was not a member of the Mafia. Jerry quickly realized he needed permission to take over the numbers. He went straight to the top man, Raymond Patriarca, by far the most powerful leader, who expanded his control to all of the New England states.

Patriarca made a few calls announcing, "Jerry's with me." That in itself was enough. Jerry quickly became a multimillionaire.

Patriarca was so impressed with Jerry's talent for making big money and as a capable organizer that he quickly placed him in charge of all gambling ventures in the greater Boston area. Jerry, along with his three brothers, Danny, Frank, and Nick, would call all the shots in Boston. Jerry was a far different gambling czar than the old "Mustache Petes" he had succeeded.

For one thing, he was a firm believer in paying taxes. He would often be heard saying, "The Jews had the right idea, they paid their taxes." Unlike the previous mob leaders, paying taxes enabled him to invest his profits into legitimate business, just as Jewish mobsters had done in the past. The old-time mob leaders would simply hide their cash, pay no taxes, but remain unable to invest. Paying taxes on gambling profits enabled Jewish gangsters of the past to invest in casinos in Las Vegas and elsewhere.

All of the Anguilo brothers were keen investors, speculating in real estate and the stock market. Jerry, in particular, watched the market daily and seldom made a bad investment. He could often be heard saying, "Don't talk to me about investing in the market when it's up." He would only buy in a down market, getting great value for his money. When Chrysler Motors was about to go under, he was one of a very few who believed the government would step in to bail them out. Jerry bought heavily in Chrysler, reaping a huge profit.

The Boston North End Mafia would retain a firm grip on gambling throughout the city. Only those connected with the Anguilos were permitted to operate. Most were involved in gambling, and no crimes of drugs or violence were sanctioned. There were no second chances for anyone who violated the rules.

When Hollywood came to the neighborhood to film a movie starring Peter Falk titled *The Brinks Job*, about the famous robbery, the movie people thought they could just come into Boston and set up shop with no problems. After all, Boston was a sophisticated city with history. They were wrong. The movie people had not asked for the mob's blessings, which they considered an act of disrespect.

On one occasion, the movie people had asked the local residents to remove their air conditioner units from their windows. They wanted to reproduce the look of the 1950s as closely as possible. Word went out from the mob not to cooperate. This would be only one of the many problems that the film people would be facing. The final act by the mob was to steal the film that had already been shot and stored away. The movie studio was forced to pay a large ransom for the return of the film. The FBI got wind of the extortion, but to his credit, the studio chief denied any extortion had taken place.

Although the Anguilos had the total say in Boston, a number of non-Italian gangsters were allowed to participate in some degree of gambling activity. One particular gang that was permitted to operate was the Winter Hill Gang. They were given the blessing to operate by Jerry Anguilo, but under tight and limited control.

Jerry was a self-educated man who had aspirations of becoming a criminal defense attorney. An avid seaman, his only vice was a fondness for luxury yachts. Days were spent cruising the Atlantic waters; nights were dedicated to dinners and meeting with gambling underlings. Bookmakers from all over Boston would meet with Jerry, often seeking permission or advice on illegal gambling activities. Jerry and his brothers controlled the daily lottery, most of the sports and horse wagering, dice games, and Las Vegas nights with casino-style gambling, using charities as a way to circumvent the law.

Getting Jerry Anguilo at any cost had been the key focus of the Boston FBI. The methods used by the government to bring down the powerful gambling syndicate would lead to one of the worst scandals in Bureau history.

Chapter 2

STEPHEN "THE RIFLEMAN" FLEMMI

Not all non-Italian gangsters were willing to be controlled by the New England Mafia.

The McLaughlin Gang, led by Bernie and George "Punchy" McLaughlin, had no intention of taking direction from Raymond Patriarca or the Anguilos. The gang dealt in gambling, loan sharking, and extortion from their base in Charlestown, Massachusetts, a blue-collar neighborhood just outside Boston.

A war between Winter Hill gangsters, led by Howie Winter, and the McLaughlins had its beginning one summer night at a Salisbury Beach night-club. A drunken Punchy McLaughlin had approached the table of two Winter Hill gangsters who were sitting with their dates. The often-feared and dangerous Charlestown wise guy began to insult a woman companion. Then, in a fit of anger, McLaughlin bit a nipple off one of the women and spit it in her face. Punchy was immediately attacked by the two men and given a severe beating. The Charlestown gangster had been left for dead.

Alexander Petricone was a participant in the beating of Punchy McLaughlin. Petricone would later go on to Hollywood and become a film star. Alex Rocco, his film name, found that a career in acting was by far a much safer occupation.

All of the Irish gangsters would now be drawn into a war. The incident that one summer night would be the match that lit the fuse that ignited the Irish gang war. The war between rival Irish gangsters would be the bloodiest period of history in sophisticated Boston since Paul Revere's midnight ride.

Punchy McLaughlin, his brother Bernie, and the Charlestown gangsters would go on a killing spree.

Howie Winter, and the extremely capable brothers James and John Martorano, would lead the Winter Hill Gang to an easy victory.

Both McLaughlins would be slain. A bloody battle between Irish gangsters would result in the death of nearly fifty hoods. Raymond Patriarca and Jerry Anguilo had supported the Winter Hill gangsters during the war. Most Mafia leaders had a dislike for the McLaughlins who refused to fall in line.

Stephen "The Rifleman" Flemmi had allied himself with the Winter Hill Gang. Flemmi's nickname was attributed to his outstanding marksmanship during the Korean War. He had twice been shot by members of the McLaughlin crew. Flemmi and his childhood pal, "Cadillac Frank" Salemme, were associated with the Bennett brothers, who had full control over the rackets in Roxbury. Flemmi and Salemme were enforcers for the Bennett mob. They had grown up in Roxbury and were well-respected by Larry Zannino for their brutality. As second in command, Zannino was responsible for overseeing mobsters not connected with the LCN.

All three Bennett brothers, Walter, William, and Edward "Wimpy" would be slain; Flemmi and Cadillac Frank were prime suspects in the murders.

After the murders, both men would make their move by quickly taking control of crime in the Roxbury area. The childhood friends were a team. However, both men would share a great deal of time in the Italian North End section of Boston. Most often, the two gangsters would be seen in the company of Larry Zannino. Cadillac Frank Salemme and Flemmi had caught the attention of Zannino and other mob leaders, including the top man in New England, Raymond Patriarca. Zannino had longed to recruit the two as members of LCN (La Cosa Nostra), meaning "Our Thing." He could offer membership into the secret organization to Flemmi and Cadillac Frank. During a late night drinking session at Zannino's nightclub, the Bat Cove, Larry made his pitch to Flemmi for induction.

Larry explained to him, "I'm going to sponsor you, and with your reputation for killing [the Bennett brothers], we won't need to verify a hit." (A hit is one of the requirements to become a Mafia member.) Flemmi could have cared less—he would show respect for the mob, but in truth, he despised them all. He knew that they stood in the way of his reaping desired profits from criminal activities. Although Flemmi was highly respected by the LCN, most notably Raymond Patriarca, Flemmi didn't share the same enthusiasm. Because of his disdain, Flemmi would become responsive to FBI Special Agent Paul Rico's proposal to become an informant for the FBI. Rico knew that the Mafia had respect for Flemmi, and had hopes of "making him." He also knew Flemmi had the trust of the mob leaders and was often in their company. The mob was impressed with Flemmi's ruthless way of murder, particularly the dumping of William Bennett's body from a fast-moving car on Harvard Street in Dorchester. He was their kind of man, an ex-paratrooper who served in the Korean War. He was also a good-looking ladies' man, often seen with young glamour girls around town. Agent Paul Rico himself was a flamboyant figure, a snappy dresser, and always well-groomed, a far cry from most of his colleagues. The two had respect for each other and shared a common goal, the dismantling of the Mafia.

Although Flemmi was born of Italian parents, his father being an immigrant from Italy, he preferred to associate with those of Irish heritage. Special Agent H. Paul Rico was often mistaken for being Italian. Many mobsters would be receptive to Rico as being one of them. However, Rico was not Italian, but rather part Irish, some Spanish.

Flemmi would agree to become an informant for Rico. The arrangement would assure Flemmi an opportunity to use the FBI to disable his enemies, enhance his safety, and with the protection offered by Agent Rico, make his own criminal activities more profitable. He would have carte blanche.

Flemmi's easy access to the LCN would have him in a position to supply Agent Rico with substantial information on the Mafia to the FBI. He would be given the title of Top Echelon Informant, one who could furnish the highest levels of information on members of organized crime. The cigar-chomping

Rico was an agent who enthusiastically embraced the FBI's new crusade against the LCN.

Flemmi was able to provide Rico with what he wanted: reliable information about leaders of the LCN in New England. Rico's suspicion that Flemmi was a murderer did not deter Rico and other agents from making him a Top Echelon Informant. Although agents had routinely promised their informants' confidentiality, Rico did not rely on that assurance alone to cultivate Flemmi. Using his personal style, Rico sought to use Flemmi by not treating him as a criminal who should be used with caution to obtain information. Instead, Rico created a sense that he and Flemmi were allies in a common cause: the destruction of the LCN. Rico promised Flemmi protection, something he was desperately seeking. Flemmi was constantly engaged in a host of criminal conduct. Now, with Paul Rico's promise of protection, it would be full speed ahead for the bold and ruthless gangster.

The development of Top Echelon Informants had been a very high priority for the FBI. The successful development of informants generally, and Top Echelon Informants in particular, has also been regarded as an important achievement for an FBI agent, with the potential to significantly progress that agent's career. Agents would be ambitious to develop Top Echelon Informants.

Before Robert Kennedy became Attorney General, it was like pulling teeth to get the Bureau to enter into investigations of the Mafia. This was due to J. Edgar Hoover's belief that there was no such thing as a national crime syndicate. The disclosures of Joseph Valachi, one of the first to come forward and give testimony concerning the Mafia, corroborated and embellished evidence developed by the FBI.

Joe Kennedy had convinced most Mafia leaders to support his son's bid for the Presidency. However, Jerry Anguilo had no reservations about the Senior Kennedy's promise of protection for the Italian mob. Jerry had voiced his objection of support to many mob leaders. He knew Joe Kennedy, who had lived in the North End, could not be trusted to deliver protection. Jerry knew the Kennedys had no great love for Italians. Once during a Senate Committee Hearing in which Raymond Patriarca was being questioned by Robert Kennedy on his role as a Mafia boss, an enraged Patriarca shot back, saying, "You don't have the brains of your retarded sister."

Jerry Anguilo was right; he knew the Kennedys were going to be poison for the mob. His plea to Mafia leaders not to support Kennedy's bid for election would fall on deaf ears. John Kennedy won a close election, thanks to the efforts of Chicago mob leaders. The Kennedys immediately began pressuring J. Edgar Hoover to dismantle the Italian Mafia. The mob had been double-crossed. There are those who believe that the pressure being exerted on key Mafia leaders, along with failed promises of protection, was cause for the assassination of John Kennedy.

The Bureau was now ready to focus its attention on the mob. However, they had a great deal of catching up to do. A special team of FBI agents was created, a strike force, whose prime responsibility was to focus on the Mafia. The newly-formed Organized Crime Unit would be given broad powers. Congress would pass the Racketeering Influenced and Corrupt Organizations Act. Often referred to as RICO, the law would be a powerful tool in the Bureau's war against La Cosa Nostra. If mobsters were convicted on RICO charges, it would mean severe prison time. Conventional crimes such as gambling and loan sharking were now subjected to heavy RICO charges and stiff prison sentences.

Flemmi would begin to convey a steady flow of information concerning the heads of the LCN to Agent Paul Rico. Rico was particularly interested in reports on Raymond Patriarca, Larry Zannino, and other LCN associates. One bit of information Flemmi would convey to Rico was in reference to Joseph "The Animal" Barboza, who had become an executioner for the mob. He was an instrument the LCN used to wipe out anyone who failed to heed their demands.

Barboza had hopes of one day being the first non-Italian inducted into the Mafia. He was Portuguese, therefore could not be a "made man." Barboza would often freelance, killing at will. He had once received a contract to kill a man, but the intended victim knew he was in Barboza's sights, therefore refused to leave his home. "No problem," The Animal said. "I set fire to his house and when he runs out, I shoot him." "His mother lives in the house with him," someone said. "No problem," Barboza replied. "When she runs out, I shoot her too."

His cavalier attitude toward senseless killings caught the attention of mob bosses. They were not pleased with The Animal. One mob leader was quoted as saying "he was bringing too much heat on everyone." Barboza would not take lightly to anyone who stood up to him, especially one who was not mob-connected. Such was the case with a tough ex-con named Edward "Teddy" Deegan, a local street thief who was getting out of line with his burglaries. One particular robbery that Deegan committed was that of a mob-connected bookie. This angered the mob leaders, and their displeasure got the attention of Barboza, who was looking for a reason to confront Deegan. Barboza knew Deegan was fair game for anyone willing to go up against the renegade.

Deegan had already made many enemies with his "I don't give a fuck for anyone" attitude. He was a tough guy who boasted of his fear of no one. Deegan's flair further infuriated Barboza; in particular, remarks describing him as a "nigger." Barboza decided it was time to go after Deegan, especially with local mob leaders upset with the burglary of a connected bookie's home. Barboza would reach out for his trusted friend, Jimmy "The Bear" Flemmi, Steve's younger brother.

The Bear had vowed to become Boston's "Number One Hit Man." Jimmy Flemmi had once told an informant that "all he wants to do now is kill people, and that it is better than hitting banks." He would oftentimes stroll the streets of Boston carrying a live hand grenade in his coat pocket. On May 4, 1964, a just-released con, Francis Regis Benjamin, had a quarrel in a bar in Uphams Corner, a suburb of Boston. The Bear shot him to death, then cut up his body. An FBI informant tells the story: "Barboza told him that he heard that Jimmy Flemmi had killed [the con] and cut off his head. When speaking to Flemmi, Barboza confronted him with this information and Flemmi's only reply was that he had heard the same thing about Barboza." A clear-cut case of mutual admiration between the two vicious murderers.

Jimmy would drive around Boston with Benjamin's head in the trunk of his car. Oftentimes, he would give a few of his trusted close friends a peek at the severed body part, saying, "Do you remember this guy?" The Bear was successfully recruited as an FBI informant by his older brother Steve Flemmi for a few months in 1965, even though other informants were telling the Bureau that he was responsible for numerous killings and that he had vowed to become Boston's "Number One Hit Man." FBI evaluation reports of The Bear's potential usefulness as an FBI mole show the chilling lengths the FBI was willing to go in its clandestine organized crime informant program. On March 10, 1965, two days before the murder of Teddy Deegan, an FBI informant told Special Agent Rico that Jimmy Flemmi was planning to kill Deegan.

"Informant advised that he had heard from Jimmy Flemmi, and Flemmi told the informant that Teddy Deegan is to be hit, and that a dry run has already been made and that a close associate of Deegan's has agreed to set him up." Agent Rico's report stated that on March 12, 1965, the bullet-ridden body of Edward "Teddy" Deegan, the ex-con who had twenty-five arrests, was found at the rear door of the Lincoln National Bank in Chelsea, Massachusetts. On the day after the murder, Special Agent Rico was given the details of the Deegan murder by an informant who named Jimmy Flemmi, Joe Barboza, Ronald Cassesso, Wilfred Roy French, and Romeo Martin as the five men who allegedly carried out the Deegan hit. Two days later, on March 15, Special Agent Rico wrote a report to then-FBI Special Agent in Charge in Boston, James L. Handley, who four days later, wrote his own report about the Deegan murder and sent it to Hoover at FBI headquarters in Washington, D.C.

After the Deegan murder, Barboza had become extremely upset with the New England mob leaders. He had been arrested for having an M-1 rifle and a .45 caliber handgun in his car. His bail was set at $100,000. Barboza was sure his two associates would raise the money and secure his release.

However, the mob leaders were becoming fearful of his random killings. He was out of control and becoming a problem. As far as the mob was concerned, he had lived out his usefulness. Arthur "Tashi" Bratsos and Tommy DePrisco were Barboza's close associates. They were going to solicit the $100,000 needed for Barboza's bail. The two associates, in an all-out effort to raise the money, began extorting local gamblers and thieves, and had raised $70,000 of the $100,000 needed for Barboza's bail. The other $30,000 was to come from the local Mafia. Tashi Bratsos and Tommy DePrisco were told to meet at a local after-hours club. There, they were to receive the $30,000.

As the two men arrived, they were greeted by five other men. They didn't receive the money. What they did receive were two shots each in the back of the head. The two bodies were placed in the Cadillac owned by Tashi Bratsos, and it was found the next morning in South Boston. The $70,000 was never located. The FBI now sensed a real chance at getting Barboza to rat on the New England mob. They had a federal grand jury indict Barboza as a repeat offender. Steve Flemmi would provide Agent Paul Rico with information to assist him in persuading Barboza to become a government witness.

Shortly after the murders of Tashi Bratsos and Tommy DePrisco, and before he decided to roll over, Barboza made an offer to the mob leaders. He wanted Phil Waggenhaim, a close associate of second in command Larry Zannino in the Boston mob. Barboza was certain that mob associate Waggenhaim was the person responsible for setting up Bratsos and DePrisco. He wanted the mob to allow him the right to kill Waggenhaim; that would even the score for the killing of his two associates. The mob had no intention of offering up Waggenhaim as a sacrificial lamb. As far as they were concerned, he had no say in any of the mob's decisions; he was an outsider who had outlived his usefulness. Their answer was a flat-out no.

After Barboza's demand for Waggenhaim was turned down, Agents Paul Rico and Dennis Condon had little difficulty in getting Barboza to lie and include four innocent men in the Deegan murder. Barboza was quoted as saying, "They screw me, now I'm going to screw them." Barboza would now seek revenge. Two years after the Deegan murder, indictments were issued by then-Suffolk County District Attorney Garrett Byrne, whose prosecutors worked closely on the case with Rico and the FBI. The list of Deegan's murderers had changed. The men now charged were Joseph "Joe the Horse" Salvati, Peter Limone, Henry Tamelo, Louis Greco, Ronald Cassesso, and Wilfred Roy French. The government would center its case on the testimony of Barboza, who had been recruited by Agent Rico to roll on these six men. Rico knew who the real killers were all along and they were not Salvati, Limone, Tamelo, or Greco.

Paul Rico and the FBI were so committed to taking down the mob and making high-profile cases in the 1960s that they had no regard if innocent people and their families were destroyed in the process. Two days before the Deegan murder, Agent Rico was told of the hit, yet he did nothing to prevent it from happening. Rico's report, later forwarded to FBI Director Hoover, had in it the names of the real killers, Jimmy Flemmi, Joe Barboza, Ronald Cassesso, Wilfred Roy French, and Romeo Martin. This report, and others, would not be turned over to the wrongfully-accused men and attorneys during their trial, as required by law. Instead, they would be secretly buried in Washington.

The secret reports would have revealed that Jimmy "The Bear" Flemmi was one of the real killers. In order to have Steve Flemmi continue as a key informant for the FBI in its intent to bring down the New England Mafia, this was a favor to Flemmi. Flemmi could not allow his baby brother to be charged with murder. Joseph Salvati was then substituted for Jimmy Flemmi's participation in the Deegan killing. Salvati had disrespected Barboza over a loan dispute earlier; it was now payback time for him. Barboza and Rico framed Limone, Tamelo, Greco, and Salvati to satisfy Barboza's quest for revenge, at the same time fulfilling the FBI's policy from Washington to bring down the mob at any cost. Cassesso and French would admit their role in the Deegan murder. In 1968, a jury found Limone, Tamelo, Salvati, and Greco guilty of the Deegan murder as well. The verdict was based solely on the testimony of Joseph Barboza.

All four men, although innocent, were sentenced to death in the electric chair. They languished on Death Row from 1968 to 1972, when the Supreme Court struck down the death penalty Shades of Sacco and Vanzetti, also victims of corrupt law enforcement. Had it not been for the Supreme Court ruling, these men would have suffered the same fate as Sacco and Vanzetti. Henry Tamelo and Louis Greco would die in prison; their pleas of innocence would be rejected by the appeals courts. When Greco died behind bars in 1995, his attorney, John Cavicchi, was so devastated he quit the law altogether, after more than twenty years as a defense lawyer. Wilfred Roy French found Jesus and became a born-again Christian. Early on, Ronald Cassesso had been offered a deal by FBI Special Agent Paul Rico. Rico had been to see him and "wanted him to corroborate Barboza's story; and if he did, he wouldn't do any time for the Deegan killing." At some point, Rico said, "We can get you together with Barboza and get your stories straightened out." According to Cassesso's attorney, he turned down the deal, telling Rico he did not want to implicate innocent men. Cassesso would die in prison in 1991, a true stand-up guy. Joseph "Joe the Horse" Salvati would receive a commutation in 1997; Peter Limone would continue to sit in prison as court after court would refuse to hear his plea of innocence. Jimmy "The Bear" Flemmi had the FBI to watch over and protect him because of his older brother's deal with them. He never had any concerns about his role in the Deegan killing, not with his big brother, Steve, in bed with the Feds.

However, The Bear couldn't stay out of trouble. On an unrelated state case in which the FBI thought better about interceding, The Bear was sent off to Norfolk State Prison. In 1976, he received a furlough, and headed immediately to his girlfriend's home. The woman feared The Bear and would make certain that she wouldn't be around to satisfy his perverted sexual appetite. When he arrived at the home, and realized that she had taken off, the enraged Jimmy Flemmi strangled her cat. The Bear decided not to return to prison, and instead went on the lam. Two years later, he was apprehended in Baltimore and charged with committing a perverted sexual act and assault on a woman. Maryland sent him back to MCI-Norfolk in Massachusetts where he died of a drug overdose in 1979.

Steve Flemmi continued to supply Agents Rico and Condon with information that Raymond Patriarca and others were very concerned about Barboza's testimony on mob activities. The mob needed to know what Barboza was going to sing about next, and who would be the potential witnesses willing to corroborate his testimony. Flemmi reported to Rico that Patriarca was incensed with Barboza's attorney, John Fitzgerald, as well. Patriarca believed the attorney could be helpful in discrediting Barboza. When the attorney refused to cooperate with the mob's request, a contract was put out on him. Steve Flemmi and his partner were given the hit.

Flemmi had an unsure relationship with the Mafia. He would at different times view them as enemies and allies. When ordered to kill Fitzgerald, he did so, thus gaining the respect and trust of the mob leaders. The attempted murder of Fitzgerald was done by placing a bomb in his car; however, the attorney was crippled and not killed by the explosion.

Flemmi had informed Agent Rico that Fitzgerald was going to be killed only days before the bombing. The Middlesex County District Attorney's office began investigating the bombing. However, neither Agent Rico nor the FBI did any investigating of their own. The fact that Rico knew Flemmi was involved in the bombing was the likely reason.

Flemmi and his loyal partner, Frank Salemme, were being investigated as suspects in the attempted murder of attorney Fitzgerald. In early September of 1969, Steve Flemmi received a call from Agent Rico informing him of pending indictments in the bombing, and suggested he and Salemme leave town. The two fled Boston together. A few days later, on September 11, they were indicted for the bombing as well as the murder of William Bennett. Agent Rico had kept his promise to protect Flemmi; however, at the same time, he violated the law by aiding and abetting the unlawful flight of a fugitive.

Cause for the car bombing indictment was based on testimony given by FBI informant Robert Daddieco. However, there is some question as to whether Frank Salemme was an actual participant in the attempted murder of Fitzgerald. Daddieco knew that Salemme and Flemmi were inseparable, making it easy to involve him in the crime. Later, Agents Rico and Condon allegedly worked on Daddieco to change his testimony, clearing Flemmi of the bombing.

Had Flemmi been prosecuted for the bombing or for the William Bennett murder, his position as an FBI informant would certainly have been disclosed, and its legal issues could have been embarrassing for Rico and the FBI. Rico would later deny that he had tipped off Flemmi of the impending indictments. Paul Rico was concerned about his method of using Flemmi as an informant. He didn't have permission to use Flemmi unless he presented evidence to FBI headquarters that the potential informant could be used without danger or embarrassment to the Bureau. This was not the case; and besides, Rico believed that Flemmi could be used again and become a valuable source for his war against the Mafia.

Although a federal fugitive warrant was issued for Flemmi's arrest for his unlawful flight to avoid prosecution, he continued to stay in contact with Rico. Rico never informed the District Attorney of Middlesex County of his continued contact with the fugitive. Flemmi would identify himself as "Jack from South Boston," a code name that the two had devised to identify each other whenever Flemmi would call. Flemmi would inquire as to what was happening, and would ask Rico how long he expected it would take to work out his problem. Rico advised Flemmi to stay away from Boston and that it would take a considerable amount of time, but to be patient. FBI policy required that all contacts with informants be recorded, yet Rico never made any record of his conversations with Flemmi while he was a fugitive. Rico never told any of the agents who were looking for the fugitive, either.

In April of 1970, Agent Paul Rico was reassigned to the Miami, Florida, office. His partner Dennis Condon would assume the investigation of Flemmi and Salemme. Condon knew that Flemmi had been supplying information to Rico in the past, and that Rico was still trying to engineer a favorable return to Boston for Flemmi, with eventual dismissal of all charges. In November of 1970, Condon received information that Flemmi and Salemme were in New York, and meeting regularly with a mobster who had been living in the vicinity of Central Park. Later on, the two fugitives would have a serious falling out and decide to separate.

Condon then contacted an FBI agent from South Boston who had been working in New York. Condon had been introduced to John Connolly by Edward Walsh, the Deputy Superintendent of the Boston Police Department. Walsh had a fanatic dislike for the Italians in Boston. He had spent many years trying to dismantle the North End mob and the Anguilos. Connolly was delighted with Condon's call, and received some general information along with several photos. The information received originated from Steve Flemmi, passed on to Condon, and then to Connolly. Flemmi had ratted out his lifelong friend and partner, Cadillac Frank Salemme.

Connolly began to focus his attention in the vicinity of Central Park, in hopes of apprehending Salemme. Months would pass without any success. Then, while walking along Third Avenue with two other agents, Connolly noticed a tall male with a well-known face. Even though the tall male's hair was longer than usual, the face was unmistakable. Connolly only made brief eye contact, not wanting to spook the fugitive. Salemme continued on his way, never noticing the FBI agent from South Boston.

Connolly turned to see if Cadillac Frank had recognized him, then informed the two agents he was with that indeed, the tall male was Frank Salemme, wanted in Boston on a fugitive warrant. "You got a piece," Connolly whispered to his partners. "You two, you got a piece." The two agents nodded then began to open their coats, while reaching for their guns. "That guy, the tall one, is wanted in Boston," Connolly told them. "We gotta take him." Salemme stopped at a storefront, giving the agents time.

"Frankie!" Connolly called out. Salemme turned reflexively. "FBI," Connolly said. "Freeze!"

At the same time, Salemme was up against a wall, his hands and feet spread apart. "I'm a legitimate fuckin' businessman," he complained. "I'm a jeweler from Philadelphia; I'm a legitimate fuckin' guy."

"You can say you're Bugs Bunny if you want. Until we prove otherwise, we're going to treat you like Frankie Salemme," Connolly told him.

Salemme would spend the next seventeen years in prison. Connolly, for his part in the arrest of the fugitive Salemme, would use this "lucky break" to ask for a transfer back to his hometown, Boston.

Careful precautions had been taken by Connolly to protect the source of his information that was responsible for the arrest. He never told of photos that had been sent to him from Boston, or the knowledge and general location of Salemme, instead calling the arrest a lucky fluke. The arrest of Salemme was accepted by the Boston mobsters as a bad break; those close to him were sympathetic to his capture. Flemmi was never suspected as the cause of the arrest. Agent Paul Rico kept his promise to protect Flemmi, and by doing so knew that Flemmi would again become a valuable FBI informant. A plan was set in motion to have Flemmi return to Boston and cleared of the charges. Flemmi, who had now relocated in Canada, was keeping a close eye on the trial of Salemme.

Salemme was found guilty of the Fitzgerald bombing solely on the testimony of Robert Daddieco. Daddieco, who was being protected by the government, testified earlier that Salemme and Flemmi had been participants in the bombing. Flemmi continued to stay in touch with Rico at the Miami office of the FBI. Rico informed Flemmi that his problems had been straightened out, and he should return to Boston.

But Flemmi wasn't in any hurry to face the serious charges, and besides, he was living comfortably in Canada. Flemmi also had reservations on just how far Rico would go to protect him. Would an FBI agent look the other way when it came to murder and the Fitzgerald bombing? Rico assured Flemmi that everything had been taken care of. He promised Flemmi that he would be released on bail, and all of the charges against him would simply go away.

On May 6, 1974, Rico made arrangements for Flemmi's return to Boston. Flemmi was met by two Boston police detectives who were close to Agent Condon. He was released on bail, although he had been a fugitive from murder and attempted murder charges for five years. The fugitive charges were dismissed that very day. The Bennett murder charges would also be dismissed, as they had been for Salemme earlier. At the urging of the FBI, Daddieco, who had testified against Salemme previously, now had a change of heart concerning Flemmi's role in the Fitzgerald bombing. Daddieco claimed that he was lying when he said Flemmi was also involved. The bombing charge was dismissed, and Flemmi was free to go about his business of crime in Boston. Paul Rico had come through for his pet rat.

Cadillac Frank Salemme would serve a seventeen-year prison sentence for his questionable role in the Fitzgerald bombing, compliments of his best friend and partner, Steve Flemmi. There would be more acts of treachery against Salemme, orchestrated by Flemmi and Agent John Connolly.

Connolly would be rewarded for Salemme's arrest in the form of a much-desired transfer to Boston. He would return to his boyhood South Boston and his childhood idol, Whitey Bulger.

Chapter 3

JAMES "WHITEY" BULGER

South Boston is a city, proud of its miles of beaches and waterfronts. The nucleus of its residents, mostly Irish-Americans, openly displays their love and loyalty for their neighborhood. A densely-populated area, often referred to as "Southie," it is comprised mostly of three-decker tenement houses. Residents can often be seen strolling up and down Broadway, shopping and greeting their neighbors.

It was a warm and close-knit community. However, in 1974 a federal court ordered black students from predominantly black neighborhoods bussed to South Boston in order to gain racial equality in the city's public schools. The residents of Southie were not receptive to the court order. Massive protests and violent confrontations with police and federal marshals would expose South Boston to the nation.

For the economically challenged Bulgers, home was the Old Harbor Housing Project in South Boston. James Bulger, the eldest son, was already building a reputation as a tough guy. "Whitey," as he was known because the color of his blond hair was nearly white, was violent and vicious. He hated the name Whitey and made certain that no one dared call him that. At the age of thirteen, Whitey had been arrested on larceny charges and quickly moved on to assault and battery. At seventeen, he was arrested for unarmed robbery; later he was charged for assault with the intent to rape. Whitey was a bully, always looking to challenge anyone who stood in his way, including the local police. He was the talk of Southie. Whitey dropped out of South Boston High and quickly pursued a life of crime, tailgating trucks in the greater Boston area. Later on, he would enlist in the Air Force, but soon after went AWOL, and was captured and court-martialed. He left the Air Force and was soon sticking up banks in Rhode Island, Massachusetts, and Indiana. It wasn't long before three members of his gang were arrested and Whitey went on the lam.

As a result of an investigation led by Agent Paul Rico, Whitey Bulger was apprehended outside the Surf nightclub in Revere, Massachusetts. He would be sentenced to twenty years in federal prison. Bulger was first incarcerated at Alcatraz, one of the nation's toughest prisons, among others. He volunteered for a government-sponsored LSD experiment while incarcerated. As a result, he received an eleven-year deduction off his original sentence for his part in the experiment.

Special Agent Rico would often visit the Bulger family when Whitey was in prison. He would see to it that they had enough money to get by. Bulger later claimed that he was inclined to help the FBI because of the favorable treatment that his family had received from Paul Rico. Rumor had it that the use of LSD while in prison only added to his vicious behavior later on.

A fitness fanatic, Whitey Bulger neither smoked nor drank hard liquor. He was involved with two women, Theresa Stanley and Catherine Greig. There were also many sexual encounters with neighborhood teenage girls. Bulger had a sick fondness for the underage daughters of South Boston, especially those from the Catholic high school. Connolly and the other kids looked to Whitey as the Robin Hood of South Boston because of his generosity to those in need. They were in awe of him.

John Connolly's childhood revolved around the South Boston neighborhood where the Bulgers resided. Although Connolly admired the gangster from Southie, he would become closer to Whitey's younger brother Billy, who was the complete opposite of Whitey. His power would come from books, not at the point of a gun. Billy would become Connolly's mentor, his hometown hero. He would encourage the younger Connolly to excel in knowledge, and would enter Billy's alma mater, Boston College.

After attending the Jesuit school, Connolly would join the FBI. He would get his big break, a transfer from the New York City Bureau to his native Boston. The arrest of Frank Salemme was a key factor to his relocation.

Connolly was the Bulgers' man, an Old Harbor Project boy. Billy Bulger would continue to move up, becoming president of the Massachusetts Senate. When a federal court ordered black students to be bussed to South Boston, Billy Bulger rose to the challenge. He was caught up in the turmoil that was tearing his beloved Southie apart. He was the voice of South Boston, traveling to Washington to voice his complaints on the issue of forced bussing. All of his efforts would fail; bussing was there to stay. While Billy Bulger was making great strides in the world of politics, Whitey was escalating as well, only his progress was in the field of crime. However, Connolly would keep a watchful eye on Whitey Bulger. The South Boston G-Man was given instructions to protect Whitey Bulger and like a good neighbor, he acted on that request.

—Chapter 4—

THE WINTER HILL GANGSTERS

In March of 1965, Whitey Bulger was released from prison and returned to Boston. Bulger was immediately caught up in the bloody Irish gang war in which Irish gangsters had been killing each other at a brutal pace. Although the feud had begun while he was safely locked up in prison, the war was still ongoing.

The Irish gang in Roxbury lost the three Bennett brothers, compliments of Steve Flemmi and associates. The Winter Hill Gang had been led by Buddy McLean, who had been killed early on in the war. After his killing, Howie Winter would become head of the gang. Winter Hill, named for the Somerville, Massachusetts, neighborhood just outside of Boston, was often referred to simply as "The Hill."

Donald Killeen and his crew of Irish gangsters had control of the rackets in South Boston. Killeen had lost two brothers fighting off their rivals, the Mullin Gang. Whitey aligned himself with Donald Killeen, serving as his bodyguard in his beloved Southie.

Early on during the Irish Gang War, Paul McGonagle, the leader of the Mullin Gang, had been battling Bulger and Don Killeen over turf in South Boston. Thomas King, a close friend of Bulger, had allied with Bulger during the conflict. The ruthless Bulger, along with King, would kill the rival Paul McGonagle. King had put his own life on the line in helping to eliminate the threat that McGonagle posed to his pal Whitey Bulger. Although Bulger and King were thought of as close friends, the two men got into a dispute at a Dorchester bar. King was not a person to back down from anyone, not even the feared Whitey Bulger. King, who could back his words with action, got the best of Bulger during the barroom brawl.

Taking a beating and lying down was not good for Bulger's reputation. The fact that King had watched Bulger's back during the violent struggle for control during the Irish War, and was a loyal friend, meant nothing to Whitey. King had committed an unpardonable act, standing up to Whitey Bulger. Any gangster worth his salt did not forgive, did not forget. Bulger, Flemmi, and the very capable John Martorano were true gangsters. They would not allow anyone to stand up to them, or question their authority. Thomas King would disappear. His close friend Francis "Buddy" Leonard would be killed by Bulger as well.

James Sousa would also have the misfortune of experiencing Bulger's wrath. Sousa was involved in a robbery that didn't come off as planned. The failed robbery angered Bulger to the extent of hunting Sousa down and killing him.

Edward Connors had knowledge of the killing of James O'Toole by Whitey Bulger. Connors would also be slain by Bulger. Investigators speculated that Connors was killed in order to prevent him from testifying against the ruthless killer. When one gangster was asked what it costs to kill someone, he replied, "How much does a bullet cost?" Bulger and Flemmi had an endless supply of bullets.

However, Bulger would keep his options open, especially after gauging the shifting of power in South Boston. Whitey's knowledge garnered from reading military history books while serving time in prison made it easy for him to determine the outcome of the bloody battle for control of the rackets in Southie. Weighing the pros and cons, he decided it was time to visit Howie Winter and form an alliance with the powerful Winter Hill Gang. Howie could straighten out the beef between the Mullin Gang and Bulger.

Bulger's betrayal would lead to Don Killeen's demise. A short time later, in May 1972, a gunman pointed a machine gun at Don Killeen, firing fifteen rounds into his body. No one was officially charged with the murder. However, rumors circulating in South Boston had Bulger as the trigger man. Whitey Bulger would take total control of crime in South Boston. He was forty-two years old.

Whitey was now aligned with Howie Winter and the Winter Hill Gang. Other top mobsters of the gang included the Martorano brothers, Jimmy and John, Steve Flemmi, and George Kaufman. Kaufman and John Martorano had rented a garage in Somerville called Marshall Motors. It would serve as headquarters for the gangsters. Whitey Bulger would frequent the garage often; there he would meet Steve Flemmi. The pair had met socially once or twice in the early days, but did not really know each other previously. They would begin to spend a great deal of time together. Whitey had an inclination that Flemmi had some degree of protection from the FBI. The charges in the Bennett murder case had been dismissed, and the witness in the Fitzgerald car bombing, who had at first testified that Flemmi was also involved, had had a change of heart. This set of circumstances paved the way for Bulger to seek Flemmi's approval on meeting with Agent John Connolly.

The meeting between Bulger and Connolly would be hastened by the investigation of an individual named Peter Pallotta, who was deeply in debt to some members of the Winter Hill Gang. Fearing for his life, he contacted the Boston office of the FBI. Agent John Connolly and his supervisor, John Morris, would participate in the loan sharking investigation. Bulger and Jimmy Martorano, along with other members of the Winter Hill Gang, were the subjects of the investigation. Agent Connolly decided this would be a good time to approach his childhood neighbor in an attempt to make him an informant. Whitey had been approached years earlier by FBI Supervisor Dennis Condon, but Whitey hadn't been interested. Condon hadn't grown up in Southie as Connolly had. Connolly would use the Pallotta investigation to approach Whitey. In an attempt to make him an informant, Connolly could promise Bulger the Pallotta problem would simply go away. Connolly also had knowledge that events were taking place between the Winter Hill Gang and Jerry Anguilo, the old school gambler. The beef was over the control of the placement of pinball machines in the bars around Boston. The Winter Hill Gang could not win in a war with the Italian Mafia. One phone call to New York, and the Boston LCN could get all the help they needed. Connolly would advise Bulger that it would be a war he and the Winter Hill Gang could not win; Bulger needed to use his friends in the FBI.

In truth, to his credit, Jerry Anguilo ran gambling in Boston very efficiently. He didn't care for the Wild West antics Bulger and the Winter Hill Gang were using—they were making too many waves. It was bad for business.

There was another issue Connolly could use to convince Bulger to become an informant. Bulger had been trying to extort a gambler named Richard Castucci from Revere. Castucci was a successful gambler with no mob ties—he was fair game for anyone, especially for the notorious Bulger. The focus of the extortion attempt was in reference to the scamming of famous rhythm and blues star Fats Domino. Castucci owned the Ebb Tide nightclub in Revere, Massachusetts, and was able to book the then-famous star to perform at his club. Domino commanded a huge fee for any appearance, and Castucci's small and unknown club could never have afforded to book the superstar. However, Castucci knew that Fats had a weakness for high stakes poker games. He, along with others, set up a rigged game and lured the unsuspecting Domino to participate. The scam worked, and Castucci was able to have the star entertainer perform at his standing-room-only club for practically nothing. Bulger caught wind of the score Castucci had made and wanted a share of the club's profit.

Castucci was not receptive to Bulger's attempt to extort him. In an effort to get Castucci, Bulger turned to Eddie Miani, Castucci's right-hand man. Bulger had threatened to kill Miani if Castucci didn't come across. "I'll kill Miani first, then you," Bulger was heard telling Castucci.

Word of Bulger's plan got to the FBI. They were well aware that he was extorting money from shylocks and bookmakers, and that Bulger was widely regarded as brutally violent. Neither Castucci nor Miani would talk to Agent John Morris about the Bulger threat. In an effort to gain Miani's cooperation in the investigation, Morris planted a fake bomb under Miani's car. He then

called the local police and alerted them to the bomb. After the device was dis-
abled, he met with Miani with the hope of scaring him into cooperating.
Morris told Miani that Bulger had planted the bomb, and he offered him the
protection of the FBI if he would become a cooperating witness.

Miani was in fear for his life, believing the bomb was real, and that
Bulger had planted it, yet he declined Morris' offer. He was a stand-up guy.
The Miani matter was one of three instances in which Morris would unsuccessfully exploit Bulger's reputation for violence in an effort to get
information for the FBI. Castucci continued to refuse Bulger's demand for
a piece of the action, something Bulger would never forget.

Bulger met with Steve Flemmi and informed him that FBI Agent John
Connolly wanted to meet with him. Flemmi knew that Bulger had some
knowledge of his previous dealings with the FBI, and he told Bulger that it
would be a good idea to meet Connolly. Flemmi was comfortable with
Bulger's suggestion to meet with Connolly. Both Flemmi and Bulger had
selfish reasons in aiding the FBI. They would reap the benefits of the void
that would be created if the Cosa Nostra were dismantled. The pair shared
an antipathy for the Italian mob leaders, a desire to profit criminally from
their destruction, and the promise of protection from the FBI.

In October 1975, Connolly met with Bulger in an effort to convince
him to play ball with the FBI. Connolly would center on the friction
between the Winter Hill gangsters and Jerry Anguilo, the wealthy gambling king pin. The agent from South Boston would point out to Bulger
that if the dispute reached a boiling point, the Boston LCN could count on
help from the Lucchese Mafia family in New York. There was also the
Pallotta investigation, with which Bulger was deeply concerned. Connolly
assured Bulger that he would avoid the upcoming indictments.

Connolly's proposal was a win-win situation for the two. Bulger could
profit by the destruction of the Mafia. Connolly would be fulfilling the FBI
objective to take out the mob at all costs. Two weeks later, Bulger would
again meet with Connolly. He would agree to accept Connolly's offer;
however, Bulger insisted on two conditions.

He wanted to be considered as a person giving technical advice, rather than an informant. Bulger was simply playing with words. He was trying to avoid the underworld word for what he was about to become, a "rat." The other condition was that his brother, Senate President William Bulger, was never to know. Connolly would agree to Bulger's demands. Whitey Bulger was in; his code name would be "Charlie."

Shortly after the Bulger and Connolly meeting, Flemmi would meet with Agents Condon and Connolly as well. The two agents knew that Flemmi had the ability to provide valuable information concerning the La Cosa Nostra. Unlike Bulger, Flemmi was often in the company of the Italian mob leaders. Steve Flemmi and Whitey Bulger would be assured by Connolly that they would be protected in the criminal activities in which they were engaged. Flemmi would begin passing information about the La Cosa Nostra to Connolly through Bulger. His FBI code name would be "Shogun." The alliance between Whitey Bulger, Steve Flemmi, and the FBI would become one of the worst scandals in the Bureau's history.

Soon after, two members of the Winter Hill Gang, James Martorano and Brian Halloran, along with five others, were arrested and prosecuted as a result of the Pallotta investigation. Although Bulger had been a key subject of the investigation, no charges were ever brought against him. Agent John Connolly kept his promise to protect his childhood idol.

Whitey Bulger and Steve Flemmi, now two top lieutenants of the Winter Hill Gang, were running wild. They and a small group of gamblers and killers, who worked out of the Marshall Motors garage, controlled a fair share of bookies around Boston. Richard Castucci, the nightclub owner, was also a clever and talented gambler and horse owner. He was having an extraordinary run of luck betting on horses with the Winter Hill bookies. Castucci's success was hurting the bookies connected with the gang. Bulger and Flemmi decided to investigate. Bulger was still angry with Castucci's refusal to pay on his extortion demand for the scamming of Fats Domino.

During the course of their investigation, Bulger and Flemmi uncovered how Castucci was able to win, betting on horses with such regularity. All the horses had been secretly owned by him. Castucci would "stiff" his horses nearly every time they ran—the jockeys were told to hold the horses back until the odds were high enough. Once the horses were entered in a race where the odds were high enough, they were allowed to win, and they won easily. Bulger told Castucci to make good on all the money he had won, or he would be killed. Castucci refused to do so, denying any wrongdoing.

But Castucci's name was already "in the hat." He had been marked for execution. It is alleged that Agent John Connolly revealed to Bulger information that Castucci had tipped the FBI that fugitives Joseph McDonald and James Sims, both members of the Winter Hill Gang, were hiding out in New York's Greenwich Village. On December 29, 1976, the body of Richard Castucci was found in the trunk of his Cadillac. Castucci had been shot several times in the head. John Martorano had been given the contract on Castucci by Bulger and Flemmi, one of the many the loyal gangster would carry out for them.

Chapter 5

ATTORNEY GENERAL LEVI'S MEMO ON FBI INFORMANTS

The former Attorney General Edward H. Levi had put guidelines into place relating to the FBI's use of handling informants. The guidelines were part of a larger effort by him and others to establish rules and regulations aimed at ending the serious abuses by the FBI. Up until then the FBI had been operating in secrecy.

The backlash of the Watergate Hearings exposed a series of incidents relating to questionable FBI activities going far beyond the illegal acts tied to the Nixon Administration. Also caught up in abuses was Dr. Martin Luther King, Jr. In an effort to discredit him as an effective leader of the Civil Rights Movement, embarrassing details were made public. In reaction to these revelations, Congress began to take a closer look at the FBI.

After Congress issued their report and Attorney General Levi adopted his FBI guidelines, FBI Director Kelly discovered that some agents had been lying and deceiving him. The agents continued to be involved with tactics to disrupt and discredit lawful domestic political activities of American citizens. The agents continued their illegal actions because they believed their work was important to national security and that they should not be governed by legal restraints or constitutional laws. Their continued use of illegal break-ins and other unlawful acts caused Congress to take a second look at the practices of the FBI. A criminal investigation by the Department of Justice led to the indictments of former FBI officials. In a statement released by former Director Kelly, it was noted that "the ability of the FBI to act in secrecy without any accountability was a major reason that such abuses were possible." The guidelines set forth by Levi were intended to diminish the need for legislation and to restrict the FBI's use of informants.

In the course of telling Connolly about the criminal activities of others, directly and through Bulger, Flemmi initially referred to his own illegal gambling and loan sharking activities. From the outset, and increasingly over time, however, Connolly was not under the illusion that gambling and loan sharking were the only, or even the most dangerous crimes in which Flemmi and Bulger were likely involved. Connolly explained: "We knew what these guys were. They didn't have a paper route when we first met them. All of them, Top Echelon Informants, are murderers. The government put me in business with murderers."

On February 4, 1976, Whitey Bulger was elevated to Top Echelon Informant status.

–Chapter 6–
BULGER AND FLEMMI IN ACTION

Through the instigating of Steve Flemmi and the engineering of Agents Paul Rico and Dennis Condon, Joe "The Animal" Barboza would continue to seek revenge against members of the LCN.

Raymond Patriarca and Henry "The Referee" Tamelo would be indicted and found guilty of conspiracy in the murder of Willie Marfeo of Providence, Rhode Island. Patriarca was one of the most ruthless crime bosses in the country and would continue to run his family while in prison.

Next to come into the crosshairs of Barboza, Flemmi, and Agent Rico would be Boston gambler Jerry Anguilo. Jerry was charged with participating in the murder of ex-boxer Rocco Di Seglio. A jury took less than two hours in acquitting the gambling czar.

Barboza had done well. Two of the three trials that he had testified in ended in guilty verdicts, including the earlier convictions of Peter Limone, Henry The Referee Tamelo, Joseph Joe the Horse Salvati, and Louis Greco. Barboza's success was the largest assault against the New England LCN thus far. He had accomplished what law enforcement had failed to do for decades. Yet, later on, the success would be tarnished when the depths to which the government had gone to achieve the results would lead to revelations of corruption and cover-ups.

As a reward for his testimony, the government cut short Barboza's original five-year sentence on the weapons charge, reducing it to a one-year prison term, including time served. In 1969, Barboza was paroled and banished from the state of Massachusetts. He relocated to San Francisco under the name of Joe Donati. It didn't take The Animal long—he promptly killed a man over a dispute involving stolen securities. In 1971, Barboza pled guilty to second degree murder for the killing, a killing he had committed while still in the government Witness Protection Program. He was sentenced to a mere five years for the murder. Barboza was able to receive this absurd sentence for the cold-blooded murder of Ricky Clay Wilson due to the efforts of FBI Agents Paul Rico, Dennis Condon, and Edward Harrington, who was head of the Organized Crime Strike Force in Boston.

The three had traveled to San Francisco to intercede on Barboza's behalf. The hit man was originally charged with first degree murder. However, Rico, Condon, and Harrington were successful in getting the District Attorney in Santa Rosa, California, to allow Barboza to plead to second degree murder. Barboza would be paroled in October of 1975, after serving only four years at the Folsom Federal Prison.

The news about Barboza was being closely monitored by concerned people back in New England. Barboza knew by now that his location was no longer a secret. He sent word back to the New England mob not to even think about retaliation or he would return to Boston and wipe out all the bosses there. This infuriated the mob leaders even more, prompting them to act quickly. A contract was put out on Barboza. An ex-Bostonian, James "Teddy" Chalmas who was also living in San Francisco, was keeping the concerned people in Boston abreast of Barboza's activities. Barboza would often visit Chalmas at his apartment. The ex-Boston wise guy was ready to set Barboza up.

On February 11, 1976, Joseph The Animal Barboza would accept an invitation to dine with Chalmas at his home. After lunch, Barboza strolled to his parked vehicle, when a white van pulled alongside the unsuspecting gangster. Barboza would be blasted in a hail of bullets from the occupant of the stolen van. The shooter was Joseph "J.R." Russo, a tall, trim, white-haired, old school Mafioso from Boston. Barboza died instantly from numerous bullet wounds. He would be the first person killed while enrolled in the government's Witness Protection Program.

Shortly after the murder, Flemmi reported to Bulger that Jimmy Chalmas had set Barboza up, and that the LCN intended to kill him to keep him quiet. Flemmi had spent a great deal of time and effort associating with the Boston underworld, and was able to discover who had been responsible for the Barboza setup. Flemmi passed this information on to Bulger, who in turn passed it on to Connolly. Connolly made certain that Bulger, his Top Echelon Informant and childhood idol, would receive the credit when preparing his 209 report. Connolly, along with Agent Dennis Condon, used this information to persuade Chalmas to admit his guilt and become a cooperating witness. It didn't take long for Connolly to convince Chalmas to cooperate, something Connolly was always good at. Chalmas would point the finger at Joseph J.R. Russo, as the triggerman in the Barboza murder.

Russo would begin receiving information that Chalmas was cooperating with the FBI. J.R. decided to leave Boston and make it difficult for the Feds to find him. It was referred to as a "semi-lam." J.R. had always been well-respected by the LCN. Other Mafia families in various parts of the country were willing to assist in keeping him unavailable for possible arrest. Russo would lay low in different parts of the country.

On one occasion, J.R. would find refuge hiding out in a hippie colony in California. He allowed his silver-white hair to grow and wore bell-bottom jeans in an effort to fit in with the others. He was extremely generous with the cash-poor group. J.R. would, at his own expense, prepare lavish Italian feasts for the entire commune on a daily basis.

In time, the FBI would make a case against Russo for the Barboza murder. However, they were in no hurry to arrest him. It is alleged that Agent Connolly had plans to use Russo and his gang as pawns to instigate a murder.

In 1976, Francis X. Green was puzzled and concerned to see Whitey Bulger, Steve Flemmi, and John Martorano at his stylish restaurant. He was well aware of their reputation as ruthless killers. More shocking to Green was the fact that Norfolk County District Attorney William Delahut was seated not far from the gangsters. Earlier, Green had observed Martorano and Delahut in friendly talk. As Green approached the table where the three gang members were sitting, Bulger got straight to the point, saying, "That money you borrowed belongs to us—it's our money."

Green had borrowed twenty thousand from Colony Finance in Boston. Green had made no attempt to pay the loan. Whitey gave Green a warning. If the money was not promptly repaid, "They would positively kill him; they would cut his ears off and stuff them in his mouth; they would gouge his eyes out."

Green, a slick con man, tried a song and dance routine with Bulger. Whitey was not impressed; he wanted the money. It didn't concern the bold gangsters that District Attorney Delahut was seated close by, no doubt something Green took notice of. If the three arrogant gangsters were daring enough to threaten Green with Delahut not far away, he didn't need a building to fall on him to understand how serious the extortion attempt was.

The terrified Green agreed to do what he could to pay them the money. He turned to Edward Harrington, a former prosecutor, who was working for a private law firm in Boston. Harrington suggested that Green present his problem to District Attorney Delahut because the extortion attempt occurred in his district, Norfolk County.

Prosecutors from Delahut's office interviewed Green and decided to turn the case file over to the Feds. The FBI was far more experienced in dealing with serious organized crime figures, and their guidelines called for far more prison time if convicted.

On October 13, 1977, Agents Thomas Daly and Peter Kennedy of the Organized Crime Squad interviewed Green. The two agents knew John Connolly; they worked together in the same office, oftentimes sharing information. Green's allegations presented a problem for Connolly.

The two agents went through the motions of interviewing Green and Delahut. They filed a report, but it remained in their files collecting dust. Later, they suggested that the case be closed because Green told the agents he was unwilling to testify. Victims of threats are often reluctant to testify; however, the Feds usually try to overcome their reluctance. As FBI

Supervisor James Ring put it, "Nobody wants to testify in these types of cases. You don't just turn around and walk away. If we did that, we'd never make an organized crime case."

Months later, when Delahut asked Jeremiah O'Sullivan, Chief Prosecutor of the Organized Crime Strike Force, what had come of the investigation, he was told, "It just didn't work out."

Harrington would later go on to become a federal judge. During the investigation of Connolly and the Boston FBI Strike Force, Harrington was asked about his role in the Green case and why it never led to any indictments. He responded, "In view of the fact that I am a federal judge and wish not to be involved in a proceeding before another federal judge, I decline to comment on the matter."

Although Daly and Special Agent Kennedy were told by Francis Green that Bulger and Flemmi had threatened to kill him in connection with their attempt to collect a debt, no effort was made to develop the reluctant Green as a witness against them. In 1979, Agent Daly would later join Prosecutor O'Sullivan in agreeing not to charge Bulger and Flemmi in the race fixing case. Looking back, the 1976 incident at the Back Side Restaurant was a turning point. An extortion case, built around a credible, cooperative witness, might have stopped Bulger and his partner, Stephen The Rifleman Flemmi from launching a fifteen-year crime spree. Instead, the FBI did nothing, sending a powerful message to two of the region's most ruthless organized crime figures: "As long as you're with us, we won't bother you."

Agent John Morris would become Chief of the Boston Organized Crime Squad. Yet, he would remain under John Connolly's spell. He was also under enormous pressure to have capable informants to assist in the war against the Italian mob. Morris was blinded by the policies coming out of Washington, to bring down the Mafia at any cost. Anything and everything was accepted, as long as it produced results.

It was easy for Connolly to have Morris see things his way. After all, they were after the same goal, destroy the LCN, and they needed Bulger and Flemmi to succeed. All Morris had to do was look the other way when it came to the informants' own criminal behavior.

Morris was from the Midwest, and the complete opposite of John Connolly. Connolly, the man about town and Prince of the City, had no problem in molding the naive Morris to his way of doing things. Morris took the street-smart Connolly's advice in accepting Bulger and Flemmi. The two agents would work in tandem in protecting their star informants. Connolly had successfully managed to dispose of the Green problem. He had resorted to a great deal of skullduggery in order to keep Bulger and Flemmi going.

No sooner had the Green problem been resolved than another surfaced. Two executives of National Melotone Vending complained that Bulger and Flemmi were extorting the company's customers. The two informants were threatening restaurant and bar owners in the greater Boston area in order to have them replace Melotone machines with those belonging to a company owned by them. The two Melotone executives wanted the FBI to conduct an investigation. Connolly would see to it that the Melotone problem would be his and John Morris'.

In meeting with the two executives, it was now Connolly's task to intimidate them. He began by telling them they were right to seek an investigation; however, there would be certain pitfalls. The two executives would most certainly have to testify against the ruthless killers. If they did come forward, their lives could be in danger. In order to fully protect the two, they would have to be in the Witness Protection Program, and relocate their families. Connolly could see they were not willing to go through it all. He would now suggest a different approach to the two—his pitch had worked. It was now "let's make a deal" time. No longer did the executives consider doing it the way they had originally intended. They would now leave it up to Connolly to straighten out their problem. He would meet with Bulger and Flemmi and advise them to back off. They would have to return the locations in dispute over to Melotone. Rather than pursue their claims of extortion and threats, or report it to other law enforcement agencies, Connolly's main concern remained that of protecting Bulger and Flemmi. He exploited the brutal reputation for violence that Bulger and Flemmi had acquired and persuaded the two Melotone executives not to pursue their charges.

In another matter, Bulger reported to Connolly about the planned imminent murder of agent Nick Gianturco, who had gone undercover posing as a fence in an investigation of truck hijackings (known as "Operation Lobster") in the greater Boston area. The agent had rented a large warehouse where he proceeded to buy stolen goods from the various gangs of hijackers. In truth, the plan was a shakedown of Gianturco and not a murder plot. Connolly had once again twisted the facts in order to strengthen Bulger's usefulness as an informant. It was pure fiction. He made no record or report to back the murder claim. Connolly continuously repeated the myth; his fabrication about Bulger's role was purely a way of protecting him from scrutiny. When asked about Bulger's role in saving his life, Gianturco didn't go as far as Connolly did. Connolly reciprocated for the alleged tip by providing Bulger and Flemmi with information that a cleaning company Flemmi was using for his loan sharking was wired in an effort to obtain evidence. Flemmi stayed away from the location and was never intercepted.

John Morris made the pursuit of the Mafia his number one priority. He understood that Bulger and Flemmi were vital in his efforts. He was fully aware that Bulger and Flemmi regarded the Mafia as mortal enemies. Flemmi, in particular, because of his acceptance by the mob, was the most important source. An Italian with a ruthless reputation, he could provide the FBI with information of the highest level regarding the LCN.

Morris would first meet Bulger and Flemmi at a dinner held at his home. This first in a series of such dinner parties included the two informants along with Connolly, Nick Gianturco, Special Agent Michael Buckley, Supervisory Special Agent James Ring, Dennis Condon, Jules Bonovolenta, and Joe Pistone. Pistone, the former New York agent, had become famous for his undercover work as "Donnie Brasco."

The dinner party was a way of treating Bulger and Flemmi as allies rather than rats. This approach was made at the urging of Connolly, and

Morris was anxious to receive the valuable assistance Bulger and Flemmi could provide. Morris had dedicated every member of his Organized Crime Squad to bringing down the Mafia.

Later, Bulger, Flemmi, Connolly, and Gianturco would meet again, this time at Gianturco's home. Bulger and Flemmi were accepted as one of their own; it was difficult to distinguish who was carrying the badge. Meeting informants in an agent's home was very unusual. Even more unusual, gifts were exchanged at some of the dinner parties. Bulger and Flemmi gave Gianturco a toy truck to commemorate Operation Lobster. He also received a glass statue and a leather briefcase. Bulger received an Alcatraz belt buckle. No record of the exchange of gifts was ever made. After retirement, when questioned about the exchanging of gifts with the two ruthless gangsters, Nick Gianturco admitted he had made a "mistake in judgment" in accepting gifts from Bulger and Flemmi.

It wasn't just Connolly and John Morris who were aware that Bulger and Flemmi were involved in a range of criminal activities. Based on information that was being provided by other informants, the FBI neither investigated nor disclosed information to any other law enforcement agencies. Connolly and Morris wanted to continue to receive the valuable assistance the two were providing on the Mafia. However, over time the end would not justify the means. The degree to which the handful of corrupt agents would go in order to protect their prized informants is disgraceful. The rogue agents would lie to other law enforcement agencies. Known crimes were covered up while ignoring FBI guidelines. The South Boston gangsters were given the identities of informants who were willing to come forward and provide evidence against them. That information was subsequently put to deadly use.

Other FBI agents knew that Bulger and Flemmi were informants. Special Agent Buckley characterized John Connolly as a close friend as well as a colleague for fourteen years. After Connolly retired, he told Connolly that a William Ierardi had accused Bulger and Flemmi of being involved in the Black Friar's Massacre in which five people were murdered. The brutal killings had taken place at the Black Friar's Restaurant in Boston during the early morning hours. A group of drug traffickers was planning a huge drug deal at the restaurant and had been slaughtered during a robbery. The city of Boston was in a state of shock at the horrible event. The cold-blooded killings bore a resemblance to the infamous St. Valentine's Day Massacre that had taken place at a garage in Chicago decades earlier. But this was a different time and a different place. This was Boston, a sophisticated and cultured city. This was another time, not the days when gangsters would kill openly with no regard for the law, as in the past.

Although William Ierardi had accused Bulger and Flemmi of being the killers in the Black Friar's Massacre, that information was never publicly disclosed. But others involved in drug dealing and other criminal activities knew that Bulger and Flemmi had committed the horrendous murders. It was no secret to those in the underworld, and it would be difficult for anyone to say no to any extortion attempt by the two. The Black Friar's killings sent a message that Bulger and Flemmi were to be feared.

Flemmi continued to supply Connolly with information on the mob. In one instance, Flemmi provided Connolly with information concerning the assassination of Federal Judge James Wood by a group of big time drug dealers. The group had feared the worst from Wood, who was the sitting judge in their case. After an attempt to bribe the judge had failed, a contract was put out on his life. Wood was shot and killed outside his home by a gunman who had been hiding behind a tree. The paid hit man was the father of the movie star, Woody Harrelson.

The FBI continued to receive information from informants that Bulger and Flemmi were involved in criminal activities, including illegal gambling and drug trafficking. John Morris was receiving reports that Bulger and Flemmi were "shaking down" independent bookmakers. The conspiracy to extort bookmakers by Bulger and Flemmi was going on for twenty years, yet the FBI made no effort to investigate when receiving information, nor did it disclose the information to any other law enforcement agencies. Connolly and Morris were only concerned with the destruction of the

Mafia, and needed Bulger and Flemmi's assistance in achieving that goal. Flemmi and Bulger were told by the FBI that "they could do anything they wanted, as long as they did not 'clip' anyone." But they would be protected even when that crime was committed. The FBI's position with regard to Flemmi and Bulger was heartless, especially to all of the victims involved. Paul Rico, John Connolly, and John Morris ignored FBI guidelines requiring them to report informers' crimes to the Department of Justice. As reports from other informants piled up, so would the bodies. John Connolly would give Bulger and Flemmi his personal and unlimited grant of immunity, which the two put to good use.

Louis Litif, a South Boston native, was one of many bookmakers paying Bulger and Flemmi for the right to operate. Litif decided he wanted to enter the fast money-making drug trade. Being a bookmaker was not as lucrative as being a drug dealer, or so he thought. He would be dead wrong. In a dispute over a drug deal that had gone bad, Louis Litif shot James "Jimmy the Juice" Matera several times in the head, in the basement of a bar he owned. The bartender, Kenneth "Bob" Conrad, had witnessed Litif and Matera go down to the basement, then saw Litif coming back upstairs alone. Soon the bartender would disappear. Conrad had been talking much too much, and far too often to South Boston homicide detectives who were investigating Matera's murder.

In 1980, Litif stabbed Conrad to death and buried his body on property he owned in rustic Deerfield, Nova Scotia. This action by Litif would infuriate Bulger. As far as Bulger was concerned, Litif had no business being in the drug trade, and no right to kill without his approval. Bulger considered himself the sole judge and executioner, and no one else. However, there was another factor upsetting Bulger. Louis Litif was an informant for none other than Bulger's childhood friend, John Connolly. Upon receiving that information, Bulger decided there was one too many, especially one who committed murder and dealt drugs in South Boston without his permission. Murder committed by other informants, even those belonging to Connolly, was infringing on Bulger's sovereignty. It was causing far too much heat.

That same year, the body of Louis Litif was found in the trunk of his car. He had been shot in the head. Brian Halloran, a Bulger associate, had gone with Litif to "the bucket of blood," Triple O's bar, one of Bulger's headquarters. Litif was to meet with Bulger there. He would not leave the same way he had come in.

In 1981, the daughter of Kenneth Conrad, Elizabeth Conrad Parent, was seeking answers to her father's disappearance. However, the revelation that she received from Agent John Connolly was not what she was hoping for.

"Honey, your father's dead. They knifed him. But don't worry; they got him good and drunk first."

But the grieving daughter would not accept the cruel explanation.

The arrogant agent added unequivocally, "I saw it."

Being bold and callous, he went on to inform Elizabeth that her father was buried in Nova Scotia. She was told not to reveal any information because the murder was being investigated, and certain persons giving information on the crime had to be shielded from exposure. Connolly was clearly concerned for Bulger, who was a suspect in the murder of her father's killer. As far as Connolly was concerned, Conrad was a nobody. His only concern was to protect Bulger. He didn't want any investigation of the Conrad murder, an investigation that could possibly uncover Bulger's role in the Litif slaying.

"Mr. Connolly, when can we get my father's body back?" she asked.

"Honey, if we dig up that backyard, you don't understand how many bodies may be there," callously responded the arrogant Connolly.

In an effort to appease the grieving daughter, Connolly would help her to collect on her father's insurance policy. Connolly didn't do it out of any moral or ethical concerns. He wanted to make certain that there would be no action that could cause any future investigation. It was the same arrogance John Connolly would show during his twenty years of protecting and nurturing Bulger and Flemmi. It was Connolly's bold and reckless disregard for life that enabled the two gangsters to kill at the drop of a hat.

–Chapter 7–
FAST WOMEN AND SLOW HORSES

Richard Castucci was not the only horse bettor taking shots at the Winter Hill bookies. "Fat Tony" Ciulla was having a great deal of success hoodwinking bookies connected with Howie Winter and the Winter Hill Gang. The six-foot-five Ciulla, who weighed over 300 pounds, didn't have the talent that Richard Castucci had with regard to the actual handicapping of a horse race. What Fat Tony did have was a genius for fixing horse races. However, he made the mistake of betting the boat races (a term used by gamblers in describing a fixed race) with a sharp bookmaker who smelled out the fix. The bookmaker, along with a member of the Winter Hill Gang, decided to have a serious talk with Fat Tony. It was at the meeting that Tony Ciulla was told to return the money won, or else he would have a problem, just as Richard Castucci had. The smooth-talking Ciulla, who could talk the balls off a pawnbroker, was able to convince the two men to participate in the race-fixing scam.

Soon after, another meeting would take place at Marshall Motors. Attending the meeting with Ciulla were Whitey Bulger, Steve Flemmi, James and John Martorano, and Howie Winter. Although surrounded by a group of ruthless killers, Fat Tony was most convincing in making his case. He knew how to work on their greed. A deal would be struck. Again, the smooth-talking Ciulla was able to convince Howie Winter and the others to participate in the race-fixing scam.

Tony Ciulla would see to the actual fixing of the races, deal with the easily corrupted jockeys, and determine what racetracks were the least likely to suspect any skullduggery. Along with cash, the crooked jockeys would also be supplied with a variety of exceptionally good-looking women. Many prostitutes were willing and eager to help out the gangsters.

The Winter Hill Gang would have access to bookmakers, and supply the necessary cash to finance the fix. The feared gangsters would also provide protection from any retaliation from disgruntled victims. The fix was in—bookies and racetracks along the East Coast would be fleeced. The gang went so far as to send Jerry Matricia to Las Vegas with a $50,000 bankroll to bet on the fixed races in the casinos there. He would blow the entire bankroll in less than a week at high stakes poker games. Matricia would be easy prey for the professionals who made their living waiting for suckers like him to arrive in town. Word on the street was to "stay away from Matricia"; that "his days were numbered."

The Winter Hill gangsters also recruited two former Bostonians, Las Vegas casino bosses Mel Golden and Elliott Price, to place wagers for them along the Vegas strip. The fix would go well when the bribed jockeys followed a prescribed script. When a particular race did not go as planned, the responsible jockeys would be searched out and given a stern warning to "pull their horses" when told to do so. However, word of the corruption and crooked races would begin to surface in the racing community. Whispers of bribes by gangsters would cause the New Jersey State Police to begin an investigation. One bribed jockey began cooperating and pointed the finger at Fat Tony Ciulla as the fixer.

Ciulla was convicted and sentenced to a long prison term. It didn't take Fat Tony long to roll. He began naming names of the others involved in the scam. The FBI was called in and Ciulla was promptly placed in the Witness Protection Program. He began supplying investigators with detailed information on others involved with him.

Bulger and Flemmi were aware of the investigation and were concerned about being indicted. Agents John Morris and Connolly had a problem with events in the race-fixing case as well. Connolly understood that his star informants could be investigated by other agents or by the State Police, and eventually prosecuted if sufficient evidence was developed. Connolly was not assigned to the investigation; instead, Agent Tom Daly would be the case agent. Connolly did not know Agent Daly, and had a problem protecting Bulger and Flemmi, who were targets of the probe.

Morris, who was Connolly's supervisor, decided to close Bulger as an informant because he was a key figure in the investigation and might be indicted. However, Connolly did not tell Bulger that he had been closed as an informant. Connolly knew that had he done so, he might lose Bulger altogether. This action by Connolly was a clear violation of FBI policy. Connolly had treated his childhood idol as a colleague, rather than an informant. He would continue his contact with Bulger and Flemmi; however, it was now off the record.

Bulger and Flemmi were deeply concerned about being indicted. They had trusted Agent Paul Rico, and now Connolly's, promises of protection. Connolly had to produce, just as Rico had done previously. Connolly would meet with Morris and plead his case on behalf of Bulger and Flemmi.

Connolly and Morris agreed they didn't want to lose Bulger and Flemmi. They wanted the North End Mafia, and its leader, Jerry Anguilo. Without Bulger and Flemmi, it would be next to impossible to accomplish this goal. Both agents decided that their value as informants outweighed the importance of prosecuting them. John Connolly was concerned about the investigation. Indictments were being assembled, and Ciulla's testimony in New Jersey would make it more difficult to protect his informants.

Morris and Connolly would meet with the hard-nosed prosecutor, Jeremiah O'Sullivan. They pleaded with O'Sullivan on behalf of the two informants. O'Sullivan would be told that Bulger and Flemmi were informants, and had agreed to help in the Anguilo investigation, a priority that the FBI and O'Sullivan shared. O'Sullivan was also told by Morris that Bulger and Flemmi were crucial to his ambitious plan to bug Jerry Anguilo's 98 Prince Street headquarters.

This disclosure violated FBI policy because the bugging had not been authorized by FBI headquarters at that time. Getting the Anguilo brothers was O'Sullivan's ticket to fame and glory—his highest priority.

O'Sullivan told the two agents he needed to speak with the case agent, Tom Daly, and would get back to them. Shortly thereafter, Morris was told by O'Sullivan that Bulger and Flemmi would be dropped from the indictment. The two gangsters were given the good news by Connolly. Flemmi asked Connolly to "thank O'Sullivan for him." O'Sullivan responded that the informants and the FBI should appreciate the special treatment.

On February 2, 1979, a RICO indictment on the race-fixing case was returned against thirteen defendants, including James and John Martorano and Howie Winter. Bulger and Flemmi were named as unindicted co-conspirators. John Martorano would be warned in advance of the coming indictments by Flemmi and Bulger. He would flee to Florida on the heels of the indictment. He was their favorite hit man, a loyal gangster whose services they would need for future killings.

After a lengthy trial, all the defendants who had pled not guilty were convicted, including those who had fled. Las Vegas casino executives Mel Golden and Elliott Price would lose their gaming licenses for their role in the race-fixing scam.

Steve Flemmi did not claim that he had an enforceable agreement with the FBI that provided him with immunity from prosecution in the race-fixing case. Rather, he recognized that he would have been indicted and prosecuted. He was grateful that Connolly and Morris had persuaded Prosecutor O'Sullivan not to indict him in order to permit him to continue to provide information on the LCN.

The Boston FBI requested and received from the Director of the FBI approval to reopen Bulger as an informant. Bulger was characterized as a source that would provide consistently excellent information, and had the ability to produce meaningful information on the Mafia in Boston.

The Director was reminded that Bulger had been closed because he had become a target of the race-fixing investigation. He was also told, however, that in the opinion of the strike force attorney handling the case, no prosecutable case would be developed against Bulger. This was not true. They were not prosecuted because Connolly, Morris, and O'Sullivan had decided that their value as informants outweighed the importance of prosecuting them, not to mention Connolly's close and personal friendship with his childhood neighbors, William and James Bulger. In any event, the Director was told that the FBI in Boston was of the opinion that Bulger had been, and would be once again, one of the most highly-placed and valuable sources of the department. With Howie Winter being sent off to prison, Bulger and Flemmi would now assume control of the Winter Hill Gang.

Chapter 8

ONE LOYAL GANGSTER

It was no wonder that Bulger and Flemmi would warn only John Martorano to flee before indictments came down in the race-fixing case. John was their loyal gangster, who could be called on anytime, day or night, to kill for them. "Johnny on the Spot," who would relocate to Florida, was their favorite hit man.

He was both rugged and handsome, with dark, wavy hair that complimented his milky-white skin. Early on, he had already established himself as a cold-blooded killer. John and his brother James were tough enough to gain respect from their peers, and would join up with Bulger, Flemmi, and the Winter Hill Gang. Their father, Andy Martorano, an immigrant from Sicily, was a high-line gambler. All throughout the baseball season, you could find the senior Martorano in the right field section of Fenway Park, home of the Boston Red Sox. Gamblers and bookies from all over Boston would gather in this one section, testing their gambling skills against one another. The group of gamblers would make odds on any situation during the ball game. They would give you the option to bet whether the next pitch would be a ball or a strike, a foul ball or a home run. This group of Damon Runyan, cigar-smoking characters was a match for any sophisticated computer at setting odds. They had knowledge as to whether the starting pitcher had been out all night and was nursing a hangover. They had memorized the statistics on every batter's success versus a particular opposing pitcher. All of the gamblers at the ballpark were aware of John Martorano's reputation for violence, so caution was exercised when doing business with Andy. Any dispute over a wager with Andy was a lost cause because they didn't want to have to answer to John Martorano.

When not at the ball park, Andy could be found at his restaurant, Luigi's. Located on Washington Street in downtown Boston, the Italian eatery sat in the heart of an area known as "The Combat Zone," which was a section of Boston comprised of endless rows of bars and clubs. Hookers would solicit their trade openly under the watchful eyes of their pimps. Aside from the regular pasta dishes, Andy would also serve alcohol, even though he had no liquor license. Luigi's was more famous as an after-hours joint. Mobsters, high rollers and party-goers would go to Luigi's to see and be seen. John Martorano would often be in Luigi's helping out his father as manager, bouncer, and host. He could identify particular mobsters and highrollers flashing huge bankrolls, and would make certain that they were given choice seating.

The senior Martorano was having an affair with Margaret Sylvester, which was oftentimes in turmoil. During an unwelcome early morning visit to the after-hours restaurant, an unruly and intoxicated Sylvester was beaten and stabbed to death by Robert Palladino. Her body was later discovered in a crawlspace above the ceiling of Luigi's. Police suspected Palladino as the murderer, and that Jimmy Martorano was an accessory after the fact. Palladino began testifying in front of a grand jury. John Martorano was concerned that Palladino would flip, and shift blame for the murder on his younger brother, Jimmy. Hit man John could not stand idly by; something needed to be done to protect his brother from a possible frame.

Robert Palladino's body would be found on Causeway Street in the North End section of Boston. He had been shot in the back of the head. It was John Martorano's first hit.

His next hit would be Tony Veranis, a former professional boxer and street thief. After pistol-whipping Veranis, Martorano shot him through the top of the head. His body was found off Route 128, outside of Boston. His third hit was John Jackson, who had tended bar at Luigi's the night Margaret Sylvester was slain. John was concerned that Jackson would shed light on events that had occurred at the restaurant. Jackson was ambushed outside his home on Queensbury Street in Boston's Back Bay section, shortly before daylight. He had been shot in the back of the head by a blast from a shotgun. The killing of John Jackson came one month before Jimmy Martorano was to be tried as an accessory to the Margaret Sylvester murder. John Jackson's name was removed from the prosecution's witness list.

Andy Martorano, along with his son John, would open a jazz club in Boston's South End district, an area mostly comprised of African-Americans. The club, named Basin Street South, would feature live jazz bands. It was no wonder that John Martorano's next victim would be black and that John would inherit the names "Johnny Sickle-Cell," "The Basin Street Butcher," and "Bwana John." The club was managed by a black man, Herbert Smith, who committed the unpardonable act of disrespecting Steve Flemmi, who had come to the club to visit with the loyal gangster, Martorano. The disrespect shown to Flemmi by Smith was not taken lightly by Martorano. John acted on his displeasure when he found Smith, along with two black teenagers, sitting in a car on Normandy Street in Roxbury one early morning. Smith felt certain he would be safe if two uninvolved teenagers were with him when confronting Martorano. Smith assumed that Martorano would not do anything rash to him, not with two witnesses sitting with him.

However, Smith would be wrong—dead wrong—and so would the innocent teenagers. Smith, along with seventeen-year-old Douglas Barrett and nineteen-year-old Elizabeth Dixon, would all be slain. The two teenagers had been in the wrong place at the wrong time, and with Herbert Smith. True to his belief, Martorano knew that dead people make poor witnesses. Robert Hicks would also be slain to prevent his testifying in the triple murder. An ex-con on parole for armed robbery, Hicks was found in his parked car. He had been shot in the forehead. In all, four bodies, all because John's friend Steve Flemmi had been disrespected—that's loyalty. Martorano killed at least a dozen or so during the Irish Gang War. He had allied himself with Flemmi during the war, then later with Bulger. He was a good and faithful soldier.

There was one sorry victim who Johnny on the Spot mistook for a rival gangster during the conflict. There was also word on the street that Martorano had killed a woman who was ready to tell police he had forced her to perform a sexual act on him. Although living in Florida as a fugitive, he was still feared.

In 1987, a Winter Hill bookmaker called "Nails," living in Las Vegas, was approached by a Providence, Rhode Island, wise guy, Anthony "The Saint" St. Laurent, and told he had to start paying protection. Nails, whose real name was Joe Snyder, was a Boston native connected with the Winter Hill gang. Snyder had been given the nickname Nails by the professional gamblers in Las Vegas, for his tenacity in dealing with point spreads on sports betting. He was considered "hard as nails" for never taking the worst of a point spread on any gambling event. If Joe favored betting on a game at one particular point spread, and the number was not available, he would not make the bet.

When St. Laurent was slow on backing off his attempted extortion of Snyder, Martorano became furious. Although The Saint was powerfully connected with the Rhode Island Mafia, Martorano was prepared to travel to Rhode Island and "whack" St. Laurent. Joseph J.R. Russo met with Steve Flemmi and assured the concerned gangster that he would contact The Saint and resolve the problem. The shakedown of Joe Nails Snyder was quickly called off.

Although living in Florida as a fugitive from the race-fixing indictment under the name of Vincent Rancourt (as in "ran from court"), Martorano could always be counted on to act on orders from Bulger and Flemmi. Just say the word, and the loyal gangster was ready to kill for them. He never once suspected that Bulger and Flemmi had an unholy alliance with the G-Men.

–Chapter 9–
THE CANDY MAN

Most residents of South Boston regarded James Whitey Bulger with respect and admiration, a courteous, gracious, and honorable man who cared deeply for those in the tight-knit community. As far as the residents of Southie were concerned, he was their protector. He could straighten out any problems in the community. Bulger was who you went to, not the police or politicians. He could get you a good job, he made things happen or problems go away.

However, while loyalists were singing the praises of their beloved gangster, Bulger was seducing neighborhood teenage girls. The South Boston Robin Hood had a bad side that few were aware of, or willing to acknowledge. "This is a whole part of Bulger's history that people in Southie don't want to even talk about," said a mental health counselor who had treated women who had sexual encounters with Bulger as teenagers. Well over 100 underage girls would fall prey to Bulger and Flemmi. Both gangsters would zero in on the Catholic high school teenagers, especially when they walked around in their school uniforms. Bulger could often be heard singing the show tune "Thank Heaven for Little Girls," while referring to them as "tasty little morsels."

Most of the teenage girls who were introduced to sex and drugs were from poor or broken homes. "They took the most vulnerable and they preyed on them," the counselor said. "They made sick kids sicker. They didn't go after girls from good families, girls who were doing the right thing. They went after girls who had nothing at home. The girls, in their early teens, were just coming into puberty and trying to answer questions about their identities, their bodies, and their sexuality. Bulger and Flemmi gave them the wrong answers," she said.

The girls would confuse love and attention with sex and drugs. They were drawn into Bulger and Flemmi's reputations as gangsters. One girl who became involved with Bulger when she was a fifteen-year-old beauty pageant winner would be in and out of drug and alcohol detoxification programs. Recently, the same woman was admitted to a Boston hospital after trying to commit suicide.

Some of the teenagers would be videotaped while engaged in sex acts. According to the counselor, many of those tapes and photographs are still circulating in South Boston. One woman the counselor knew as a friend growing up was lured at the age of fourteen into a sex and drugs morass by Bulger's gang and like many others, became the subject of pornographic pictures. The woman she described as "beautiful, absolutely beautiful" as a young girl, struggled for years with heroin addiction and shame. When the woman was in her early twenties, the counselor said her then-boyfriend was at a friend's house where they were showing pictures of some of Bulger's young conquests. The man saw his girlfriend in the photos and quickly ended their relationship. "He told her she was trash," the counselor said. The woman returned to heroin and several years later died of AIDS, according to the counselor.

For years, Bulger's myth as the Robin Hood and protector of South Boston was promoted by a handful of politicians obligated to Whitey's brother, Senate President William Bulger. Billy Bulger, in tandem with Agent John Connolly, would sell the Whitey Bulger fantasy to the public. No one was willing to stand up to the powerful William Bulger in discrediting Whitey, or, for that matter, John Connolly and the FBI. Whitey also had the full support of the local press. Former *Boston Globe* columnist Mike Barnicle often portrayed Whitey Bulger in a positive light. According to Barnicle, who referred to Bulger as "Jimmy," the name used by Whitey's friends and relatives, he "had more integrity than the FBI."

One would certainly question how much integrity it took to prey on underage girls and steal their innocence.

When Bulger claimed a share of a $14 million lottery ticket in 1991, Barnicle wrote, "Knowing him [Bulger], he probably already has handed out money to St. Augustine's." Bulger, along with Flemmi, would hand out money, but not to the church. According to sources, Bulger and Flemmi handed out cash, expensive clothes, jewelry, and free vacations to their young girlfriends. "The street became their sanctuary and here, there were guys who dressed them, gave them jewelry, sent them on cruises," a mental health counselor said. "They were fifteen years old, and they were getting on planes for the Bahamas. They went after kids they knew wouldn't or couldn't say no."

In the case of some girls, Bulger and Flemmi also bought their parents' silence with gifts, including cash and furniture. Some families were given entire living room sets. At one point in the early 1980s, Bulger even gave the family of a thirteen-year-old South Boston girl living in public housing a triple-decker home in the fashionable City Point section, sources said. The family of another girl was given a trip to Hawaii. Some families were too petrified to complain, knowing full well of Bulger and Flemmi's reputations as killers.

A woman formerly of South Boston said one particular family became a feeding ground for Flemmi. She said there were six girls in the family and Flemmi had sex with all of them. The family had an apartment full of furniture delivered to them, courtesy of Flemmi. "The parents knew what Flemmi was doing," the woman said. "He bought their silence." The youngest daughter, who the woman said was impregnated by Flemmi, is now a drug addict and a prostitute living in Quincy, Massachusetts.

Bulger and Flemmi would help themselves to anything they wanted: teenage girls from the neighborhood, money from extorting drug dealers and bookmakers. They even took the lives of their enemies. The South Boston gangsters had no concerns for any consequences. They had John Connolly and the FBI running interference for them.

–*Chapter 10*–

98 PRINCE STREET

In 1980, Howie Winter had been sent off to prison for his part in the race-fixing case, and the old headquarters, Marshall Motors, would give way to a new location. Front man George Kaufman, who had operated the old location in Somerville, now would set up shop in Boston for Bulger and Flemmi. The pair were not the least bit grieved for Winter and instead, viewed his absence as an opportunity to further their own ambitions. Situated in downtown Boston, the Lancaster Street garage would be an ideal location for extortion and loan shark payments to be dropped off. Every wise guy in the city would find the new location convenient to drop in and huddle with Bulger and Flemmi. The Massachusetts State Police would soon take notice that both LCN and non-LCN crime figures were frequenting the garage, and it was obvious that a considerable amount of illegal business was being. conducted. The Massachusetts State Police began to investigate Bulger and Flemmi.

The State Police would meet with Federal Prosecutor Jeremiah O'Sullivan to discuss obtaining authority for electronic surveillance of the garage. They believed that Bulger and Flemmi were indeed informants, and insisted that the FBI not be informed about the planned bugging. The State Police were particularly concerned about Connolly and Morris compromising their effort to investigate Bulger and Flemmi. Morris, however, was told about the State Police conducting electronic surveillance at the garage. Early on, Special Agent James Knotts had met with Morris in an honest effort to obtain information that the State Police could use in order to establish probable cause necessary to obtain a warrant to bug the Lancaster Street garage. Authority was granted to bug the garage, which proved to be extremely fruitful. The state troopers had set up shop across from the garage, in a dirty, rundown, cold-water flat. The garage would reveal meetings between Bulger, Flemmi, and the "who's who" of the Boston underworld, coming and going. After only two weeks, it soon became evident to the State Police that Bulger and Flemmi had been tipped off. Talk of criminal activity at the garage ended abruptly.

The Massachusetts State Police wrongly believed that Supervisor John Morris was the source of the tip to Bulger and Flemmi. Flemmi had actually received the initial tip about the bug from an associate, John Naimovitch, of the same State Police. Flemmi immediately discussed the bug with John Connolly, who later confirmed the garage was indeed bugged, and all criminal activity ceased. Later on, Flemmi would accuse Morris, stating that Morris received the information from Connolly. Flemmi would continue to protect Connolly at the expense of Morris.

When learning that the investigation had been blown, Colonel O'Donovan of the Massachusetts State Police began pointing the finger at the FBI. He was convinced that Bulger and Flemmi were rats, and being protected by the Feds. Newly appointed Special Agent in Charge (SAC) Sarhatt was concerned that a promising criminal investigation of Bulger and Flemmi had been compromised. There was also concern that if the mob had gotten wind that the two were rats, this fact could get them killed. This would put in question the ability of the Feds to protect its sources. Sarhatt was also aware that Bulger and Flemmi could be prosecuted for other crimes, even murder. He would now consider whether Bulger and Flemmi should be targeted for investigation, or whether to continue to use them as informants.

Sarhatt would meet with Connolly and Morris. They urged him to continue to use Bulger and Flemmi. Connolly would point out the fact that information supplied by Bulger and Flemmi would be used to establish the probable cause necessary to obtain a warrant to bug 98 Prince Street. In addition to the Anguilo brothers, other information picked up on tape would furnish evidence to establish probable cause to bug locations frequented by Illario Zannino, the number two man in the Boston Mafia, as well as other organized crime figures. Sarhatt knew that the targeting of 98 Prince Street was the highest priority of FBI headquarters in Washington, D.C. Connolly and Morris together continued to remind Sarhatt of the important roles Bulger and Flemmi played in the plan to bug 98 Prince Street, in which the Boston FBI had a large investment. They strongly urged Sarhatt that Bulger and Flemmi should not be closed as informants.

Sarhatt was not completely satisfied and decided to meet with Jeremiah O'Sullivan, now Chief of the Boston Organized Crime Strike Force. He wanted to know O'Sullivan's position in regard to Bulger and Flemmi being used as informants. He was not aware that O'Sullivan already had knowledge that the two were informants. O'Sullivan was on the same mission as Connolly: He wanted Jerry Anguilo. He too urged Sarhatt to continue using Bulger and Flemmi as informants, saying, "It is crucial that the FBI continue this source (Bulger) inasmuch as the information he is currently furnishing is crucial to a Title III application (wiretap) of LCN members in Boston." O'Sullivan stated that he "did not feel there was any improper conduct on behalf of the FBI in continuing the informant relationship with Bulger." He stated that there was "sufficient justification for continuing him, regardless of his current activities, to be able to eventually prosecute LCN members."

Sarhatt would go one step further. He decided to meet Bulger himself. He still was not convinced as to whether Bulger and Flemmi should be continued as informants, or whether the FBI had blown the State Police's Lancaster Street garage investigation. Sarhatt determined the only way to get the answers to these troubling questions would be to meet with Bulger.

On November 25, 1980, it was at this unusual meeting that Bulger conveyed his fondness for Agent Connolly based on the fact that they both grew up in South Boston and shared common roots. Bulger also expressed his "deep hatred for the Boston Mafia," a similar feeling shared by the FBI.

What Bulger failed to convey to Sarhatt was the profitable position he and Flemmi would be in, due to the vacuum caused by the destruction of the LCN. In typical fashion, Bulger would protect Connolly, lying to Sarhatt that he had not received any warning about the Lancaster Street garage investigation from the FBI. Sarhatt warned Bulger that the Massachusetts State Police knew he was an informant for the Bureau and that his life could be in danger if that information should fall into the wrong hands. Bulger was not the least bit troubled for his own safety because the thought that a vicious criminal, with a brutal reputation such as his, would be part-ners in crime with the FBI was too extraordinary and too incredible to be believed. Bulger felt certain the Boston mob would never buy into that story; instead, they would assume it to be a ploy to cause trouble between him and the LCN.

Bulger went on, telling Sarhatt that with respect to his association with Colonel O'Donovan of the State Police, he had "met him on some occa-sions, especially one in which he made disparaging and derogatory statements about the professionalism of FBI personnel," to which he had "taken great umbrage, inasmuch as his association with the FBI had been nothing but the most professional in every respect."

Bulger's snow job was obvious to Sarhatt. He was still considering whether to use Bulger and Flemmi as informants, or to target them for an investigation. Sarhatt had concerns about their usefulness, causing Connolly and Morris to come up with a bit of skullduggery. Their plan was to give Bulger and Flemmi some importance in their role for the planned bugging of 98 Prince Street. Sarhatt decided to continue Bulger and Flemmi as informants rather than targeting them for investigation. The bugging of the Anguilo headquarters would now become paramount. Jerry Anguilo was the key. He and his organization were the prime targets of the new directive out of Washington. The Boston FBI would dance with the devil to get the bold and defiant Jerry Anguilo.

Although the Boston FBI had already taken steps on the government's request for electronic surveillance of 98 Prince Street, the application had made no mention of Bulger and Flemmi as a source for the request. Connolly and Morris had to find a way to give Bulger and Flemmi credit in the bugging attempt in order to satisfy Sarhatt and keep them going as informants.

The plan was to ask Bulger and Flemmi to make a contribution: assist in the bugging of 98 Prince Street, code named "Operation Bostar." For years, Gennaro Jerry Anguilo had presided, along with his four brothers, over the day-to-day activities of the gambling enterprise from this location, known as the "Dog House" to insiders. Aside from the Anguilo brothers, there were other heavy hitters. Only insiders were allowed to participate in the lavish dinners served there. They were always prepared by Donato "Danny" Anguilo. Danny, often called "Smiley," was a bona fide tough guy who would deal with the likes of Bulger and Flemmi. Discussions about daily gambling activities were often carried out here. Disputes would be resolved, and frequently Bulger and Flemmi's names would surface.

During one particular conversation, Jerry Anguilo expressed his dismay about a $200,000 loan Bulger and Flemmi had incurred when they took over the Winter Hill mob. Although they had acknowledged their responsibility to Anguilo, they never made any attempt to repay him. Bulger and Flemmi were asked by Connolly and Morris to go to 98 Prince Street, take a close look at the office, and provide information concerning the doors, locks, and security devices.

Bulger expressed concern with this request. He had never been invited inside 98 Prince Street. Unlike Flemmi, he was Irish and considered an outsider, and did not trust the Italian Mafia. He was afraid he might be "clipped." Flemmi also expressed concern for his safety. Although he was Italian and had always been well-liked and respected, his fear was with merit. After the bugging, John Morris had Bulger and Flemmi listen to a tape on which the number two man, Illario Zannino, also known as "Larry Bione," and his right-hand man, Dominic Isabella, discussed looking for the right spot to kill the two.

Another concern expressed by Flemmi was the possibility that some of their own criminal activities would be intercepted on the bug. Morris and

Connolly assured Bulger and Flemmi that they would not be prosecuted for anything picked up on tape. With that assurance, Bulger and Flemmi decided to go for it. On January 9, 1981, the government applied for, and received, a warrant to bug 98 Prince Street. Bulger and Flemmi were two of the sources whose information was used to establish the legally required probable cause. Connolly now had his justification to continue using his star informants.

They were successful in getting some information concerning the mob headquarters; however, the credit for the success of Operation Bostar belonged to the FBI. The bugging of 98 Prince Street was a remarkable feat, done by a group of agents with great technical know-how. Although Bulger and Flemmi had provided some information, the experienced team of agents, acting on instincts, was the sole reason for the success. In a matter of only a few hours, the agents were able to plant two microphones that would transmit a scrambled signal to thwart any scanners from intercepting the bug. The scrambled signal was important in intercepting conversations without detection. After only a short time, Jerry Anguilo was intercepted voicing his suspicions that the office had been bugged. Information on mob activities discussed at 98 Prince Street was somehow finding its way to the Feds. He decided to send for Mickey Caruana in order for him to "sweep" the office for bugs. Not only was Caruana the mob's drug kingpin, answering only to Raymond Patriarca, but an electronics expert, of sorts, as well. FBI agents who were listening to Anguilo's suspicions that the office was bugged didn't have any concerns about possible detection. The sweeping device used by Caruana was no match for the sophisticated equipment used by the crack team of FBI electronics experts. The bug was never detected, revealing all the FBI expected and more. A video camera was installed in an air-conditioning unit that was sitting in a window directly across from the office. Mob members were videotaped as they entered the Anguilo headquarters.

Even though Bulger and Flemmi had stayed away from 98 Prince Street for fear some of their criminal activities would be intercepted on tape, their names would be brought up by Anguilo and Zannino. Flemmi's name would be mentioned in connection with his part in the killings of the three Bennett brothers. Another intercepted conversation contained Jerry Anguilo's assertion that Bulger and Flemmi were extorting bookmakers of weekly payments for the right to continue to operate.

Though Bulger and Flemmi had avoided 98 Prince Street, they were deeply concerned. Morris and Connolly reassured them that the tapes would not be used against them. With that, Flemmi agreed to assist with interpreting the tapes. His assistance enabled the FBI to develop a strong case against Jerry Anguilo and his associates. He also made known to the FBI the name of an individual who, if targeted, would testify against Anguilo.

On February 1, 1983, Flemmi told Connolly that Jerry Anguilo could be found at Francisco's restaurant on Monday, Tuesday, and Friday nights. Jerry and his three brothers, along with members of his crew, would partake in the lavish meals served in the private back room of the North End eatery. Flemmi himself would at times join in the feast, often in the company of a young, good-looking woman. However, his sole purpose was to "case" the establishment for the FBI in their anticipated arrest of Jerry and his brothers. Flemmi furnished a drawing that he had made of the restaurant, including the back room where Jerry Anguilo held court. Flemmi also told Connolly that Larry Zannino regularly met members of his crew on Monday and Tuesday evenings at the Bella Napoli restaurant. Flemmi again provided a diagram of the layout, indicating where Zannino sat while conducting mob business. Flemmi informed Connolly that Zannino would talk in riddles, using coded phrases that only other mobsters would comprehend. However, Zannino would speak freely while riding in Dominic Isabella's (his right-hand man) automobile. Flemmi and Bulger would be used as sources for a warrant to bug Isabella's car in August of 1983. The bug would prove to be highly successful. Conversations picked up by the bug would expose Zannino's dislike for Jerry Anguilo and include talk about Bulger and Flemmi. In truth, Jerry Anguilo was by far a better leader, and ran the enterprise extremely well. He had more talent in the overseeing of the vast gambling enterprise and did a far better job in profitability and efficiency than any corporate CEO. Zannino, on the other hand, was hot-tempered and extremely crude, especially to those associated with him.

In May of 1981, FBI Chief John Morris arranged to meet with Bulger and Flemmi at the Colonnade Hotel outside of Boston. There, Morris played for them a taped conversation that was intercepted at 98 Prince Street. In the course of the meeting, the three drank wine. Morris had so much to drink that Bulger decided to drive him home. Flemmi kept the tape. Bulger and Flemmi would begin referring to Morris as "Vino."

In September of 1983, Jerry Anguilo, along with his brothers Frank, Donato (Danny), Mike, and Jerry's son Jason, were indicted on Federal RICO charges. A team of FBI agents, including Connolly, would converge on Francisco's to make the arrests, blocking both exit and entrance doors. Stunned patrons would pause from enjoying the Italian cuisine at their tables to watch the live show that was taking place before their very eyes. The raid was like something only seen on the big screen. When Jerry was approached by Agent Connolly and told of the warrant for his arrest, he replied, "Mr. Connolly, we finally meet." Jerry had been fully aware of Connolly's successes and of the agent's determination to "get that grease-ball from Prince Street," as Jerry was often referred to by many of those in law enforcement.

As the lavish dinner for Jerry and his associates was ready to be served, he offered the agents an invitation to join in the feast; they declined with thanks. He assuredly ordered the waitress to, "Keep my food warm, I'll be right back." However, he would not return to enjoy his dinner that night. He would be held without bail until his trial. His brothers, along with his son Jason, would in time receive bail, but not until after months of battling with prosecutors during bond hearings. All of the Anguilos anticipated indictment. They had an opportunity to flee before their arrest with an endless supply of cash to ensure a comfortable life as fugitives. But they were not going to "take it on the lam." It just wasn't their style. Instead, they were determined to face the charges against them.

In the fall of 1983, Connolly and Morris had dinner with Bulger and
Flemmi at Flemmi's parents' home in South Boston. The dinner party was
a celebration of the Anguilo indictments. The rogue agents and their
prized informants toasted to their success in the Anguilo arrests, mocking
Jerry Anguilo in particular for his statements in addressing Agent Connolly
when he was being arrested. Absent from the celebration was Connolly's
supervisor, James Ring. Ring had participated in two dinner parties earlier
and was appalled at the manner in which Connolly was treating Bulger and
Flemmi. Ring felt it was inappropriate for Connolly to be treating the two
as friends or consultants rather than informants. In particular, Ring was
upset that Connolly was giving Bulger and Flemmi information, which he
deemed inappropriate. Rules set forth in the FBI manual required that all
contacts with an informant be recorded on a 209 report, yet no record of
the meetings that Ring attended was made. Ring later met with John
Morris to discuss the Attorney General's guidelines for informants to commit crimes. The guidelines required that discussions and disclosure of the
informant's identity be made. Morris told Ring that seeking authorization
was not worth the aggravation of doing so. Ring knew that Bulger and
Flemmi were committing crimes without authorization and that they
would be subject to prosecution if caught. Ring never told Bulger and
Flemmi that they had immunity, or would be protected. They would continue to provide information to John Connolly; the unholy alliance would
escalate. Bulger and Flemmi had John Connolly, and he could supply all
the protection required.

Chapter 11

THE BEANTOWN HIT MEN

When FBI Agent Paul Rico retired in 1975, he landed a position as Security Chief of World Jai Alai in Florida.

Thirty years earlier, Rico had recruited Stephen The Rifleman Flemmi into one of the most productive informants in FBI history.

Roger Wheeler owned World Jai Alai, which had facilities known as *frontons*—a hybrid of squash and lacrosse—in Florida and Connecticut, where it was legal to gamble on the jai alai matches. Wheeler was a Tulsa businessman and a self-made millionaire. Earlier, as CEO of Telex Corp., Wheeler had built a fortune on magnesium and oil.

Born in Reading, Massachusetts, and the father of five children, he decided to invest in the highly lucrative legalized gambling operation. He received his financing for the jai alai operation from the First National Bank of Boston, through the efforts of accountant John Callahan. Part of the financing deal required Wheeler to keep Paul Rico as head of security, and Callahan as president of Wheeler World Jai Alai. Callahan was responsible for Rico acquiring the position. He was from Winchester, Massachusetts, and closely associated with Brian Halloran of the Winter Hill Gang, with strong ties to Bulger and Flemmi and hit man John Martorano. Wheeler was not aware of former Agent Paul Rico's association with Steve Flemmi. He began suspecting that Callahan was skimming money from World Jai Alai for the Winter Hill gangsters. Under the watchful eyes of former Agent Paul Rico, millions of dollars were being skimmed. Callahan had created a scheme to siphon money from the company, funneling the proceeds into the hands of Bulger and Flemmi.

Wheeler decided to fire Callahan, along with his financial officers, and replace them with his own people. He would order an audit in order to determine how much Callahan and the Winter Hill gangsters had actually stolen from his company. An audit would have dreadful consequences for Callahan. He had been living the high life, often in the company of gangster and drug dealer Brian Halloran. The showy Callahan would often be found in the Boston nightlife scene, "Putting on the Ritz." A long stretch in prison would be a likely scenario for the flamboyant accountant. He needed to take action before the audit could expose the enormity of the scam orchestrated by him and the Winter Hill gangsters.

His plan was to have his close associate, Brian Halloran, a local tough guy who was dealing drugs for Bulger, whack Roger Wheeler before the paper trail could be discovered and lead to fraud charges against him. In early 1981, the plan to kill Wheeler was discussed at a meeting at Callahan's ocean front luxury apartment. Bulger and Flemmi listened as Callahan put forth his plan to murder Wheeler. He assumed his drinking partner Halloran would be willing to kill Wheeler.

Bulger thought otherwise. He had little use for a drug-dealing stumble-bum who was using too much of his own product. Bulger knew that Halloran was out of his league. Killing Roger Wheeler required a professional. Bulger and Flemmi would contact their favorite hit man, John Martorano. Although Martorano was a fugitive, fleeing to Florida to avoid arrest for his role in the race-fixing case, he could still be called upon to kill for the two gangsters.

However, Bulger had reservations about killing a legitimate businessman, and Roger Wheeler was certainly a legit guy. Bulger had killed before, but a legitimate guy was something he had avoided in the past. Yet, there was no choice. The gangsters had the FBI running interference for them. There was too much at stake. Roger Wheeler had to go. Bulger and Flemmi would make arrangements for the Wheeler murder by telephone to John Martorano in Florida. Roger Wheeler would have a rendezvous with death.

In exchange for the slaying, Martorano would receive a contract to run a lucrative parking lot concession at World Jai Alai in Miami. Bulger and Flemmi would gather the guns needed, then send the weapons for the Wheeler killing on a bus bound for Oklahoma. Martorano and Joseph McDonald flew from Florida to Oklahoma City where they rented a vehicle, and then the Beantown hit men proceeded on to Tulsa.

McDonald was more than willing to assist Martorano in the murder. Early on, Martorano had killed Richard Castucci after learning that he had informed on McDonald's location while he was a fugitive. The pair set up their base at the Trade Winds West Motel. They began scouting the best place to kill Wheeler. His home was too risky, and his corporate office at Telex had a security camera.

Weeks before the murder, Martorano had met with John Callahan in Miami. During the meeting, according to Martorano, Callahan slipped him a note detailing a description of Wheeler and his work habits. Callahan claimed it had been written by ex-FBI Agent Paul Rico. The Beantown hit men decided to set up Wheeler at the Southern Hills Country Club, where they had spotted his Cadillac.

On May 27, 1981, upon completing a round of golf with friends, Roger Wheeler headed to his vehicle. Martorano and McDonald had been painstakingly waiting for Wheeler to exit. The professional killers were in no hurry; they knew it was only a matter of time before the murder contract would be fulfilled. As far as "hits" went, this was an easy one. Not at all similar to others during the Irish Gang War where the intended victim or victims were dangerous criminals. Wheeler was a "legitimate sucker," a "square," an easy target.

The men observed Wheeler approaching his vehicle; they had parked close by. Martorano sprang into action. As Wheeler opened his car door and started to slide in, he was stopped by a beefy, bearded man in sunglasses, who jerked the door from Wheeler's hand. Though Wheeler raised his left arm in defense, Martorano fired a single shot from a .38 caliber revolver, hitting Wheeler between the eyes. He never had a chance to reach for a gun kept under the seat. Four live cartridges were left inside and around Wheeler's car by Martorano, perhaps a signature of his trade. No one reported seeing the murderous act, but some heard a firecracker sound. It was over for Roger Wheeler. The brown car containing the Beantown hit men sped in the direction of a back gate.

Tulsa Homicide Detective Michael Huff was the first to arrive at the Wheeler murder scene. It didn't take long for Huff to discover that John Callahan and the Bulger Gang were responsible for the killing. The Massachusetts State Police had given him a great deal of information that led Huff to that conclusion. He didn't need to go any further than Bulger and crew, along with John Callahan.

However, Huff could not get any help from the Boston FBI. The office in Boston was successful in keeping agents from other agencies and local law enforcement officials from speaking to Bulger and Flemmi. The Bureau in Oklahoma City was interested in exploring Callahan's relationship with Brian Halloran; the two were often seen socializing. The FBI's Boston Organized Crime Squad opened an investigation to support Oklahoma City's effort to solve the Wheeler murder. At John Morris' request, Connolly interviewed Callahan as part of that investigation. The Boston investigation was then quickly closed, which came as no surprise.

The FBI was receiving, but not investigating, reports concerning criminal activities in which Bulger and Flemmi were engaged. The Bureau was advised that bookmakers were being extorted to pay the two gangsters for the right to operate, and that the two were involved in cocaine distribution with an individual named Brian Halloran in South Boston.

One particular report that John Morris received was information that Bulger was getting a piece of the cocaine action in Southie. Bulger, who was thought to be anti-drug and a protector of his beloved South Boston, was smack-dab in the middle of all drug dealings. Without Bulger's blessing, no drugs were sold in the neighborhood.

Not only was Halloran handling cocaine distribution for the two, but he was also responsible for ripping off any drug dealers not connected to Bulger. Anyone dealing drugs had to give Bulger and Flemmi a piece of the action. Morris and Connolly would simply file the reports, but no action was taken. Bulger would continue to promote himself as the Robin Hood of South Boston, and an anti-drug gangster.

After the murder of Roger Wheeler, Brian Halloran became aware that he could have a serious problem. He knew that Bulger and Flemmi were responsible for the Wheeler murder through his association with John Callahan. Although Callahan still regarded Halloran as a trusted associate, Bulger had little regard for the drug addict. Halloran continued his drug dealing and extortion, even though he did so without Bulger's authorization. His continuing drug use was out of control, something the Winter Hill gangsters had taken notice of. Now Halloran was on the outs; no longer was he to be trusted, especially when it came to having knowledge of the Wheeler murder.

Halloran's problems would continue to escalate. He and a local drug dealer, George Pappas, were having a serious dispute over a drug deal at a Chinese restaurant in Boston. Prior to Pappas' arrival, Jack Salemme had been sitting with Halloran having an after-hours cocktail. Jack was the brother of Cadillac Frank Salemme, who was still behind bars for the Fitzgerald bombing, compliments of Steve Flemmi and Agents Dennis Condon and John Connolly. Halloran informed Jack Salemme that he was waiting for Pappas and that the two were having a problem over a drug dispute.

After hearing the drunken Halloran's side of the story, Jack wisely decided he didn't want to be any part of the problem and left before Pappas arrived. The restaurant was a favorite with party goers. Many locals would be seen drinking their favorite mix served in teacups long after the bars had been closed. Shortly after Jack Salemme exited the restaurant, George Pappas arrived and joined Halloran, who was by then highly intoxicated. A heated argument quickly ensued between the two men. Neither was willing to back down and tempers began to escalate. Suddenly, without any warning, Halloran pulled a gun and fired a shot across the table, killing George Pappas. Halloran quickly exited the restaurant as patrons looked on in disbelief. The killing of Pappas would compound Halloran's problems. He now had a murder charge to contend with, along with Bulger's distrust of him.

Homicide detectives arrived at the restaurant. Glasses that had been used by Halloran, Pappas, and earlier, Jack Salemme, were taken and fingerprinted. Salemme would now be a suspect in the killing along with Halloran. The Boston mob had reason to fear that Halloran would implicate Salemme, if not as an accessory, quite possibly as the actual triggerman. The mob's concern that Halloran would shift the blame for the murder of Pappas onto Salemme was with merit. They didn't want one of their soldiers, especially the brother of a well-respected stand-up guy, involved in the shooting with Halloran. Halloran wasn't one of them; he was Irish, and involved with drug dealing.

After receiving a severe tongue-lashing for his association with the likes of Halloran, and for being in the wrong place at the wrong time, the mob would begin to protect Salemme. They owed that much to his brother Cadillac Frank. Jack Salemme was ordered to stay low, until the problem could be taken care of. Halloran also stayed low, but only for a brief period of time.

In late 1981, he began to make arrangements for bail, and to surrender to local authorities. Halloran continued with his cocaine use while facing the murder charge. But he was on the outs with Bulger and the local Mafia. He was a problem for everyone. Bulger quickly decided on a strategy. The cunning gangster put out word that the mob wanted Halloran killed to prevent him from being a witness against Jack Salemme, while putting the entire blame for the murder on Salemme. Bulger would make certain that Connolly's 209 reports reflected this information.

It was a perfect situation for Bulger. Send the local cops looking to someone else, not at the real killer. The deception would have Bulger and Flemmi in a position to kill Halloran and not be suspects. The Boston mob would take the heat for the murder. But Brian Halloran, who had learned to survive the mean streets of Boston by getting in the first blow, as was the case with Pappas, also had a plan. Give the FBI information on Callahan, Bulger, and Flemmi's participation in the skimming from World Jai Alai, and the murder of Roger Wheeler. In exchange for the information, Halloran would seek the FBI's help in getting a reduced sentence for the Pappas murder.

In January 1982, Halloran began cooperating with the FBI in Boston. Special Agents Leo Brunnick and Gerald Montanari, two members of the Boston FBI's Labor and Racketeering Squad, were assigned to work with Halloran. Halloran began "spilling the beans." He gave the two agents details concerning the skimming from World Jai Alai and information on Bulger and Flemmi's role in the Wheeler murder. Halloran also revealed that former Agent Paul Rico, who was head of security at the company, was deeply involved with the events, including the Wheeler murder. Brunnick consulted with Supervisor John Morris and asked him for his take on Halloran's claim, and to get his assessment of Halloran's reliability as a potential witness. Morris realized that Halloran posed a serious problem for him and John Connolly. They had gone out on a limb for Bulger and Flemmi. Now, Halloran's revelations could expose their shocking alliance with the gangsters.

Morris was still relishing the successful bugging of Jerry Anguilo's 98 Prince Street mob headquarters in which he had played a key role. He was enjoying a romantic affair with Debbie Noseworthy, a secretary who worked in his Organized Crime Unit. Morris realized that Halloran's allegations threatened Bulger and Flemmi's future as FBI informants. It was the Bureau's policy to close any sources that it was investigating. Morris and Connolly did not want to lose their prize sources that were important to their war on the Mafia, and to their own status and future careers in the Bureau.

Morris and Connolly had selfish reasons for protecting their two prize rats. Morris advised Special Agent Brunnick that Halloran's claim was bogus and inaccurate, that Halloran was an unsavory character, that no jury would believe the ravings of a drug-dealing maggot. A few agents sided with Halloran and were not pleased with the decision not to utilize his allegations concerning Bulger and Flemmi. However, they were no match for Connolly's skullduggery in protecting Bulger and Flemmi.

Halloran was hung out to dry, even though Agent Fitzpatrick knew that not allowing Halloran into the Witness Protection Program could be fatal. Fitzpatrick, the Assistant Special Agent in Charge of the Boston office, was concerned that word of Halloran's cooperation could get him killed. Yet, his plea fell on deaf ears. Halloran was shown the door. In early May of 1982, the FBI denied Halloran's request to be placed in the Witness Protection Program and told him that his relationship with the FBI was terminated. Although the FBI in Oklahoma City had expressed interest in Halloran, no information was given to the Oklahoma City Bureau. Halloran's revelations would be an in-house matter, known only to a few in the Boston FBI office. Halloran had to somehow survive on his own.

Morris told Connolly that Halloran had been talking with FBI Agents Brunnick and Montanari, and of the information he was providing about Bulger and Flemmi. Morris expected that Connolly would tell Bulger and Flemmi about Halloran's charges. He knew that doing so would endanger Halloran. Connolly did exactly what Morris assumed; he told Bulger and Flemmi about Halloran's cooperation and claims. The two agents, who had pledged to serve and protect, would take a page from the mobsters—dead men make poor witnesses. Several weeks after telling the FBI that Bulger and Flemmi were involved in the Wheeler murder, Halloran would suffer the same fate as Wheeler. On May 11, 1982, Halloran ran into Michael J. Donahue at the former Topside Café on Northern Avenue in South Boston. Donahue, a thirty-two-year-old truck driver from South Boston, and a neighbor of Halloran, offered him a ride home. Before Donahue could drive out of the parking lot, several gunmen, including Bulger, opened fire. Brian Halloran would be slain, along with the innocent Michael Donahue. Donahue was not a gangster, but a hard-working family man who had the misfortune of offering his neighbor a ride. The brutal slayings reflected the personalities of individuals who had no concerns for any consequences.

Years later, in a series of interviews with *The Boston Herald* and the CBS news program *60 Minutes*, Edward J. "Eddie Mack" McKenzie, Jr. detailed his decade of work for Bulger as an enforcer and cocaine dealer in the 1980s. According to McKenzie, the murders of Halloran and Donahue in front of a South Boston bar in broad daylight were not that particularly brazen. Bulger said the attack was really not that risky. "Big Brother was watching our back on that," Bulger reportedly said. McKenzie said he didn't understand at first. "What do you mean by 'Big Brother'?" he asked. "Connolly, the FBI," Bulger replied. "We had them with binoculars, we had walkie-talkies. He [Connolly] gives us two clicks, we whack 'em on the spot, all clear. One click, that's it, don't move. Don't move 'til you get the two clicks." McKenzie's account of his conversation with Bulger bolstered *The Boston Herald* report that Steve Flemmi told at least two other reputed gangsters that Connolly was in the area when Halloran and Donahue were gunned down. The associates Flemmi told came away from the conversations with the impression that because he was in the area, Connolly likely knew of the plan to kill Halloran and may have been serving as either "backup" or as a lookout, sources told the newspaper.

Later on, long-hidden FBI reports obtained by *The Herald* revealed that three eyewitnesses saw a dark sedan on Northern Avenue opposite the Topside before, during, and after the shooting. Each witness described a man in business attire alone in the sedan. One witness, a since-deceased Newton, Massachusetts, police sergeant, told the FBI she saw the unidentified man peering at the Topside Café through binoculars approximately thirty minutes before Halloran and his friend, Donahue, were cut down in a hail of gunfire just after leaving the establishment. McKenzie had no doubt Connolly was involved. "Connolly was the lookout," he said. "I was told right to my face that he [Connolly] was the lookout for the Halloran and Donahue murders."

Kevin Weeks served as a lookout while Halloran and Donahue were shot, and disposed of the weapons used in the shooting. A local detective at the murder scene claimed that Halloran identified Jimmy Flynn as one of the shooters before he died. It was a ploy to focus attention away from Bulger and Flemmi. Although Flynn was a suspect, Supervisor John Morris believed that Bulger and Flemmi were responsible. Morris did not hesitate to take advantage of the information he supplied to Connolly concerning Halloran's claim. He recalled that Connolly once told him that Bulger and Flemmi really liked him, and "if he ever needed anything, he should let them know."

After the Halloran murder, Supervisor Morris was sent to Glencoe, Georgia, for special training. Morris would need something from the two gangsters. He had begun having a serious affair with his secretary, Deborah Noseworthy, even though still married. Morris decided it would be a perfect opportunity for Noseworthy to visit him. However, Morris lacked the funds needed to purchase her plane ticket. Remembering Connolly's message from Bulger and Flemmi, "if he ever needed anything . . . ," Morris would allow Connolly and the gangsters to corrupt him. He would come cheap—$1,000. Morris had to know that accepting the money was wrong, but rationalized that it was all part of the effort to destroy the LCN. As far as the Halloran murder, it would be accepted as collateral damage. Morris proceeded to ask Connolly to solicit the funds necessary from the two gangsters to buy Noseworthy's plane ticket. Connolly delivered $1,000 in cash to a surprised Noseworthy, telling her it had come from Morris and that he had saved the money and wanted her to have it.

Two years later, Charlestown bank robber Jimmy Flynn was indicted by the Suffolk County District Attorney's Office in Boston for the Halloran and Donahue murders. Flynn's arrest was based solely on the questionable statement made by Halloran before he died. However, Morris knew that Connolly had told Bulger and Flemmi of Halloran's efforts to cooperate with the FBI. He also knew this information would be relevant to any investigation of the Halloran murder, yet he never came forward with the facts. Instead, he was willing to have Flynn, an innocent man, found guilty of the murders. Fortunately, Flynn would be acquitted of the false charges.

John Morris had allowed himself to be corrupted. He had been bought and paid for by Whitey Bulger and Steve Flemmi. During the day, Morris would portray himself as the good agent, yet by night, he would socialize with the ruthless gangsters. He was morally weak, and was on the verge of losing his marriage and his career in the FBI.

The Halloran murder was becoming a problem for the Boston Bureau, urging a meeting at FBI headquarters in Washington, D.C. The Feds had to come to grips with Bulger and Flemmi as useful informants or targets in the Wheeler and Halloran killings. Representatives agreed to coordinate the Wheeler and Halloran murders. Also in agreement were O'Sullivan, the Organized Crime Force Chief in Boston, and the U.S. Attorney in Oklahoma City. A decision was made to continue Bulger and Flemmi as informants, unless information was uncovered implicating them in the murders. Never were the Attorney General's guidelines governing the use of informants discussed. No mention was made as to whether to inform local law enforcement agencies in Boston or Oklahoma, which were also conducting an investigation of Halloran's claim that Bulger and Flemmi were responsible for the Wheeler murder.

Clearly, the Boston office of the FBI was allowed to control the flow of information, and the decisions to be made concerning its prize informants. Scheduled meetings between Oklahoma authorities and the Boston FBI were called off.

Special Agent Gerald Montanari continued to investigate whether Bulger and Flemmi were involved in the Wheeler murder. The files of his investigation were being reviewed by Connolly. Montanari suspected that Connolly was passing on information from his investigation to Bulger and Flemmi. Montanari took his complaint to Robert Fitzpatrick, who locked the files in his own office. Not only was Fitzpatrick concerned that Connolly could not be trusted, he did not want anyone outside the Boston office to have access to Bulger and Flemmi. When the Oklahoma FBI sought authority to question Bulger and Flemmi, Fitzpatrick denied their request. He wanted to prevent information concerning the two informants from reaching other agencies. The agents from Oklahoma City were completely frustrated by Fitzpatrick's decision preventing the two suspects from being interviewed. The FBI in Boston also took measures to make it almost impossible for others to review or evaluate reports containing Halloran's accusations relating to Bulger and Flemmi. This was done by not properly indexing reports containing allegations with reference to their names.

Tulsa Homicide Detective Mike Huff was in charge of the Wheeler murder investigation. Through information he received from the Massachusetts State Police, Huff immediately suspected that John Callahan, along with members of the Winter Hill Gang, was involved. Callahan was also getting attention from the Connecticut State Police long before the Wheeler murder. They began an audit of World Jai Alai and were now focusing on Callahan as a possible link to the murder.

Detective Huff and the Tulsa FBI were becoming more and more interested in Callahan. A reluctant John Morris agreed to question Callahan at the request of the Tulsa Bureau. Morris' choice to seek out information from Callahan was his sidekick, John Connolly. Morris knew that Connolly had a great deal of skullduggery and would be far more likely to thwart the possibility of any outside investigation. This Connolly did successfully, defending Bulger and Flemmi as non-participants with Callahan. Bulger and Flemmi began to question whether Callahan could stand up to the pressure heading his way. The audit of World Jai Alai would most certainly reveal his criminal involvement, and he could implicate them in the Wheeler murder. As far as Bulger and Flemmi were concerned, there was no choice.

On August 4, 1982, the bullet-ridden body of John Callahan was found stuffed in the trunk of his Cadillac at the Miami International Airport. He had been dead for several weeks. Bulger and Flemmi had called upon the loyal gangster John Martorano to handle the Callahan problem.

Homicide Detective Mike Huff had begun to zero in on the World Jai Alai accountant. He knew that Callahan was the go-between in the

Wheeler murder. However, the gangsters had beaten him to the punch. The straight-shooting middle-American would soon learn the depths that the G-Men and gangsters would go to against anyone who could pose a problem to their unholy alliance. The handful of corrupt agents, led by John Connolly, would hang tough against any investigator.

Although still legally married to Jeannette McLaughlin, and living with Marion Hussey, his common-law wife, Steve Flemmi had an insatiable appetite for seducing young girls.

Debra Davis was a naive seventeen-year-old glamour girl who in 1972 would have the misfortune of meeting Steve Flemmi while working behind the counter at a suburban jewelry store. The shapely, long-legged blonde would be no match for the streetwise Flemmi. She would be easily taken in by the smooth-talking con man. Flemmi began to shower her with lavish gifts. When Steve The Rifleman Flemmi took aim, whatever he wanted, he would get. Nothing was off-limits to the bold gangster, not the taking of life, money, or a young girl's innocence.

After two years of dating, the two began living together in Brookline and Randolph. Debra was living in the lap of luxury, and the two became an item. True to form, Steve Flemmi wasn't satisfied with Debra Davis— no, he wanted more. He began sexually molesting Debra's young sister, Michelle, at the tender age of thirteen. This devil knew no parameters; nothing was sacred to him.

After seven years, the itch began to set in with Debra. The once naive girl had grown up and wanted out of the relationship. No longer was she infatuated with the older mobster who was already married, and had a common-law wife as well. After returning from a family vacation in Mexico, she told friends and family members that she intended to leave Flemmi. Debra had given her heart to someone new.

Flemmi was not going to be dumped for another man. He had always had his way, either as an FBI informant or as a ruthless killer. He and Bulger decided on a plan to lure Debra Davis to the home of Flemmi's mother. On September 17, 1981, the two gangsters would strangle the life out of the sweet young beauty. Debra Davis was twenty-six years old when her mother filed a missing persons report with local authorities. Olga Davis was interviewed on numerous occasions by FBI agents about Flemmi's relationship with her daughter. "It felt for a long time that our family was being shoved aside," said Robert Davis, Debra's brother. Whenever FBI agents questioned the family about Debra's disappearance, they seemed more interested in getting information about Flemmi or his cohorts than in finding her body. The agents were most likely doing all they could to fend off any investigation of Flemmi.

Although a prime suspect in Debra's disappearance, Flemmi continued to console the Davis family while sexually molesting the younger sister, Michelle. "We kept peace with him, because I feared what could happen to my other children and grandchildren," Olga Davis said. The body of Debra Davis would be buried by Flemmi and Bulger, with the assistance of gang member Kevin Weeks, along the shore of the Neponset River in Quincy, Massachusetts. Her body would be buried three feet away from Thomas King, who early on had gotten the best of Bulger in a barroom brawl. However, it would not be the final resting place for either of the two. Steve Flemmi would continue as an FBI informant.

Arthur "Bucky" Barrett was a genius at defeating burglar alarms, and an expert safecracker. If you needed to bypass an alarm, you would call on Barrett. Bucky was more than a consultant, he was a hands-on person who would personally participate in the heist. Such was the case with his involvement with Jerry Quimette's crime organization based in Cranston, Rhode Island. Quimette and his crew, with the assistance of Barrett, pulled off one of the most daring burglaries in Rhode Island history.

For his part in the score, Barrett had become the focus of Vincent Vespia, the former police chief in South Kingston, Rhode Island. When Vespia was called to testify in the Rhode Island case, he described Barrett as "one of the best in New England." Bucky had a colorful career. He was convicted of breaking into the famous Parker House Hotel in Boston and rifling safety deposit boxes. He was also responsible for the theft of precious stamps from Regis College in Weston, Massachusetts.

But Bucky was even more famous for orchestrating a daring burglary in a 1980 Memorial Day weekend robbery, where $1.5 million in cash and jewelry was stolen from Depositors Trust in Medford, Massachusetts. He and five others, including three policemen, rifled 714 safety deposit boxes in the bank. Less than a week after the heist, Bulger and Flemmi were seen threatening Barrett at the Lancaster Street garage for a share of the burglary. Bulger had received information that Barrett had duffel bags full of precious stones taken from the robbery. Barrett agreed to placate the two gangsters with a "piece of the action." But Bulger wasn't satisfied with only a piece of the score—he wanted it all. He informed Agent Connolly that Barrett had pulled off the daring bank heist, hoping to get Barrett caught in a vise. One way or another, Bucky Barrett was going to pay.

Connolly and John Morris, acting as Bulger's errand boys rather than sworn agents, wasted no time in seeking out Barrett. He would be given an ultimatum—rat on the participants in the robbery, accept the government's protection, enrolling in the Witness Protection Program, or deal with Bulger. Barrett was told that it was no secret that he had masterminded the heist, and that Bulger was going to come at him for a larger piece of the action, and in all probability, all of it.

Barrett turned down the offer from Connolly and Morris—he was a stand-up guy. On July 26, 1983, Barrett left his home on Oceanview in Squantum and went to a bar he co-owned in Boston. Later that day, he was lured to East Third Street in South Boston, home of a longtime Bulger associate. Here, Barrett was confronted by Kevin Weeks, Bulger, and Flemmi. In an effort to get Barrett to turn over his share of the heist, Bulger began torturing the helpless Barrett. While grasping a set of pliers, Bulger began to extract teeth from the confined Barrett. The extraction of teeth would not only inflict pain on the victim, but would make it impossible to identify the remains through dental records. Bulger and Flemmi would often resort to cutting off the fingertips of their victims as well, making it impossible to check fingerprints. Barrett had no choice but to give in to the relentless torture by Bulger. He phoned his wife, instructing her to take the children and leave their home. Barrett's share would then be retrieved from the home by the gang. The pitiless Bulger showed no mercy to Bucky. Instead of being satisfied with Barrett's share, he promptly murdered him. Barrett's body would be buried in the cellar of the Third Street home by the group. He was forty-six. It would not, however, be the final resting place for Arthur Bucky Barrett.

The bugging of the Lancaster Street garage and the constant harassment by the State Police forced Bulger and Flemmi to find a new location. They had been in the process of searching out a new headquarters needed to conduct their illegal businesses. Although the garage was ideally located in Boston's North End, it had brought far too much heat. The comings and goings throughout the day by various organized crime figures had not gone unnoticed by law enforcement officials. Also, Bulger's hatred of the Italian wise guys caused him to yearn for his home turf, South Boston. As far as he was concerned, Southie was a better fit. Bulger knew every alley and side street, and he knew most of the faces there. He felt more insulated and protected in the community where he had lived his entire life. These set of circumstances would not be good for Stephen and Julie Rakes.

In late 1983, Stephen Rakes, more commonly known as "Stippo," came across an abandoned service station on Old Colony Avenue in South Boston. Stippo knew immediately that the location was perfect for a package liquor store. He and his wife Julie wasted no time; they acquired the property, along with a liquor license. The couple were on their way to fulfilling their lifetime dream—a business of their own. Julie had two daughters and this new source of income, which she and her husband were counting on, would secure their future.

With the task of renovating the service station into a liquor mart completed, the couple was ready for the grand opening in time for the holidays. Friends and family had sent flowers and cards for the occasion. However, Bulger and Flemmi had taken note of the newly renovated store. The two jackals kept circling the property; they were impressed with Stippo's liquor mart.

The new location could serve as a front for Bulger and Flemmi to laun-
der proceeds from drugs and as a drop-off for loan shark payments. The
liquor mart would be a perfect setup, a legitimate business, something
Bulger and Flemmi had never had, but desperately needed. Julie and
Stephen Rakes would be given an offer they could not refuse. The two
gangsters, along with Bulger's sidekick and surrogate son, Kevin Weeks,
would pay a visit to Stippo with an offer to purchase the liquor mart.

Never did the two gangsters take into account that the Rakes had no
intention of selling. They had taken note of the Rakes' schedule, and knew
that Stippo would be at home baby-sitting. As the trio entered the Rakes'
home, Bulger got right to the point, telling Stippo he had no right to open the
liquor mart without first clearing it with him. Stippo had shown no respect for
Bulger, nor to the competition, who were also connected to Bulger.

"I have a way out for the disrespect you did to me. I'm going to buy you
out," Bulger said.

"We don't want to sell it," replied Rakes.

"How much did you put into the store?" Bulger asked, ignoring Rakes'
statement.

"Sixty seven thousand dollars, but it's not for sale," Rakes replied.

An infuriated Bulger shot back, "You don't understand, do you? You
have no choice—I could kill you, and then take the store."

Flemmi left the home and quickly returned with a brown paper bag containing $67,000. The two gangsters then handed Stephen Rakes the bag of
money. Stephen Rakes was reluctant to take the money when his two
daughters entered the kitchen. They had been awakened by the conversation of the gangsters. Flemmi then sat down at the kitchen table, pulled
one of Rakes' blonde-haired daughters onto his lap, and set a gun on the
table in front of her. The curious toddler picked up the gun and playfully
sucked on the handle.

"It would be a shame not to see your children grow up," Bulger said. The
Rakes could surrender their store, or turn their children into orphans. One
way or another Whitey and his jackals were going to be "merchants."

A horrified Stephen Rakes called his wife at the store and told her to pack up all their belongings and come home. Just two weeks after the store opened, the hapless owners were forced at gunpoint to turn it over to Bulger and Flemmi for $67,000 stuffed inside a brown paper bag. The following day, Kevin Weeks was at the store, ringing up liquor sales behind the counter, even though no actual passing of papers had occurred. Soon the front sign was changed from STIPPO'S to the SOUTH BOSTON LIQUOR MART, and a large green shamrock was painted on the storefront.

There is extortion, the type that involves taking possessions from drug dealers, safecrackers, and bookmakers. This was different. The Rakes were legitimate folks who would be so emotionally scarred that time would not heal their wounds. It would destroy a marriage and a family. Their hopes and dreams for a better life for them and their children had been taken away from them at gunpoint by Bulger and Flemmi, with the help of a rogue agent. The extortion succeeded; Stephen and Julie Rakes reluctantly sold their liquor mart. On May 11, 1984, the ownership of the liquor store was transferred to Kevin Weeks. Five days later, two new names were added to the ownership papers, those of Bulger and Flemmi's mother, Mary. The call was made for Julie Rakes to talk to her Uncle Joseph Lundbohm, a Boston police detective, for help. Lundbohm knew that Bulger and Flemmi were reputed to be dangerous members of organized crime. He felt that the FBI would be the most appropriate law enforcement agency to investigate the ongoing extortion. He had no idea that Bulger and Flemmi were FBI informants, or that Connolly was their handler. Lundbohm knew that he was involved in investigating organized crime and decided to meet with Connolly in an effort to prompt an FBI investigation.

Although Lundbohm knew that John Connolly had grown up in Southie, he was not aware of Connolly's allegiance to Bulger. Lundbohm was warmly received by Connolly. He related to the rogue agent all the details his niece and her husband encountered with the extortion. Upon hearing all the facts, Connolly knew he had a problem. It was National Melotone Vending all over again: Bulger and Flemmi using threats of violence to have their way.

Connolly had successfully protected the pair then, stopping any investigation dead in its tracks. He would now use the same approach by intimidating the victims by informing them of the danger involved. He explained that they would be asked to wear a body wire and participate in the Witness Protection Program and relocate. Connolly would use the same song and dance routine that had been successful in the past. He never had any concerns that the Rakes were a hard-working young couple, struggling to get a small share of the American dream.

Although Connolly had received reliable information from Detective Lundbohm concerning the extortion by Bulger and Flemmi, he took no action. He made no report, and did not submit any of the information to the Supervisor of the Organized Crime Squad, James Ring. Although Connolly never made it a point to interview the Rakes or conduct any type of investigation, he didn't hesitate to tell Whitey Bulger about his meeting with Detective Lundbohm.

Within only a few days of the meeting between Connolly and Lundbohm, Bulger and Flemmi spotted Stephen Rakes while crusing the streets of South Boston. Bulger, who was behind the wheel, pulled the vehicle alongside the terrified Rakes. The shaken Stephen Rakes was given a stern message to "back off." Rakes reported his encounter with Bulger and Flemmi to Detective Lundbohm, who realized that the message to back off indicated that Bulger had been tipped off to his meeting with Connolly. He smelled a rat, and the rat was Whitey Bulger. The Rakes had no choice but to surrender to Bulger's threat.

Years later, on December 8, 1989, Weeks and Flemmi sold out to Bulger for $40,000, giving him sole rights to the property. The same day Bulger purchased the property, he sold it for ten times what he paid for it, to the Shamrock Realty Trust. The trustees of the trust, which financed the $400,000 purchase by taking a mortgage from Bulger, were Bulger allies Kevin O'Neil and Gordon McIntyre. Payments of $4,672.90 were made monthly, using deposit slips left by Bulger. Soon the FBI was patronizing

Bulger's store. The large discounts the Feds received made the trip from downtown Boston to the South Boston liquor mart worthwhile.

A 1990 raid on the liquor mart by the Drug Enforcement Administration, the Suffolk County Organized Crime Squad, and the IRS uncovered a receipt indicating liquor was purchased by Agent Dick Baker, a friend of John Connolly, a Christmas party organizer.

Later, Connolly did not deny the FBI bought liquor at the store, but said "the piece of paper with his name on it was planted by Detective Frank Dewan during the raid." Connolly had a hatred for Dewan, who tried unsuccessfully to investigate his friend Bulger on a host of criminal activities in South Boston. Dewan, an honest cop who refused to fall in line, would receive his justice.

Brian Halloran was not the only informant Connolly allegedly identified for his two prize rats. Through disclosures received from other agents, Connolly was able to keep Bulger and Flemmi abreast of several other informants.

On the surface, Whitey Bulger was leading two lives, one with Teresa Stanley, the other with Catherine Greig. Neither woman knew that Bulger was unfaithful to her. It wasn't only the women Bulger would betray, but his beloved South Boston as well.

Bulger had total control of the drug trade in Southie. No drugs were sold without first clearing it with Whitey, from nickel bags to huge shipments of cocaine. He extorted a piece of every drug deal in the community. Through his brother, Senate President William Bulger, and some of Billy's whiskey-nosed cronies, Whitey was portrayed as a protector of Southie, and anti-drugs. It would take years before Bulger's involvement in the drug trade would be exposed; for many it would be too late. Teenage addicts were dying, while addicted young girls would turn to prostitution. Families would be torn apart by addicted mothers and fathers.

Through it all, never were the FBI's guidelines taken into account. Bulger's key role in the drug trade was a clear violation of the rules governing the use of informants. Connolly and Morris could have cared less about the guidelines; they wanted the information on the mob that Bulger was clearly not delivering.

However, the same mob that the FBI was so intent on delivering at all costs, including turning a blind eye to murder, extortion, and drug dealing, refused to get into the big money drug trade. Although Jerry Anguilo had numerous offers to enter into the fast-and-easy money-making drug trade, to his credit he withstood all attempts to influence his anti-drug position. He was content to make his money the old-fashioned way. The way the old-time men of honor had done before him. Jerry made certain that those seeking to borrow large sums of money from him did not use it to finance drug deals. He kept a watchful eye on those associated with him, making certain they were not involved in the drug trade. Not only was Bulger falsely portrayed as an anti-drug gangster, but an IRA sympathizer as well. This myth would also be shattered.

In mid-October of 1984, John McIntyre began cooperating with Detective Richard Bergeron of the Quincy Police Department. McIntyre, who had been arrested on an unrelated charge, began spinning a tale to a mesmerized Bergeron. McIntyre revealed that he was the engineer of a fishing trawler named the *Valhalla*. The *Valhalla* was secretly owned by a big-time drug dealer, Joseph Murray. He also revealed to the astonished detective that the ship had been used in an attempt to deliver guns and ammunition from Gloucester, Massachusetts, to the Irish Republican Army in Ireland. He informed Bergeron that Murray was closely connected to Whitey Bulger, and that Bulger, through his associates Kevin Weeks and Patrick Nee, was involved in the *Valhalla* arms shipment. Steve Flemmi was also mentioned as being involved.

Nee's role was to travel to Ireland and meet the shipment of arms and weapons. But the *Valhalla* would never make it to Ireland. It had been seized at sea, along with the cache of weapons, off the Irish coast. Bulger's history of playing both sides was clearly evident. After receiving payment for the guns, Bulger would betray the IRA, just as he had his beloved Southie. Many believed he was the informant responsible for the capture of the *Valhalla*. McIntyre was willing to tell it all, but was fearful of the people involved.

Detective Bergeron realized he had a bombshell. He needed help; he needed the heavy hitters. Bergeron arranged for agents of the DEA and the United States Customs Service to participate in the debriefing of McIntyre. He also informed FBI Special Agent Roderick Kennedy of McIntyre's charges against Bulger.

Kennedy knew that Bulger and Flemmi were Connolly's informants. They belonged to him. Connolly revealed to Kennedy that Bulger had told him that he had extorted $60,000 to $90,000 in storage fees from Murray. Murray was storing marijuana in a warehouse in South Boston, Bulger's turf. Agent Kennedy had participated in the raid on Murray's warehouse, along with the DEA. Kennedy did not share Connolly's disclosure with the DEA, government prosecutors, or anyone else at the FBI. Kennedy knew that Connolly expected confidentiality concerning the information Bulger had provided.

Kennedy, along with agents from Customs, interviewed McIntyre on October 17, 1984. He never disclosed that Bulger and Flemmi were FBI informants. McIntyre told Kennedy that, "An individual named Whitey, who operates a liquor store in South Boston, had become partners with Joe Murray." Kennedy was also informed by McIntyre of the story of the arms shipment. Kennedy reported the information he had received from McIntyre to the Special Agent in Charge.

Agents Kennedy and Connolly would often exchange information. The fact that Kennedy never disclosed information regarding Murray's warehouse to interested parties, and protected Bulger and Flemmi in an extortion investigation, suggests strongly that he may have told Connolly about McIntyre's claims regarding Bulger. Although McIntyre was willing to cooperate and blow the lid off a spectacular case, the FBI did not investigate any of McIntyre's claims against Bulger and Flemmi, nor did it discuss with the DEA or Customs anything regarding any investigation they might wish to conduct.

The FBI did not in the course of its investigation, ask the DEA whether it had any evidence linking Bulger and Flemmi to the *Valhalla*. Had the FBI asked, the DEA could have reported that electronic surveillance it conducted in 1984 and 1985 "showed that Bulger and Flemmi shipped guns and ammunition to the IRA in Ireland." An electronic surveillance recorded that upon seeing a news report that the *Valhalla* had been seized, Bulger exclaimed, "That's our shipment. That's ours!" Bulger and Flemmi were not charged in the *Valhalla* case.

A police bulletproof vest registered to Michael Flemmi, the younger brother of Steve Flemmi, was recovered aboard the *Valhalla*. McIntyre continued to cooperate with Quincy Detective Bergeron. He offered an enormous amount of information regarding Bulger and his gang's involvement in drug dealing and gun running. This was Bergeron's big chance to rocket to the top of the heap. He was not, however, aware of the skullduggery that was taking place behind the scenes.

Bergeron had hitched a ride on a rocket that was about to explode. On November 30, 1984, after only a few weeks of cooperating with law enforcement, John McIntyre disappeared. McIntyre, who was thirty-two when he vanished, was to meet with Bulger associate Patrick Nee. He had suffered the same fate as others who were planning to inform on Bulger. But, unlike Brian Halloran, whose bullet-ridden body was in plain view, lying on a South Boston street, McIntyre was never seen again. McIntyre, who was planning to go to South America with money given to him by his father, was last seen with Patrick Nee.

He had been lured to the same Third Street home as Bucky Barrett had been, and murdered by Bulger and Flemmi. McIntyre's body would be buried in the cellar of the home, next to the remains of Bucky Barrett. Assisting in the burial arrangement was Bulger's surrogate son, Kevin Weeks. However, it would not be the final resting place for John McIntyre.

When Detective Bergeron learned that McIntyre was to meet Patrick Nee, he became suspicious of Bulger's role in the disappearance. He had heard that Bulger and Flemmi were informants, but tended to brush aside those rumors. He knew Bulger and Flemmi were stone-cold killers, saying, "he didn't think that somebody at that level, doing what they [Bulger and Flemmi] were doing could be informants for the FBI." His logic was correct; however, time would expose the depths of the FBI's sleaze.

Later, while lying in a hospital bed, John McIntyre's father received a visit from two members of Bulger's gang who delivered a threatening message not to investigate his son's disappearance. The two strangers warned the senior McIntyre that he "still had one son."

In 1984, after the murder of John McIntyre, the DEA, Quincy Police, and the FBI began an investigation targeting Bulger and Flemmi. The DEA suspected that the pair were FBI informants, and had concerns that the FBI would compromise their investigation. The DEA preferred to go it alone, and not join forces with the FBI. However, they needed the Bureau for authorization to conduct electronic surveillance on the two drug-dealing gangsters.

James Ring, who was supervising the FBI's role in the investigation, believed that Bulger and Flemmi had no immunity and that they would be on their own if the DEA could make a case against them. But the task of making a case would be next to impossible for those involved and trying to do the right thing. It is possible that John Connolly received information from those close to him in the Boston Bureau, regarding the investigation and electronic surveillance. Bulger and Flemmi were warned of the investigation; "Operation Beans" was doomed from the start.

There is reason to believe that Agent John Morris was one of Connolly's sources regarding the DEA's investigation of Bulger and Flemmi. All roads led to John Morris, who had received his first $1,000 from Bulger and Flemmi in 1982, after informing Connolly of Brian Halloran's revelations. It was likely he was one of the sources who told Connolly about the investigation. Morris received a second $1,000 payment, along with a case of expensive wine, from the two informants. The timing of the "gifts" suggests that they may have been made as an act of appreciation for Morris' part concerning the tip about the DEA investigation.

Special Agent Kennedy was also a likely source in warning Connolly of the investigation. Kennedy would often warn Connolly that if Bulger or Flemmi were arrested, they would most likely divulge their relationship with Connolly and the FBI. Connolly would shrug his shoulders, saying "he did not have to worry because they were too smart to get caught." But Connolly was not relying on the ability of the street-smart criminals to avoid any arrest.

The arrogant Connolly was sure that he could keep an eye out for his two prize informants. He was receiving information from many in the Boston Bureau when it came to any investigation of Bulger and Flemmi. After all, he was John Connolly, the Prince of the City. He was the one who could get tickets to the local sporting events; he was the one who could get agents good jobs after retirement, most likely through the powerful Senate President Billy Bulger.

Bulger and Flemmi knew that they were under investigation and surveillance. Their reaction to the joint DEA, Massachusetts State Police, and Quincy Police investigation is significant. Flemmi did not complain to Connolly or James Ring that his agreement with the FBI gave him immunity from being investigated by other agencies or from being prosecuted if that investigation was successful. Flemmi understood that it would be legally permissible for him to be prosecuted as a result of the investigation that was being conducted. Flemmi believed that the FBI was obligated to protect him by providing him with information about investigations that he could then use to frustrate the proceedings in one way or another. Flemmi understood the warnings he received regarding any investigation of him were part of both the FBI's promise to him and its fulfillment—never was he told that he had immunity from prosecution. In no way did Flemmi's agreement constitute immunity, something that he would fail to realize later on.

In April 1985, Connolly, Morris, Dennis Condon, Bulger, and Flemmi met for dinner at Morris' house in Lexington, Massachusetts. The dinner was held several weeks after Bulger had found a bug in his car and it had become obvious that the investigation led by the DEA would not succeed. The dinner was evidently planned to celebrate the failure of the effort to investigate Bulger and Flemmi. At the dinner party, Morris told Bulger and Flemmi, "You can do anything you want just as long as you don't clip anyone."

However, Bulger and Flemmi would be protected, even when it came to murder. Later, Morris would testify that he did not recall telling Bulger and Flemmi that they could do anything they wanted as long as they didn't clip anyone, and doubted he had done so. But Flemmi's characterization of Morris' statement was that he did have immunity from prosecution.

Shortly before they left Morris' home, Bulger told Flemmi he wanted to loan Morris $5,000 to help him out with some financial problems the Fed was experiencing. (Morris was having problems due to medical expenses in his family.) Bulger gave Morris $5,000 in cash, which Morris never repaid.

In 1984, Raymond L.S. Patriarca, the boss of the New England Mafia, passed away. Steve Flemmi reported to Connolly that Raymond "Junior" Patriarca would be named to succeed his father. The Russo and Ferrara factions of the Boston Mafia were upset with the choice. In particular, Russo had little respect for Junior, due to the fact that he had inherited the position as boss, without earning it. Junior had never "made his bones" (an act of murder).

Flemmi also told Connolly that Russo, who was a fugitive as a result of the Barboza murder, was living in Montreal but was being urged by his crew to return to Boston. The old LCN had been depleted, and a struggle for control by the Russo-Ferrara Gang was on the horizon. The appointment of Junior Patriarca as head of the New England LCN was hotly contested by the Boston faction of the LCN, led by Joseph J.R Russo and Vincent "The Animal" Ferrara. After a bitter struggle for control, they reluctantly accepted Junior's role as leader of the New England LCN; however, they remained poised to make their move against Junior and his allies.

In June of 1985, the Anguilo trial began and ended with the convictions of all the Anguilos. At the onset of the trial, Joe Pistone, a former agent from New York, was in Boston to review some documents in preparation for possibly testifying as an expert in the case. Pistone, who had left the FBI, was renowned for infiltrating the New York LCN as Donnie Brasco, and for testifying in many Mafia prosecutions. After retiring from the Bureau, Pistone wrote a book. *Donnie Brasco: My Undercover Life in the Mafia* would become a best-seller. Later, Hollywood would make a movie titled *Donnie Brasco*, starring Al Pacino.

As a result of Pistone's infiltration of the LCN in New York, a $500,000 contract was put out on his life by the mob. Although precautions were being taken to assure the secrecy of Pistone's location and activities, the arrogant Connolly invited him to dine with Bulger and Flemmi. Connolly felt certain that his two trusted informants would do nothing to endanger Pistone. Being invited to dine with Pistone, the two ruthless murderers would regard themselves as honored members of the government's team combatting the LCN, not the pitiless killers that they actually were.

Bulger and Flemmi had also supplied information to the FBI that would be used to get a warrant to bug Illario (Larry Bione) Zannino's social club at 51 North Margin Street in Boston's North End. The number two man, Zannino, was convicted and would later die in prison.

Through all of the murders, drug dealing, and extortion, Steve Flemmi still found time for seducing young girls. This time the sadistic gangster would zero in on Deborah Hussey, the daughter of Marion Hussey from a previous relationship. Deborah was an infant when Flemmi began his affair with her mother. He had raised her as though she was his own. Flemmi's common-law affair with Marion would produce two sons and a daughter. Deborah thought of Flemmi as her real dad, just as her step-brothers and sister did.

But at the tender age of fourteen, Flemmi made his move on Deborah, stripping her of her innocence. After twelve years of acts bordering on incest, the feelings of guilt were beginning to take hold on Deborah. She decided that she was going to come clean; it would be the first step in feeling good about herself. She intended to reveal to her mother the truth about her affair with her stepfather. This was a big problem for Flemmi. He didn't need the headache, especially having to answer to Marion Hussey. It had been fun for twelve years, but now the party was over.

Flemmi would seek out his partner, Whitey Bulger, for a solution. The answer was a simple one for the ruthless killers. It wasn't as though they had any reservations about killing; what was one more body, anyway? In early 1985, the unsuspecting Hussey would also be lured to the same Third Street home as Bucky Barrett and John McIntyre before her. Once there, the ever physically fit Bulger wrapped his powerful hands around the tender neck of Deborah Hussey, squeezing all the sad life out of her. With most of the victims, fingertips, and in some cases, teeth were removed, making it difficult to identify the body through fingerprints or dental records. Her body would be buried in the cellar of the home next to the remains of Barrett and McIntyre. Assisting in the burial once again was Kevin Weeks. It would not, however, be the final resting place for Deborah Hussey. She was twenty-six when she drew her last breath; the same age as the other young captivating blonde before her, Debra Davis. Steve Flemmi would deny any knowledge of Deborah's disappearance to Marion Hussey, at the same time consoling their three children together.

In October 1985, Bulger, Flemmi, and Weeks would begin the gruesome task of dredging up the remains of Bucky Barrett, Deborah Hussey, and John McIntyre. The bodies that had been previously buried at the Third Street home of a Bulger associate had to be exhumed and reburied because the house was being sold. Fearing the remains might be discovered, the bodies were removed and taken to a new grave site. The grisly task of digging up and reburying the remains of the three victims came easy for this sinister group. Bucky Barrett, Deborah Hussey, and John McIntyre would be buried in a gully alongside the Southeast Expressway across from Florian Hall in Dorchester, Massachusetts. It would not be their final resting place. Bulger and Flemmi would continue on with their criminality without any remorse for the victims. The digging of graves came with the price of doing business.

–Chapter 12–
NEW LCN (MAFIA) LEADERS EMERGE

By mid-1986, Anguilo and his codefendants had been convicted and Larry Zannino, the number two man, was ill and incapacitated while awaiting trial. The mob in Boston was in disarray, creating a vacuum. Bulger and Flemmi decided it was a good time to make their move and expand their own criminal activities. The two believed that their unholy alliance with the FBI provided an opportunity to take over "the turf" in Boston that had previously been controlled by the Anguilos. It was an ideal situation for them—they had John Connolly and the FBI protecting them. Their bargain with the FBI was to supply information; in return, they were given carte blanche to "rip and tear."

One of John Morris' informants reported that bookmakers who were once connected with the Anguilos were receiving very little direction. They didn't know who was in charge or running the show in Boston. Bulger and Flemmi had stepped in and were taking over the mob's bookmakers, and the LCN was unable to do anything to stop them. The new mob leaders were well aware of Bulger and Flemmi's reputations and were not ready to go to war with them.

Although the Boston Bureau was aware of Bulger and Flemmi's plan to take control of the rackets, nothing was done to stop them. In order to placate him, the LCN offered to "make" Flemmi a member of "Their Thing," La Cosa Nostra. But Flemmi wanted no part in being a made man. An informant told Connolly that Flemmi would not want membership inasmuch as he was an independent person and would not want to be subject to the rules of the Mafia. Flemmi did not need the headaches and he, along with Bulger, were their own bosses, with their own things going for them.

Connolly and Supervisor James Ring, along with others in the Boston Bureau, were ready to target the successors of the Anguilos. Flemmi would be an asset in bringing down the "young bucks" set on taking control. Flemmi wasted no time in reporting to Connolly on the activities of Joseph J.R. Russo and Vincent The Animal Ferrara. Russo and Ferrara were the new leaders of the Boston mob, along with Robert Carrozza, Angelo "Sonny" Mercurio, Dennis Lepore, and Biagio Digiacomo. Flemmi also reported to Connolly information on the members of the Providence, Rhode Island, mob, including Raymond Patriarca, Matthew Gugliametti, and Anthony The Saint St. Laurent. Flemmi explained to Connolly that the emerging new leaders wanted to meet in order to form a relationship with him and Bulger. The LCN leaders wanted to discuss the payoff on the illegal numbers and other gambling matters.

Sonny Mercurio, who had been friendly with Bulger and Flemmi, took a leading role in bringing them together. Mercurio urged the LCN members to get together with Bulger and Flemmi in order to form a cooperative relationship. Mercurio had recently been released from prison and had been extremely bitter toward the Anguilos. He felt that the Anguilos had no concern for him during his stretch in prison. They made no effort to help him financially. Instead, Bulger and Flemmi would send $100 a week to Mercurio's family while he was incarcerated.

Flemmi would agree to meet with the new mob leaders several times. The meetings were held in a storeroom of Vanessa's restaurant, owned by Mercurio. The back storeroom at Vanessa's was a perfect location for meetings and "sit downs." The restaurant was located in the Prudential Plaza in Boston's Back Bay section. The trendy shopping center had an underground garage, making it easy for those attending the meetings to feel secure that they were not being tailed.

Connolly was kept abreast of the meetings and what was being discussed. Flemmi reported to Connolly the LCN's plans concerning illegal football cards, changing the payoff odds on the illegal numbers racket, and the extortion of bookmakers. One extortion in particular was a scheme to shake down Harry "Doc" Sagansky. Sagansky started off as a young graduate of Tufts Dental School. He quickly gave up his practice for the lucrative numbers racket. Not only was he a numbers bookie, but he became known as the top layoff man in the city. When far too much money was gambled on certain numbers, Doc would take the layoffs from all the other bookmakers. Doc became a millionaire and was regarded as Boston's biggest bookmaker.

As was the case with Meyer Lansky and the New York crime families, Doc became a financial advisor to the Anguilos. Not only was he respected for his genius with numbers, but Jerry Anguilo had a fondness for the grandfatherly Doc. Sagansky was given the right to operate by Jerry and for years conducted his bookmaking operation without paying a street tax to the mob. But with Jerry and his brothers behind bars, Doc was now on his own. He would be fair game for the new breed of mobsters. At the age of eighty-nine, he should have been in Florida enjoying his few remaining years in the sunshine. Instead, he was given a choice—"pay or die."

Flemmi would often meet with the new mobsters at Vanessa's. While sitting in on one of the meetings, talk about the attempted extortion had been discussed. The mobsters spoke openly with no concern for Flemmi's presence. After all, he was a highly-respected killer and could certainly be trusted. They were wrong. Flemmi wasted no time reporting the planned extortion of Doc Sagansky.

The FBI promptly decided to target Vanessa's for electronic surveillance. Connolly wanted Flemmi to provide the FBI with a detailed diagram of the back storeroom at Vanessa's, and other logistical information. Flemmi and Bulger were used as the sources necessary for the application for a warrant. Flemmi understood that the FBI was about to bug Vanessa's and as a result, he and Bulger would now stay away from the restaurant.

On October 31, 1986, Judge William Young authorized the electronic surveillance of Vanessa's. The bug was extremely productive. Among other things, the extortion of Sagansky was of significant importance. The conversations that were picked up on the bug revealed the extortion of Sagansky. He was ordered to come up with $500,000 for all the years that he had operated during the Anguilo reign without paying "rent." Now the party for Sagansky was over. Doc and his associate, Moe Weinstein, who had accompanied him to the storeroom, were given a choice—either Doc paid the $500,000, or he would never see his lifelong friend, the seventy-eight-year-old Weinstein, again.

Sagansky and Weinstein, although surrounded by dangerous mobsters, cried poverty. In return, the mobsters expressed their need for the money. There were lawyers that needed to be paid and other mob associates were in trouble. Sagansky still refused to pay. "I'm not going to give you guys a bankroll," he said firmly. The mobsters had heard enough. Moe Weinstein would be taken and held as a hostage. It would be up to Doc to determine the fate of his long-time friend and partner.

Sagansky knew the men were serious; he knew of their reputation. With his back against the wall, and true to his ethnic heritage, he would begin to bargain. Paying $500,000 was out of the question; he had never paid retail for anything. A 50 percent discount would be the best he could do, he thought. "I'll pay $250,000; the other $250,000, you will have to wait for that. I don't know how long it will take to get it."

The following day, the $250,000 was paid to the mobsters. It was delivered to Vanessa's by Moe Weinstein, who was videotaped by the agents as he carried in the large plastic bag. Also, the cut-up of the money, along with the accompanying dialogue, was recorded on tape. There was one bit of conversation of particular interest to the Feds.

During the distribution of the $250,000, talk between the mobsters centered on how to keep Junior Patriarca from finding out about the extortion. As the new boss of the New England mob, Junior was entitled to a share. Those present had no intention of giving up anything to Patriarca. In fact, their lack of respect for the new boss would become even more evident when one of the men called him a "bonehead."

Another conversation showed the concerns the mobsters had over drugs. Sonny Mercurio was intercepted saying that he "was really glad to have that $400,000"—his share of the extortion, and that—"he would like to buy his daughter a house." She was apparently on welfare. Vincent Ferrara responded, "Well, you know, your top priority is going to be to go someplace where the schools are good and there are no drugs." The talk continued with reference to the fact that you could not find any schools these days that were absent of drug dealers or users. Connolly most certainly listened to the tapes from Vanessa's, in particular the talk confirming the mobsters' disdain for drugs, and the fact that drugs were everywhere.

One might question how Connolly could continue his alliance with Bulger. It was no secret that his idol had polluted their beloved Southie by allowing drugs into their community. The cut-up of the $250,000, along with the accompanying dialogue, was now on tape. John Connolly and the FBI had enough to successfully prosecute Russo, Ferrara, Mercurio, and the others in the Sagansky extortion. The government received a series of extensions, and the storeroom at Vanessa's was bugged until June of 1987.

The electronic surveillance of Vanessa's was terminated after Mercurio found the bugs. He reported to Bulger that he, Ferrara, and the others had begun making exculpatory statements in an effort to clean up their criminal talk and the Sagansky extortion. Later on, Sagansky would be offered immunity in exchange for his testimony in the extortion. Although victimized, he refused to rat out the mobsters. The eighty-nine-year-old bookmaker would sit in a jail cell until he was willing to come forward and testify for the government. But the old-time bookmaker would not talk— he was truly a stand-up guy.

Russo, Ferrara, Mercurio, and others knew the Sagansky-Weinstein extortion was a big problem for them. Mercurio did not want to return to prison. The fruits of the wiretap gave the FBI powerful leverage in its efforts to convert Mercurio into an informant. The information reported to Flemmi on Vanessa's and the Sagansky shakedown would prove extremely beneficial to him and Bulger. It was a way to keep the new breed of mobsters from taking control and keep the FBI on their backs, while he and Bulger could have free sailing in their effort to control the criminal activities in Boston.

In November 1986, James Ahearn became the Special Agent in Charge of Boston. Two months earlier Larry Potts had become the assistant to Ahearn. Potts was responsible for matters relating to the Organized Crime Squad. Later on, he would hold several of the highest positions in the FBI, serving as the Assistant Director in Charge of the Criminal Division, and as acting Deputy Director in 1995. John Morris had proposed to Potts that "Bulger was no longer providing information of sufficient value to maintain his relationship as an informant, and should be considered as a subject of investigation, rather than as a confidential source." Morris was on the hook to Bulger and Flemmi, having received $7,000 from the two. He was becoming troubled by reports of their criminal activities. Morris wanted out of his association with the two murderers, but wanted someone else in the department to go after them, rather than do it personally.

Potts ran Morris' request by Ahearn, who asked Potts to conduct a suitable review of Bulger and Flemmi. In conducting his review, Potts did not consider the range of factors prescribed by the FBI manual. He knew that Bulger and Flemmi were engaged in a host of criminal activities, yet he merely sought to evaluate their productivity. He never weighed their value against the seriousness of the crimes he knew they were committing. He never once took into account the FBI's guidelines on the handling of informants.

Connolly, along with others, supported the FBI's position with regard to continuing the use of the murderers as informants. Connolly in particular brought to Potts' attention Vanessa's, and Bulger and Flemmi's roles in support of the electronic surveillance. Potts advised Ahearn that "the information in Bulger's informant's file was of substantial value" and, in his opinion, "Whitey Bulger should be maintained as an informant rather than as a target."

Later, Potts would do the same thing for Steve Flemmi. Ahearn went along with Potts' recommendations. In conducting his interview, Potts was aware of the FBI manual requiring that FBI headquarters review at least annually the determination by a field office that an individual was suitable to serve as an informant. But Potts' advice to Ahearn was given orally and Ahearn's decision to continue Bulger and Flemmi as informants was not reported in writing at that time. Thus, it was never reviewed by FBI headquarters. Potts was comfortable with the decision not to report to FBI headquarters. He knew that headquarters had never reversed a field office decision on whether or not an individual was suitable to serve as an informant. The reports that Potts reviewed regarding Bulger and Flemmi were favorable to the gangsters due to Connolly, who had been "cooking the books." Potts interviewed several agents, all of whom were pro-Connolly, leaving Morris the only one to voice objections.

Bulger and Flemmi would begin to approach Mercurio in an effort to recruit him, a "made member" of the LCN, as a Top Echelon Informant. Meanwhile, Russo, Ferrara, and others knew they had a serious problem with the Sagansky extortion. They all anticipated indictments. Joe Russo would not wait around Boston to be arrested; he decided it was time to go on the lam. Mercurio would remain in Boston, and soon he would be given an "offer he could not refuse" by Flemmi and Bulger, and later by John Connolly. Following the conclusion of the electronic surveillance of Vanessa's, Steve Flemmi would be designated a Top Echelon Informant in December of 1987.

After approving Potts' review and Ahearn's decision regarding Flemmi, headquarters congratulated the Boston office on developing such a "fine informant." The lengths to which the FBI would go to protect Bulger and Flemmi because of their value in bringing down the LCN, as opposed to targeting them for prosecution, would be demonstrated in the manner in which the Bureau dealt with the murderous criminals' victims. Time after time, cries for help from their victims were completely ignored.

In 1986, Raymond Slinger, a real estate broker in South Boston, was introduced to Kevin O'Neil, a Bulger gang member. O'Neil would often have Slinger discuss the booming real estate market in South Boston with Bulger and Flemmi. Slinger knew that Bulger and Flemmi were reputed to

be violent criminals but thought that he could benefit from their relationship. In early 1987, O'Neil asked Slinger to come to Triple O's, a bar that
served as Bulger's headquarters. Slinger thought this was his chance, with
Bulger's help, to cash in on the local real estate market. He was aware of
Bulger's way of getting things done, not to mention his brother's, Senate
President William Bulger, connections. Slinger thought that this could be
the start of something big. But he was wrong.

As he entered Triple O's, which was often referred to as "the bucket of
blood," he was ushered to a private room on the second floor. He was again
introduced to Bulger, who looked at Slinger sternly. Bulger got right to the
point. "I was given a contract to kill you," Bulger said to the now-confused
Slinger. It was not what Slinger had been expecting. He began looking for
answers as to who and why. He certainly didn't wear any halo, but who
would go so far as to want him dead? Bulger would not shed any details. He
couldn't. It was merely a ploy to shake down the terrified Slinger. There
was no contract on him, but Slinger could not be certain that one did not
exist. "You can buy your way out of it by paying me instead," Bulger said.

The fearful Slinger replied, "I can give you $2,000." Bulger scornfully
rejected the offer of two grand, saying, "My boots cost more than that. I
want $50,000." Slinger placated Bulger; he would agree to anything to get
out of the bar with his life.

After leaving Triple O's, Slinger called his friend, Boston City
Counselor James Kelley. He told Kelley of the extortion attempt by Bulger
and O'Neil, describing the details of his meeting at Triple O's. Kelley told
Slinger that he knew Bulger and O'Neil and would speak to them. Later,
Kelley told Slinger that he had spoken to someone and that he should have
no further problems, but, if he did, Slinger should call the authorities.

A week or two later, in March 1987, Kevin O'Neil again called Slinger
and told him that Bulger wanted to see him at Triple O's. This time, Slinger
took his assistant, Arlene Lehane, and a hidden handgun with him. Upon
arriving at Triple O's, Slinger was separated from Lehane and forced to the
same second floor by Kevin Weeks and Kevin O'Neil, where Bulger

awaited his arrival. Bulger and his two associates began to search Slinger for a body wire, only to discover the hidden handgun. The three hoodlums began to beat Slinger badly and berated him for talking to Kelley about the shakedown. Then Bulger took Slinger's loaded gun, placed it on top of Slinger's head and said, "If I shot you from this angle, there would be no blood spatter." Bulger then ordered Weeks to get a body bag. The horrified Slinger nearly wet his pants. After a brief moment, Bulger said, "I'll give you another chance to get the $50,000, quickly." Once again, Slinger would agree to anything, as long as he could walk out alive. He left Triple O's with Arlene Lehane, who had remained downstairs. He was badly swollen, and his shirt had been ripped during the search for a body wire.

The three gangsters had no concern that a witness was with Slinger, and could testify as to his condition. Bulger had John Connolly and the FBI in his pocket. He could get away with anything, even murder if he chose to. A short time later, Slinger borrowed money from his sister and wife and made an initial payment of $10,000 to O'Neil. He was then forced to make weekly payments of $2,000, a total of $25,000, by May 1987. Being unable to pay anymore and fearing the worst, Slinger called the FBI.

Special Agent Rod Kennedy was assigned to investigate the extortion of Slinger and asked Agent John Newton to accompany him. Kennedy and Newton interviewed Slinger at the Old Harbor Real Estate office. Slinger told the two agents what had occurred. When asked if he was willing to testify, Slinger said that he would.

Special Agent Newton thought that the Slinger matter looked like a great case, the kind of case that agents dream about. Newton's squad had the jurisdiction to investigate the Irish mob, and Bulger was its leader. Bulger was the number one priority of the squad, and Slinger was the first of Bulger's victims to provide Newton with any hard facts. Slinger was not only willing to testify, but agreed to wear a wire to record incriminating conversations. The FBI had an opportunity to conduct an interview with Arlene Lehane, and to record O'Neil's phone conversations with Slinger. But Newton knew that Bulger belonged to John Connolly, and that a high-level decision would need to be made if Bulger was to be investigated. If the decision was made to give Bulger a pass, then Newton knew Slinger needed to be protected.

Larry Potts was the Acting Special Agent in Charge. He decided that there would be no investigation of Bulger. Slinger was not interviewed again by the FBI, and Arlene Lehane was never asked about Slinger's extortion, even though she had witnessed his badly swollen face and torn shirt. Slinger's revelations and his willingness to testify provided a case for either referring Slinger's allegations to state or local law enforcement, or reporting the desire not to do so to FBI headquarters and the Assistant Attorney General.

The guidelines were utterly ignored. Requirements set forth in the FBI's manual and standard FBI practices were overlooked; no FBI 302 or other written record was made of the interview of Slinger. Agent Newton realized there was a problem with the continuing extortion of Slinger. Just as in the case of the National Melotone matter a decade earlier, the call was made by the FBI to Bulger to "lay off." The message given to Bulger was delivered by Agent John Connolly. The day after the FBI interviewed Slinger, O'Neil told him that he would not have to pay the remaining $25,000 he still owed. Some sport, this Whitey Bulger.

In 1980, a special squad known as C-2 was formed. The responsibility of the squad was to investigate non-traditional organized crime groups, such as the Winter Hill Gang. Although Bulger and Flemmi were the leaders of the Winter Hill Gang, they were never investigated. James Blackburn was a member of this special squad. He had been working with the DEA and other law enforcement agencies in 1986 in a combined effort to investigate a top-ranking drug dealer, Hobart Willis. Blackburn had received information that Willis was paying tribute to Bulger for the right to operate. Blackburn knew that Bulger was an informant for Connolly.

Connolly was made aware of the investigation by Blackburn, who told Connolly that an electronic surveillance was conducted, but Bulger was not intercepted. Connolly had Blackburn believing that Bulger was not extorting money from bookmakers, drug dealers, loan sharks, and others who could not complain to the police without incriminating themselves.

Connolly told Blackburn that although Willis was a drug dealer, Bulger was not extorting him. Connolly easily convinced Blackburn that Bulger was not receiving any money from Willis. Although Blackburn was continuously receiving information that Bulger was indeed extorting Willis, the FBI never investigated Bulger's connection to Willis. One informant told Blackburn that Bulger and Flemmi were receiving $4,000 to $6,000 per month from Willis for the right to operate in South Boston. No information regarding Bulger's connection with Willis was shared by the FBI with other law enforcement agencies.

On August 5, 1990, one of Blackburn's sources reported that Willis expected to be indicted along with Bulger within the next two weeks. Willis and a number of other drug dealers in South Boston were indicted. Bulger, however, was not charged.

Flemmi continued to supply the FBI with information that the new LCN faction in Boston was concerned about the FBI developing a powerful case against them. Russo, Ferrara, Carrozza, and Mercurio knew that the extortion of Doc Sagansky and Moe Weinstein was about to go to a grand jury, and indictments would be coming down soon. Mercurio in particular, who had been released from prison in 1986, feared returning. He didn't want to do anymore time, and would be ripe for the taking. Bulger and Flemmi, as directed by Connolly, would try to exploit Mercurio. They began making plans to serve up Mercurio to Agent Connolly, who had a special talent for getting mobsters to "roll."

Mercurio would be easy for Connolly to turn. He had become disenchanted with the Mafia because "no one in the LCN did anything for him while he was away." Mercurio remained close to Bulger and Flemmi, who had sent his girlfriend $100 a week while he was in the "can" (prison). Bulger reported to Connolly that Mercurio would go on the lam before he would go to prison again. Connolly and his supervisor, Ring, decided to try to exploit Mercurio's discontent with the Mafia and his fear of returning to prison by recruiting him as an informant.

Connolly would meet with Bulger and Flemmi in order to get a run-down on Mercurio that he could use in his effort to recruit him. All he needed was a bit of information on the subject, just enough to get his foot in the door. With a profile provided by Bulger and Flemmi, and with the blessing of Ring, Connolly would make his move on Sonny Mercurio. He knew that Mercurio wanted to take off before the indictments, and Connolly could provide him with a head start. Connolly was studying for a master's degree in public administration at Harvard, and would meet Mercurio at the prestigious school. Meeting at Harvard would ease Mercurio's fear of being seen by any of his peers talking with Agent Connolly.

Mercurio was receptive to Connolly. In return for information on the mob, he would be alerted as to when he was about to be indicted. Mercurio needed to be "on the street" for as long as possible. He had shylock money to collect as well as other pending illegal deals.

In October 1987, Mercurio began providing information to the FBI and was soon opened as an informant. Connolly would take great pride in recruiting Mercurio, a "made" member of the LCN. Angelo Sonny Mercurio would be another informant whom Connolly would add to his ever-growing list.

In 1988, Frank Salemme had recently been released after serving fifteen years in prison for the Fitzgerald bombing, compliments of his best friend, Steve Flemmi. Even though Salemme did not suspect that Flemmi was responsible for his arrest, Flemmi was deeply concerned. Flemmi conveyed his concerns regarding Salemme to Agent Connolly, who requested that Flemmi begin to provide information again on Cadillac Frank. Flemmi would begin to reestablish contact with Salemme.

In the spring of 1988, John Morris was the Supervisor of the White Collar Crime Squad. An investigation of a bookmaker, John Baharoian, who was suspected of bribing several Boston police officers for protection, was underway. Baharoian was also making protection payments to Steve Flemmi. Agents from Morris' squad were preparing an application for electronic surveillance of Baharoian, which targeted Flemmi as well. Morris was concerned that Flemmi would be intercepted on the wiretap. If Flemmi was caught on tape, arrested, and indicted, it could be a problem for Morris. He didn't know how loyal Flemmi would be if faced with a prison sentence. The thought of Flemmi giving him up in exchange for leniency crossed his mind. He needed to protect Flemmi from being intercepted.

Morris asked Connolly to warn Flemmi and Bulger to stay away from Baharoian. Morris also conveyed to Connolly that Bulger and Flemmi should not do anything to Baharoian because he "did not want another Halloran." Morris knew that his revelation of that investigation had caused Bulger and Flemmi to murder Halloran.

Baharoian's telephone was wiretapped from June 22 to September 25, 1988. The wiretap led to the indictments of Baharoian and several Boston police officers. Because of the tip from Morris, neither Bulger nor Flemmi was intercepted, nor was either charged. But Morris was not comfortable about warning the two informants about the wiretap. He realized that he had broken the law; he had obstructed justice. Morris wanted out of his relationship with Bulger and Flemmi. He felt completely compromised and vulnerable. Bulger and Flemmi would not be able to continue to skate on thin ice forever; at some point they would fall through. Then his alliance with the two would be revealed.

Morris decided that he was going to do whatever he could to stop Bulger and Flemmi, short of admitting his crimes. He had tried earlier to get his supervisor, Ring, to close out Bulger as an informant; telling Ring that Bulger had outlived his usefulness. But Ring was blinded by his desire to bring down the mob at any price, not to mention Connolly's role in defending Bulger's usefulness. Now it was time for Morris to take matters into his own hands. He would begin to rekindle rumors that Bulger was an informant, and that disclosure could get Bulger killed. Morris would attempt to provoke another Brian Halloran, who had been murdered when information surfaced that he was an informant.

In June 1988, Morris spoke to Gerald O'Neil, a reporter for *The Boston Globe*. He told O'Neil that Bulger was an informant for the FBI. Morris wanted the mob to kill Bulger. Having tried unsuccessfully to get Bulger closed as an FBI informant, he felt he had no other way to go. He had accepted money and gifts from them, and he had obstructed justice and broken the law. Morris believed that an article reporting Bulger as an informant would be enough to get him killed. The Mafia didn't need an official inquiry, or any 209 or 302 reports. They didn't need proof. Morris wanted the mob to end any risk that Bulger might "put the finger" on him.

The Boston Globe Spotlight Team was planning to write a series of articles indicating that Bulger had been an FBI informant for many years, and he had been tipped to electronic surveillance and was being protected from investigation and prosecution. The Globe Spotlight Team began focusing on the race-fixing case in which Bulger and Flemmi were not indicted, the Lancaster Street garage investigation, and the DEA investigation in 1984–85.

As part of his research, Richard Lehr, a member of the Spotlight Team, sent a letter to Anthony "Fat Tony" Ciulla, the star witness in the race-fixing case, who was being protected by the government. Lehr wanted Fat Tony's take on the events concerning the race-fixing case. On July 19, 1988, Tom Daly, who was the lead FBI agent on the race-fixing case, called Kevin Cullen, another member of the Spotlight Team. Daly informed Cullen that he was aware of the letter sent to Ciulla by the reporter, and expressed regret that Cullen had not called him first. Daly was curious as to what extent the newspaper would be willing to go.

Cullen was up front with the agent. He told Daly that the Spotlight Team was preparing an article that would report that Bulger was an FBI informant, that Bulger had the protection of the FBI and as a reward for his role as an informant, was not indicted in the race-fixing case. Daly denied that Bulger was not indicted in the race-fixing case because he was an informant. Daly also denied that Bulger ever was a source for the FBI. Daly questioned Cullen: "Do you know what you're doing?" He wanted Cullen to understand the danger of reporting such a story in the paper.

Daly proceeded to tell Cullen that he had spoken to Fat Tony Ciulla, who had a message. Bulger was a very dangerous man who would think nothing of

"clipping" anyone who wrote the kind of story Cullen described. Daly empha-
sized that in his opinion, Cullen was especially vulnerable because it was
well-known that he lived in South Boston. South Boston was Bulger's turf,
and he would not take lightly to anyone who would write a story which would
cause him embarrassment, especially in that tight-knit community.

Cullen knew of Bulger's reputation as a cold-blooded killer. The blood-
stains on Northern Avenue where Brian Halloran and Michael Donahue
had been slaughtered had remained visible for some time after, serving as a
daily reminder to anyone who dared to cross Whitey Bulger. Cullen
believed that Daly's comments constituted a threat intended to discourage
The Boston Globe from publishing the story it was planning.

The FBI in Boston decided to go one step further. Not feeling comfortable that *The Globe* would back off from running the story, it was now time
for the Boston Bureau to bring in the heavy hitters. Special Agent in
Charge James Ahearn would speak to the Spotlight Team on the record.
The FBI did not want any nosy reporters to expose their unholy alliance
with Whitey Bulger. James Ahearn was unequivocal when asked if Bulger
had relations with the FBI that left him free from its scrutiny. "That is
absolutely untrue," said Ahearn. "We have *not* developed anything of an
evidentiary nature that would warrant it and, if we ever do develop anything of an evidentiary nature, we will pursue it. We specifically deny that
there has been any special treatment of this individual." Cullen met with
his colleagues and editor to discuss Agent Daly's warning. They all agreed
that Daly's tactic was to intimidate the Spotlight Team from running the
articles. *The Boston Globe* and their reporters stood their ground.

The Globe did what any responsible newspaper would do—the story was
going to run. To its credit, *The Globe* did what *The Washington Post* had
done when it was under pressure in the Watergate days; it "ran that baby."
The Globe did, however, take the threat to Cullen seriously. Shortly before
the series was going to run, *The Globe* paid to have Cullen and his wife
relocated. Still concerned for his safety, Cullen returned to South Boston
after a short time. On September 20, 1988, *The Boston Globe* published its

article on Whitey Bulger. The article detailed the special treatment Bulger had received from the Bureau in Boston. Receiving particular attention was the race-fixing case in which Bulger was not indicted, the warning to him of the Lancaster Street garage bug, and the DEA investigation. The article indicated that Bulger had avoided arrest for years by providing the FBI with information on the Mafia, a quid pro quo.

However, the desperate plan by Morris to get Bulger killed would fail. It would fail due to one simple fact that Morris had not considered. It was too unbelievable for the FBI to have a relationship with a ruthless killer like Whitey Bulger. Hoover's "fair-haired boys" would never sink so low as to allow Bulger to commit murder, extortion, and drug dealing in order to bring down a Mafia family. That was how the new mob leaders interpreted the newspaper articles. No, the mobsters would not buy the story that Whitey Bulger was a rat; it was too unbelievable. The new mob heirs interpreted *The Globe's* articles as an attempt to embarrass Whitey's brother who had many enemies.

At Ahearn's request, the FBI conducted an administrative inquiry focusing primarily on whether Morris had leaked the fact that Bulger was an informant to *The Boston Globe*. Special Agent in Charge Ahearn, along with Connolly, suspected that John Morris was the person who had supplied the information to *The Globe*. Morris lied under oath during the course of the investigation, denying he had been the source of *The Globe's* story. He refused to take a polygraph test as well. Morris did admit to inadvertently confirming Bulger as a source. However, Morris would stand firm in his denial of other allegations. As a result of the investigation, he received a censure and a fourteen-day unpaid leave. Later on, he would become Chief of the Training and Administration Section at the FBI Academy in Quantico, Virginia.

The article published in *The Globe* was troubling to both Flemmi and Bulger. They had concerns for their safety. Agents in the Boston office began to distance themselves from Bulger and Flemmi; they had far too much "heat" on them. However, the bold and arrogant John Connolly stood firm. He advised the two informants to "hang in." He was certain the Bureau could deflect *The Globe's* story. Connolly told Bulger that Morris was indeed the person who had leaked information to *The Globe*, and that he and Flemmi should lay low for awhile, which the two agreed to do.

However, another problem had surfaced. Flemmi was extremely paranoid with Cadillac Frank Salemme; he was very concerned that Salemme could soon discover his role as an informant. More importantly, Flemmi was deeply concerned that Salemme would discover that he was the one responsible for his capture while on the lam for the Fitzgerald bombing. Connolly asked Flemmi to report to him on Salemme's activities. The G-Man and the gangster would begin to lay out a plan for the elimination of Cadillac Frank once and for all.

Flemmi would seek out Salemme in order to provide information that the FBI wanted concerning the LCN, and on Salemme in particular. Flemmi reported that Salemme had allied himself with Raymond Patriarca in the struggle for control of the rackets in New England. Flemmi kept Connolly informed of the rising tension between Salemme and the Boston faction of the LCN as well.

Sonny Mercurio was also aware of the trouble brewing between the Russo-Ferrara faction of the LCN and the Patriarca-Salemme crew. He also had concerns due to his role in the Sagansky extortion.

Mercurio told Connolly that he wanted the FBI to seek an early termination of his parole. He was told by Supervisor Ring that the request for early termination would involve generating documents describing his status and value as an informant, which would be maintained outside the FBI. Nevertheless, Mercurio told Ring to "go for it." Mercurio had no concerns; he was planning to skip town anyway. All he needed was the warning from Connolly of the coming indictments. Sonny Mercurio had been promised a head start. The Strike Force head, O'Sullivan, sent a letter to Benjamin Baer, the Chairman of the Parole Commission, requesting that Mercurio be granted early termination of his parole. The letter was based on information that O'Sullivan had received from John Connolly. The information used claimed that Mercurio had provided data to support applications for electronic surveillance, which was not true. O'Sullivan's letter alone was not sufficient to persuade Baer to terminate Mercurio's parole. Baer requested that the FBI provide a letter supporting O'Sullivan's request. The FBI did just that.

The FBI indicated that Mercurio would be indicted with other mob members in the near future. It added that the early termination of his parole would ensure that at the time of his arraignment, Mercurio would be afforded bail, and not otherwise remanded to a federal holding facility, which could jeopardize his physical safety. This was not true, either. The reason that Ring and Connolly were requesting the early termination of Mercurio's parole was to ensure that when he was arrested, he would be released on bail, thus allowing him to flee Boston.

Ring told James Summeford, who was the Chief of the FBI Informant Unit, that when Mercurio was indicted, his cooperation would be made known to the court. Again not true—the government never had any intention of exposing him as an informant. His exposure would have raised many legal issues, which the government didn't want raised. Mercurio's parole was terminated in February of 1987.

A few days later, Mercurio told Agent Connolly that he, Ferrara, and those involved in the Sagansky extortion, planned to take off before being indicted. Connolly's 209 reports received by Ring included this information.

By May 1989, Ring realized that when Mercurio was indicted, his dual status as an informant and defendant would present an awkward dilemma for the government. As Ring understood it, Mercurio's involvement with his codefendants after their indictment would implicate their Sixth Amendment Rights to the confidentiality of joint discussions of defense strategy, and dealing with this issue would entail the risk of disclosing that Mercurio had been cooperating with the government.

Mercurio had been furnishing information to Connolly on the defense strategy being provided by Ferrara's attorney, Anthony Cardinale.

However, the plan all along was to warn Mercurio in advance of any indictment. He would be given the opportunity to flee, thus avoiding the possibility for disclosure of his role.

In May 1989, Mercurio was upgraded to Top Echelon Informant. His code name was "Ness," a name chosen in recognition of the famous crime buster of the past, Elliott Ness.

On June 5, 1989, Mercurio told Connolly that he, Russo, Carrozza, Ferrara, and other gang members felt under pressure because of their anticipated indictments, and were angry at Salemme, who was poised to take over after they were indicted. They were also upset with Charlie Quintana, who had allied himself with Patriarca and Salemme. Mercurio added that it was believed that Salemme, Quintana, and mob leader Billy Grasso from Connecticut would kill Ferrara, if they could set him up. Vinny The Animal Ferrara was one of the most dangerous members of the up-and-coming new Boston mobsters. Mercurio explained that the Boston LCN was planning to murder Salemme and those associated with him first.

The following day, June 6, 1989, Flemmi provided Agent Connolly with information that Raymond Patriarca had given his blessings to Salemme to become the boss of the Boston branch of the LCN, and that Cadillac Frank was "moving and shaking" all over the city.

Patriarca and Salemme were anticipating the imminent federal indictment of the Russo-Ferrara mob. The Russo crew was furious with the appointment of Salemme, and might try to kill him if they had the time to do so before their indictment for the Sagansky extortion. Russo in particular was extremely upset with Patriarca's selection of Salemme to head the Boston mob. Russo and others felt that they should have control of the rackets in Boston, not Salemme. They were good and faithful soldiers who had "paid their dues."

Flemmi continued to convey his concerns regarding Salemme, who was considered extremely street-smart. In time, it was possible he would unravel all the various sets of circumstances concerning himself and

Bulger. Salemme could become a threat to their unholy alliance. It was time for Connolly to stir the pot.

On June 13, 1989, *The Boston Herald* published an article by Shelley Murphy headlined, *Ex-Con Seen as Hub Mob's Heir Apparent*. The article cited "law enforcement sources" and consisted mainly of information that closely tracked the contents of 209 reports prepared by Agent Connolly based on his discussions with Mercurio and Flemmi. The article by Murphy consisted primarily of information that could only have come from Connolly's 209 reports. The newspaper article accurately reported that Joseph J.R. Russo, Robert Bobby Carrozza, Dennis Champagne Lepore, Vincent The Animal Ferrara, and Angelo Sonny Mercurio would soon be indicted.

It appears that the leak to *The Boston Herald* may have had the predictable effect, if not the idea, of provoking the attempt to murder Salemme. If Salemme had been murdered by the Russo faction, the FBI would have been spared the necessity of developing a prosecutable case against him. In addition, Flemmi and Bulger would have received one of the benefits of their bargain with the Bureau, an enhanced opportunity to profit from the vacuum created by the decimation of the LCN in Boston.

But the most important factor would be the elimination of the threat that Salemme posed to unraveling Flemmi's role as an informant, and being revealed as the person who had betrayed him. After serving nearly eighteen years in prison due to Flemmi's betrayal, the street-smart Salemme was beginning to get a pulse on criminal activities in Boston.

It would only be a matter of time before Cadillac Frank would come to the conclusion that Flemmi had something going for him. Far too often, Flemmi had avoided indictments when others had not, even though he and Bulger were involved in a host of criminal activities. Salemme was far too clever. In time, he would begin to see through it all. Flemmi was well aware of this, and it concerned him deeply.

Three days after the article was published, Salemme's rivals went into action. As planned, Shelley Murphy's article would inflame an already volatile situation. It was not just the mobsters who wanted Salemme eliminated, but another group of criminals, carrying badges, and acting in the name of justice, as well.

On June 16, 1989, Cadillac Frank Salemme was lured to a meeting at the International House of Pancakes on Route 1 in Saugus, Massachusetts, by Sonny Mercurio. Mercurio had requested the meet on the pretense of discussing important mob matters. Once again, Cadillac Frank would be dealt a round of treachery and betrayal.

Mercurio, who had allied himself with Flemmi, Bulger, and Agent Connolly, would serve up Salemme for execution. The elimination of Cadillac Frank would be a huge relief for all, and Steve Flemmi in particular. After realizing that Mercurio would not be on time, the now-aggravated Salemme left the restaurant. Wearing a sweat suit, just having completed a workout at a nearby gym a short time earlier, he decided to wait for the tardy Mercurio outdoors. It was a beautiful summer day and Salemme thought he would catch a few rays, assuming Mercurio would show up at any moment.

However, Mercurio would not keep the appointment with Salemme as prearranged. Instead, a stolen car carrying Vincent "Gigi Portalla" Marino and three other masked men took aim on Salemme with high-power automatic weapons, firing off a hail of bullets from their moving vehicle into a crowded shopping center. The shooters had total disregard for the safety of innocent bystanders. As Salemme ran from his attackers, they sprayed the area with automatic weapon fire. Salemme was hit four times before stumbling into a nearby pizza shop. After being rushed to a nearby emergency hospital, and undergoing hours of intensive surgery, Cadillac Frank would survive the attack.

On June 27, 1989, Mercurio told Agent Connolly that the murder attempt on Salemme was planned and carried out by the Russo faction of the Boston mob. Mercurio specifically named J.R. Russo, Vincent The Animal Ferrara, and Robert Carrozza as the persons who handled most of the details of the Salemme "hit." But Connolly's 209 reports conveniently made no reference to Mercurio's role in the shooting. Once again, the arrogant agent, as he had in the past, would manipulate the official report to his satisfaction.

On August 2, 1989, an informant whose supervisor, James Ring, regarded as highly reliable advised him that Mercurio had played a central role in the Salemme shooting. The informant told Ring that Mercurio was indeed the person who had set up Salemme, and that Mercurio had fled after the shooting had failed. The informant also reported that Patriarca was urging the Russo-led faction to settle their problems with Salemme peacefully. However, Mercurio was against any peace agreement. As long as Salemme remained alive and involved with the LCN, he was still a threat to his and Flemmi and Bulger's alliance with Connolly and the FBI. Mercurio was also fearful of retaliation for his role in setting up the extremely dangerous and capable Salemme.

Cadillac Frank Salemme was one of the most loyal and respected members of the LCN. He had always conducted himself in the ways of the old-time Mafia dons; he was a man of honor. Flemmi and company rightfully feared Salemme would detect their alliance with the FBI. Flemmi knew it would only be a matter of time before the very resourceful Salemme would see through it all.

Supervisor Ring knew that Mercurio had set up Salemme. He also knew that the Attorney General's guidelines provided for a special review process if an FBI field office wanted to keep an informant open after it learned that he had participated in a serious act of violence or any other serious crime. The Attorney General's guidelines also required that state or local law enforcement authorities be informed of the evidence concerning the informant's crime or that FBI headquarters and the Assistant Attorney General be promptly consulted. Ring was also told by a highly reliable informant that Mercurio had played a central role in the murder of Connecticut mob figure Billy Grasso.

The serious acts of murder and attempted murder were never reported to FBI headquarters or the Assistant Attorney General. FBI headquarters and the Assistant Attorney General should have been advised of the information. Instead, the Boston Bureau continued to use Mercurio as an informant, despite knowledge that he had been involved in a murder and attempted murder while an FBI informant. The war on the mob was paramount, and once again the Attorney General's guidelines would be ignored by an arrogant FBI.

Later, when Prosecutor Diane Kottmeyer learned of Mercurio's role in the Salemme shooting, she asked Ring whether it presented a problem. She was concerned that the Attorney General's guidelines had been compromised. Supervisor Ring told her that using Mercurio was not a problem. Again, the FBI completely ignored Attorney General Levi's guidelines requiring authorization of criminal activity and reporting of unauthorized crimes committed by informants. The established standards and procedures aimed at ending abuses by the FBI were disregarded.

Chapter 13

A MAFIA INDUCTION CEREMONY

After the failed attempt on Salemme, Raymond Patriarca, fearing the worst in a struggle for control of the LCN, called for a truce. One of Patriarca's lieutenants, William Grasso, had been slain earlier by the rival mobsters and they had nearly succeeded with Salemme. Junior Patriarca had been given a responsibility he found difficult to maintain, nor was it one which he actually desired.

In 1981, when his late father had become seriously ill, Junior was given the task of running the family. However, he quickly designated others to the position of overseeing the business of the LCN. Junior was quoted as saying he "could not stand being his father's agent."

In September 1989, J.R. Russo and others had threatened to kill Junior if he did not step down. Yet, out of respect for his father, a Mafia legend, Junior was given a "pass." Russo had consulted with organized crime bosses in New York before he made his move on Patriarca. Junior's power had been diminished, but out of respect for the Patriarca name, he still remained boss, although he gave Russo a great deal of power as well. He was not as strong as his father, who would have received all the help needed from the New York Mafia during a "war."

Junior Patriarca had concerns that the Russo faction would continue to kill more of those who had allied themselves with him. In a move to avoid any further bloodshed, Russo would be given the position of consigliere of the family. However, Russo wanted to strengthen his control, insisting that fifteen new members of the family be "made," including three or four immediately.

The fifteen proposed for induction to La Cosa Nostra would be those loyal to Russo. Patriarca would agree to Russo's demand, but it was only a stall. Junior was counting on the anticipated federal indictments to eliminate the necessity of "making" new members loyal to Russo. Beginning in June 1989, Mercurio was among those telling the FBI that there might soon be a ceremony to "make" new members of the Patriarca family.

During the summer of 1989, informants also reported that Russo and other members of the LCN were meeting at a variety of new locations and would at times talk while walking outside. Physical surveillance conducted by the FBI confirmed this to be true. In response, Supervisor Ring instructed prosecutor Diane Kottmeyer to draft criminal complaints, and have them available if necessary to arrest Russo and his crew. Ring also discussed with Kottmeyer the possibility of getting a roving bug warrant. Ring was not yet aware of the location of the induction ceremony, thus the need for this type of electronic surveillance.

The roving bug is the most intrusive device of wiretapping. It is not to be used in situations where traditional investigative techniques can achieve the same results. What makes the roving bug different than a traditional form of wiretapping is not its size—no bigger than a dime—but that it uses the location's own power lines to transmit conversations from within. Some legal experts say that its use is a clear violation of Fourth Amendment protection against unreasonable searches.

Congress made it clear that when using the roving bug, "The government is obligated to disclose to the court all the information it possesses relevant to the need when using this form of bug."

The roving intercept provision replaces the usual practice that the location to be searched be identified in a warrant by an address with a description of that place. When requesting a roving wire interception, you must establish that the specifically targeted subjects use various and changing facilities for the purpose of avoiding electronic surveillance, and that the locations in question are unknown. The FBI would make no effort to obtain the testimony of Mercurio about the induction ceremony, nor ask him to record it. Had the FBI done so, there then would have been no need for a court-ordered bug. The FBI preferred to allow Mercurio to flee and avoid any indictment, and in so doing, the FBI would be relieved of the risk that the prosecution of Russo, Ferrara, Carrozza, and their codefendants would be jeopardized by the issue that would have been presented by Mercurio's dual status as a defendant and an FBI source with regard to the induction ceremony. The lengths to which the FBI would go did not stop with intrusive wiretapping.

The Bureau continued to use Mercurio, even though they were aware of his role as the set-up man in the attempted murder of Frank Salemme. The FBI showed no concern that Mercurio was part of the plan to murder an individual in broad daylight, with the possibility that some innocent bystanders could be killed, including women and children.

The FBI was keenly aware of the fact that Mercurio was leading the call to finish off Salemme. He was extremely fearful that Salemme at some point in time would come at him, seeking revenge. Clearly, Mercurio should have been indicted for his role in the murder plot. Instead, he was continued as a Top Echelon Informant.

Mercurio's flight would also cover up the violations of the Attorney General's guidelines committed by Supervisor Ring and his colleagues when they decided to continue Mercurio as an informant, despite his role in the Salemme shooting, without consulting FBI headquarters and the Assistant Attorney General. But the plan all along was to have Mercurio go on the lam; thus, the FBI would be relieved of responsibility for any of these issues.

Throughout the summer and early fall of 1989, Supervisor Ring worked hard to prevent the U.S. Attorneys who would be prosecuting the Russo faction from discovering that Mercurio was an informant and from reviewing his FBI file.

Jeffrey Auerhahn and Greg Sullivan were the Strike Force attorneys presenting the case against Mercurio, Russo, and the others to a grand jury. When they learned that Mercurio's parole had been terminated early, they suspected corruption and wanted to investigate. Prosecutor Kottmeyer knew that Mercurio was an FBI informant and discussed the matter with Ring. Kottmeyer felt that it was essential that Auerhahn and Sullivan be advised of Mercurio's role as an informant, and be permitted to review his FBI informant file to determine whether it contained any information or evidence that the defense could raise with issues concerning whether Sixth Amendment rights had been violated because an informant was reporting putative defendants' discussions with their attorneys, among other things. Even though Kottmeyer raised these issues with Ring, he still refused to permit Auerhahn and Sullivan to be told that Mercurio was an informant, or to review the file. Ring was not concerned with Sixth Amendment rights violations, as was the case with Kottmeyer. He knew that Mercurio would not be around; he would be given a head start prior to the issuance of indictments.

On September 1, 1989, a frustrated Kottmeyer sent a memorandum to David Margolis, the Chief of the Organized Crime and Racketeering Section of the Criminal Division of the Department of Justice, seeking support for her insistence that her two Strike Force attorneys be permitted to review Mercurio's informant file. Kottmeyer explained her concerns about the possible authorization defense Mercurio might assert based in part on the successful effort to have his parole terminated and foreseeable Sixth Amendment issues that could arise when Mercurio was charged. The FBI's battle to keep Auerhahn and Sullivan from reviewing Mercurio's informant file continued throughout October of 1989. It was finally resolved by an agreement between high level officials of the Department of Justice and the FBI in Washington.

On October 25, 1989, it was agreed that Sullivan would be permitted to review Mercurio's informant file in the presence of an FBI agent, but he could not take any notes or make any copies of any documents. The following day, on October 26, Sullivan read Mercurio's informant file. He was not allowed to disclose any information contained in the file without the approval of the FBI. The effort by Supervisor Ring and the FBI to keep the prosecutors from knowing that Mercurio was an informant was designed to minimize the risk that his role would be disclosed to the court, thus avoiding any legal issues which might be brought to play by the defense.

In October 1989, Sonny Mercurio would meet John Connolly at Harvard College in Cambridge, Massachusetts, outside of Boston. Through the efforts of some powerful politically-connected friends, Connolly was able to enroll at the prestigious school, although not qualified to do so. Connolly was preparing to use his ill-gotten degree from Harvard, along with the aid of some South Boston politicians, to secure a high-paying job after retirement. While on recess from one of his classes, Connolly would be given the names of four members of the Patriarca family who were to be inducted into "Their Thing." As the two stood by the statue of John Harvard, Mercurio told Connolly that Vincent Federico, Richard Floramo, Carmen Tortora, and Robert DeLuca were going to be "made."

Mercurio also informed the agent that Vincent Ferrara had told him that the ceremony would have to be conducted while Federico, who was in prison, was on a furlough. Mercurio said the ceremony would be held somewhere in the vicinity of the Howard Johnson's Restaurant at Wellington Circle in Medford, Massachusetts. He related that he would be one of the persons designated to drive those attending from the restaurant to the site of the ceremony. Connolly knew he was onto something big. All along, the FBI wanted to prove to disbelievers that there was a Mafia. Intercepting a Mafia induction ceremony would prove once and for all the existence of the "secret society."

For years, criminal defense attorneys had argued that there was no such Mafia; the bugging would silence those critics. The taping of an induction ceremony, including the pricking of a trigger finger while a holy card burned in cupped hands, would be of immense value in future government prosecutions and Congressional hearings. Connolly and Supervisor Ring continued to ask Mercurio to provide them with more information concerning the ceremony. Although Mercurio promptly provided them with the information he received, no record was made of the information he furnished to the FBI.

A week before the ceremony, Vincent Ferrara told Mercurio that Vinny Federico had received a furlough for Sunday, October 29, 1989, and that the induction ceremony would be held then.

Vinny Federico had been incarcerated on an attempted murder charge. He was a close and loyal friend to Ferrara, who was proposing him for induction into "Their Thing." Massachusetts had allowed inmates with good conduct, who were about to complete their sentences, a furlough from prison. The purpose of the furlough was to visit with and strengthen family ties. On his application, Federico accurately listed "family business" as the reason for wanting the furlough.

Mercurio wasted no time reporting the new information to the FBI, assuring them that a ceremony was a "definite go" for October 29, 1989. Mercurio was not given the address of the ceremony; however, being one of the drivers of the participants to the event, he and the FBI knew that he would have to be told of the location in advance.

Prosecutor Diane Kottmeyer met with Supervisor Ring and two of his assistants and was told that the Patriarca family would be conducting an induction ceremony in the near future. Kottmeyer, who was the Strike Force Chief, knew that Mercurio was an informant, due in part to her role in having his parole terminated early. She was asked to prepare the necessary application and supporting affidavit. Ring made no mention of the information he and Connolly were receiving from Mercurio. The withheld information would have given Kottmeyer notice that the application was false and misleading.

On October 27, 1989, a warrant was drafted for a roving bug deemed necessary because it was impractical to specify the location to be bugged. The FBI desperately wanted to have an actual Mafia induction ceremony on tape. The Bureau had never succeeded in recording such an event. The opportunity for overhearing and recording a baptism ceremony would give the government a valuable tool to use at other Mafia trials across the nation, for years to come.

At the same time, Mercurio received the information that Ring and Connolly desperately wanted knowledge that the ceremony would be held at 34 Guild Street, Medford, Massachusetts, on October 29. Ring knew that there would be at least one informant, Mercurio, at the ceremony. But the FBI sought a warrant for a roving bug that could be used at multiple, unidentified locations rather than authorization to bug 34 Guild Street alone. This step was taken in order to protect its source, Mercurio. The FBI had no intention of using that warrant to intercept conversations more than once. They now had solid information that the ceremony would be held at 34 Guild Street several hours before Kottmeyer met with the judge to obtain the warrant authorizing the roving surveillance based upon representations that it was then impractical to identify the location to be bugged.

The court was misled by the government. Not only was the issuing judge lied to, but no effort was made by the FBI to obtain Mercurio's testimony concerning the induction ceremony. Had they asked him to record the event, there would have been no need for a court-ordered bug. The FBI had Mercurio over a barrel. They could have tried to persuade him to cooperate by threatening him with prosecution for his role in the Salemme shooting as well as the Sagansky extortion. Instead of taking these steps, Ring and Connolly would give Mercurio a pass; he would be permitted to flee before any indictments. The government lied to the judge in obtaining the warrant authorizing roving surveillance, stating it was impractical to identify the location to be bugged. In reality, the FBI was concerned that while participating in the induction ceremony, the discovery of Mercurio's dual role as a codefendant and a government informant could jeopardize the prosecution of Russo, Ferrara, Carrozza, and others.

Allowing Mercurio an opportunity to flee would cover up for many years to come the violation of the Attorney General's guidelines committed by Ring and Connolly when they decided to continue him as an informant, despite what they believed to be Mercurio's involvement in the Salemme shooting.

Those guidelines directed the FBI not to take any action to conceal a crime by one of its informants. If the FBI learned that one of its informants had committed a serious crime, and did not disclose that information to the appropriate law enforcement officials, then the Bureau was directed to inform the Department of Justice. The decision as to whether to continue the informant or close, and subsequently subject the individual to prosecution, would then be made by the Justice Department.

In any event, the Attorney General's guidelines were ignored once again. While the Justice Department has historically respected the right of the FBI to maintain the secrecy of its informants from other law enforcement agencies and federal prosecutors, courts have recognized their duty to compel disclosure of an informant's identity when it has been demonstrated that such information is relevant or helpful to the defense of an accused or essential to the fair determination of a case. But, with Mercurio being given a head start to flee the pending indictments, Ring and Connolly felt certain that they would not have to contend with the matter of disclosure, and thus, they would avoid opening up a "Pandora's Box."

Knowing that Vincent Federico, one of the persons to be "baptized," had applied for a prison furlough, Ring obtained Federico's furlough application. The application indicated that on October 29, Federico was planning to go to 34 Guild Street. Ring then sent several FBI agents to conduct a surveillance of that address. Ring intended to arrest Joseph J.R. Russo, Vincent The Animal Ferrara, and Robert Carrozza at the conclusion of the forthcoming induction ceremony. Ring would be overruled by the head of the Organized Crime Section. There was concern that those arrests would result in the prompt disclosure of an ongoing electronic surveillance being conducted in Connecticut.

At 12:50 P.M. on October 27, excited FBI agents observed J.R. Russo, Vincent Ferrara, and informant Mercurio arrive at 34 Guild Street with the owner of the property, Stephen DiStefano. The agents had been watching 34 Guild Street from the home of Agent Stan Moody, who lived two houses down. Stephen DiStefano had no idea that Moody, his neighbor, was an FBI agent. The Moody home was perfect for surveilling the comings and goings at the Guild Street home. The group of agents watched intently; they knew they were part of a history-making event, the impending recording of a Mafia induction ceremony.

Inside 34 Guild Street, Russo and Ferrara were also excited. The murder of Billy Grasso in Connecticut and the attempted murder of Cadillac Frank Salemme had prompted Raymond Patriarca to seek a truce. The four new men to be inducted into "Their Thing" were loyal to the Russo faction. In response to the agreed truce, Patriarca appointed Russo as consigliere, a person who would settle disputes and render decisions. But the agreed truce by Patriarca was only a stall. He was buying time until the anticipated indictments of Russo and his crew came down. Once that occurred, he would again take full control of the New England Mafia.

After leaving the 34 Guild Street house, informant Mercurio returned to Vanessa's restaurant and called Supervisor Ring. "Vinnie Federico will go to 34 Guild Street, his brother-in-law's house, on Sunday, October 29, and the making ceremony will begin at that location around 11:00 A.M. Federico's brother-in-law and sister will leave the house on Saturday afternoon. The sister knows nothing about them using the house, but the brother-in-law does," Mercurio reported.

"Are you certain they are going to use the 34 Guild Street house?" asked Ring.

"I'm sure that's where the ceremony will take place," Mercurio said.

"I had some agents observing you, Russo, and Ferrara at 34 Guild Street," Ring said.

"I figured that," Mercurio responded.

Ring then spoke to Prosecutor Kottmeyer and provided her with information from other sources, particularly Federico's furlough application and the FBI agents' surveillance of 34 Guild Street, but he did not share with her the information provided by Mercurio before the application for a roving bug was filed.

The failure to provide Kottmeyer with information Ring received from Mercurio, or the mention of Mercurio at all, prevented her from considering on a fully-informed basis whether it continued to be legally permissible to omit any reference to the induction ceremony from the application which had not yet been approved by the Department of Justice or formally submitted to the court. Ring's plan was to exclude knowledge of the induction ceremony, and not acknowledge the status of an informant—Mercurio—attending the event.

In the late afternoon of October 27, 1989, Mercurio met Agent Connolly and Supervisor Ring in a hotel room and reaffirmed that the ceremony was a definite go for 34 Guild Street on October 29. No report was made of the meeting with Mercurio, a violation of FBI policy and practice.

Later that same day Kottmeyer received approval for a roving bug from Federal Judge Nelson. Although the government had received reliable information indicating that the ceremony would be held at 34 Guild Street, that information was withheld from the application.

On the afternoon of Saturday, October 28, 1989, FBI agents who were surveying the Guild Street residence observed the DiStefano couple pack their suitcases in their car and leave their home as Mercurio had said they would. Later that evening an FBI locksmith, along with a group of sophisticated electronic technicians, made entry at the Guild Street home. Within a short period of time, the necessary installation was in place, ready to intercept any verbal communication.

The following day, October 29, events were developing as anticipated. Mercurio would meet some of the mob members at the Howard Johnson restaurant at Wellington Circle. He would then proceed to drive the participants to 34 Guild Street.

Inside the home, a total of seventeen known mob members of the Patriarca crime family were already present. The "who's who" of the New England LCN included J.R. Russo, Vinnie The Animal Ferrara, Robert Carrozza, Matthew L. Gugliametti, Jr., Pasquale Gallea, Louis Failla, Dominic "Slats" Marangelli, Gaetano Milano, Biagio Digiacomo, Charles Quintana, and Raymond J. Patriarca, along with others. Patriarca, the reigning Mafia boss in New England, would begin by saying, "The problems we had in the past have been straightened out. We are here to bring four new members into Our Thing. Vinnie Federico, Bobby DeLuca, Richie Floramo, and Carmen Tortora are here today to become made soldiers in our family."

The Russo faction was feeling fairly secure. The four new members about to take the oath of "Omerta" (code of silence) belonged to them. The plan was to add an additional dozen or so new members also loyal to the Russo crew at a later date.

In an effort to avoid an all-out war between the two mob groups, Patriarca reluctantly agreed to the present four new members. Cadillac Frank Salemme would not be attending the baptism ritual. He was against the "making" of the mobsters, especially those loyal to the Russo-Ferrara faction. He was still bitter at Mercurio for his role in setting him up for assassination. Salemme felt certain that Mercurio, out of fear of retaliation from the very capable Salemme, would not feel safe until Salemme was killed. However, Mercurio would be no match for a prepared Salemme, and Mercurio knew it.

Instead, Mercurio was making plans to flee Boston shortly. But the cagey Mercurio would commit one more act of treachery shortly before fleeing.

Salemme had tried to persuade Patriarca to refuse the proposed "making," noting that "the books," membership into La Cosa Nostra, had been previously closed. However, Patriarca decided to go along with Russo's demand. Also absent was Anthony The Saint St. Laurent, a crude and unpopular gambler, who would eat dinner in the most elegant restaurants using only his fingers. Later on he would be suspected of being an FBI informant.

Before the ceremony was to begin, Raymond Patriarca told the newly-proposed men that the Mafia membership was "not a ticket to abuse people."

Biagio Digiacomo, a native of Sicily, would be the master of ceremonies. He began speaking to the four in a strong Sicilian dialect. Joe Russo would

repeat Digiacomo's words in English, in order that they might fully comprehend. Mercurio would calmly approach the television set, turning down
the volume. He wanted to make certain the voices of the participants could
be clearly recorded.

One by one the four would be asked, "What if I told you your brother or
your kid was a rat, and was going to hurt one of us by ratting, what would
you do?"

"Then he's gotta go," they each replied.

"If any one of us here asks you to do that, would you kill him?"

"Yes," they replied.

"What if your mother, father, brother, or sister, were on their death beds,
but we needed you right away. Would you leave them for us?"

"Yes, I would leave them," they answered.

"You know the severity of this Thing of Ours?" they were asked.

"Yes."

"You want it that badly, that desperately?"

"Yes," they replied.

Following other tests of loyalty, Federico, Tortoro, Floramo, and DeLuca
were instructed to draw blood from their trigger fingers with a knife. While a
holy card with a picture of a saint burned in their cupped hands, the four men
would swear the Mafia creed: "As burns this saint, so will burn my soul, I enter
into this organization alive, and leave it dead," said the four men.

After the ceremony, the four new "made" men would be given the rules
of La Cosa Nostra by Consigliere Russo and the Capo Regimes (captains),
Ferrara and Digiacomo.

Russo would begin, "You now are in this Thing of Ours, you are soldiers
and must obey any orders given to you by the Capo Regimes. When you
have a problem with another made guy, don't make any moves on your
own, you come to me with your 'beef.' I will hear both sides, then rule on
who's right or wrong. That's the way we straighten out any problems."

Then Ferrara added, "You are not supposed to tell another guy that you belong to Our Thing unless another 'made' guy introduces you as one of us."

After the ceremony, the Mafiosis would leave 34 Guild Street in small groups, avoiding unnecessary attention. Mercurio, Ferrara, and Russo would remain to discuss the upcoming Doc Sagansky extortion indictment. After a brief weighing of their options, Mercurio would "advocate the lam." He made his choice clear to Russo and Ferrara, telling them that there was no other way to avoid a long prison term. He would not do anymore time. As far as Mercurio was concerned, fleeing was his best bet. In doing so, he believed that his role as an informant would go undetected. He had not one ace in the hole, but two—Connolly and Ring. He could have cared less about his two close Mafia friends, Russo and Ferrara, or any of the others. The rat had eaten the cheese.

Later that evening, Mercurio called Supervisor Ring, who told Mercurio that he was aware that he had turned the volume on the television down. He also admonished Mercurio not to mention the matter to anyone else because it could jeopardize his safety. Ring believed that Mercurio was saying goodbye and that he would not hear from him again.

The following day Mercurio spoke to Agent Connolly who told Mercurio that he had been tracked by airplane while driving from Wellington Circle to the 34 Guild Street ceremony. During the conversation, there was a strong assumption that Mercurio was told it was time to leave town. Mercurio's departure from Boston occurred at about the same time Steve Flemmi returned from Asia, where he had attended a reunion of Korean War vets. Flemmi was a member of the International Association of Airborne Veterans.

On November 13, Mercurio told Ring that Russo, Ferrara, and Carrozza were all in the Boston area. Due in part to Mercurio's tip, Prosecutor Kottmeyer obtained complaints authorizing the arrests of Russo, Ferrara, Carrozza, Mercurio, and Lepore for the Sagansky extortion.

Kottmeyer knew that Mercurio had left Boston and could not be located. However, Ring and Connolly could easily have contacted Mercurio by simply calling Vanessa's restaurant and leaving a message. Mercurio had always returned Connolly's calls, and met with him and Ring whenever asked. The FBI made no effort to contact, meet with, or arrest Mercurio.

Ring established separate teams of FBI agents to arrest Russo, Ferrara, and Carrozza. No team was established to try to find Mercurio or arrest him. Mercurio had been given a head start by the FBI; he was a fugitive, but no one was out to find him or arrest him. With Mercurio on the lam, the FBI and the government did not have to contend with the legal issues arising from Mercurio's role as an informant and a defendant, an issue about which Prosecutor Kottmeyer had concerns.

On November 16, 1989, Russo, Ferrara, Carrozza, and Mercurio were indicted. The task of finding the fugitive Mercurio was given to Special Agent Carter. Carter knew that Mercurio was an informant who was responsible for the interception of the Mafia induction ceremony at 34 Guild Street. Carter also knew that Connolly and Supervisor Ring were Mercurio's personal handlers, and that they had a special interest in Mercurio. Although Agents Carter and Connolly were close friends, Carter never asked Connolly for help in locating Mercurio. In fact, Ring and Connolly told Carter that they did not know where Mercurio was. Carter was never told that they had always been able to contact the fugitive by simply calling Vanessa's and leaving a message. Mercurio continued to call Connolly. He wanted to keep abreast of events concerning Russo and the others, and be assured his role in the bugging of the induction ceremony remained undetected. Connolly never told Carter about Mercurio's calls.

In December of 1990, Special Agent John Connolly retired on short notice. Connolly had had a very successful run, climaxing with his best effort yet—the taping of a Mafia induction ceremony. He received a plush job as head of corporate security at Boston Edison, a company that was obligated to the powerful Senate President William Bulger.

Earlier that year, Supervisor of the Organized Crime Squad Ring had also retired. Ed Quinn, another close friend of John Connolly, would succeed Supervisor Ring. With Connolly's retirement, Bulger and Flemmi would be administratively closed as informants.

They, along with Mercurio and Connolly, had brought down the new pretenders to the New England mob. Most of the Mafiosi would plead guilty to the RICO charges. Raymond Patriarca received an eight-year sentence, J.R. Russo was given sixteen years, and Vincent The Animal Ferrara was dealt the stiffest sentence, a twenty-two-year prison term. A portion of the sentences for Russo, Ferrara, and their allies was tacked on due to their refusal to admit being part of a secret society (LCN), or even knowledge of its existence. Judge Wolf expressed to the men that he admired their loyalty to the oath of Omerta; however, he had no choice but to add the additional years to their sentences. The men accepted their punishment honorably. They would be the last of the stand-up guys.

Joseph J.R. Russo also pled guilty to murdering Joe Barboza, and was incarcerated at the Lompoc Federal Prison in California. There, he and long-time friend New York mob boss Carmine Persico, would spend their days cultivating roses. Later, he would die in prison of lung cancer.

Whitey Bulger and Steve Flemmi were on the sidelines, "licking their chops." They would step in and profit from the vacuum created by the downfall of yet another band of mobsters. Now they would have free sailing throughout Boston. They no longer would have to contend with any local Mafiosi. Their extortion of drug dealers and bookmakers would reach a new high. Mercurio had avoided the fate of his lifelong friends. He was on the lam, enjoying some form of freedom, thanks to Ring and Connolly. Most criminals would consider themselves lucky to have escaped a federal indictment, and would lay low. Not Mercurio. He would continue to deal drugs from Florida to California. He knew he could count on the FBI for protection, if caught. Mercurio had now acquired the same supreme arrogance that Agent Connolly had displayed throughout his career with the FBI.

In December 1990 or January of 1991, a Massachusetts Millions State Lottery entry was purchased by Michael Linskey at Whitey Bulger's Rotary

Variety Store, and registered in his name. Linskey's entry would then automatically participate in drawings over the following year. In July 1991, Linskey's entry won, and was worth approximately $14.3 million before taxes, payable in annual payments over a twenty-year span beginning in July 1991, and continuing through July 2010. Michael's brother Patrick was a close associate of Whitey Bulger. It didn't take long for the greedy Bulger to muzzle his way into a piece of the winnings. Bulger would make an offer that Michael Linskey would not refuse. Whitey would be kind enough to leave the ticket holder half the proceeds. Michael Linskey had a partner whether he wanted one or not.

Out of the goodness of his heart, Bulger paid Michael Linskey $700,000, in blood and drug money, for a one-sixth share worth nearly $2 million. Shortly before the first disbursement of the winnings, papers were provided to the State Lottery Commission indicating that Whitey Bulger, Patrick Linskey, and another Bulger gang member, Kevin Weeks, were by prior agreement entitled to equal shares of a one-half interest in the winnings. Michael Linskey would receive half of the winnings; the other half would be divided by Bulger, Patrick Linskey, and Kevin Weeks, or one-sixth each. Arrangements were made with the South Boston Savings Bank to assist in distributing the winnings. In July of each year, beginning in 1991, the winnings, less taxes, were paid to Michael Linskey, who deposited them in his account at the South Boston bank. The bank would then distribute the funds. Bulger's share of the winnings would be deposited in a joint checking account he held with his brother, John.

Events could not have been going better for Bulger, Flemmi, and Connolly. Bulger had recently made a score with the lottery, Flemmi was making a killing with real estate, and Connolly had a big job with Boston Edison. Call it the luck of the Irish, but the leprechaun along with his magical powers would soon evaporate.

−Chapter 14−

AN EXTENDED VACATION

After Connolly's retirement, a new brand of agents had quietly begun replacing the old regime. The terrain was changing, not only with the Boston Bureau, but with the United States Attorney's Office in Boston as well. There was a new sheriff in town. Fred Wyshak had arrived in Boston with a reputation as a hard-nosed, no-nonsense prosecutor. It wasn't long before he came to the conclusion that Whitey Bulger had been living a charmed life of crime.

The thirty-seven-year-old had acquired a reputation for making big cases, and Whitey Bulger was a big case to make. Getting Bulger would become an obsession with him. He didn't want to hear that Bulger could not be taken, or wasn't worth the effort. The determined Wyshak was not about to have anyone do his thinking for him. He was puzzled as to why someone had not gone after Bulger, and why so many in the Boston Bureau were reluctant to do so.

In 1992, the United States Attorney's Office began a grand jury investigation targeting Bulger and Flemmi. The two Winter Hill wise guys had put the arm on most of the local bookmakers. Bulger and Flemmi had for many years extorted bookies to pay tribute, better known as monthly rent payments, for the right to operate. Burton "Chico" Krantz was one of the top bookmakers caught in the jaws of Whitey Bulger.

Chico had been paying Bulger and Flemmi $3,000 monthly for the right to take action throughout the greater Boston area. Krantz was an extremely sharp odds maker who would make large bets, and take large bets on all sporting events. The much-talented Krantz would become very successful in the world of sports betting. He was well-known throughout the gambling community. The mastermind of sports betting caught the attention of the State Police.

The heat was on Krantz—it was time for a vacation. He had grown tired of the cold and snow, and the never-ending demand for more money from Bulger and Flemmi.

Chico decided to try and relocate to Las Vegas, a new frontier, where sports betting was legal, and there would be no wise guys with whom to contend. He began bargaining to buy Gary Austin's sports book, located on the famous Las Vegas Strip. Chico dreamed of having a legitimate sports book of his own. He believed that he was sharper than the local gamblers, and was ready to match his sports gambling knowledge against the Vegas high rollers. He had already picked out a name for his sports book, "Boston Blackie's." He was ready to go up against the many talented gamblers who migrated to Vegas from all over the country. After meeting with a very powerfully connected Las Vegas attorney, Chico was given the bad news. He was told that he would not be able to obtain a gaming license due to his legal troubles in Boston, to where the dejected Krantz would return.

Shortly after his return, an investigation would lead to his arrest. During a search of his home, keys to a safety deposit box were found. Over two million in cash was discovered stuffed in oversized boxes belonging to the high roller Chico. The two million not only represented a problem with the government, but Chico had a more serious cause for concern with regard to Bulger and Flemmi. He had lied to the gangsters when he was being assessed a street tax, crying poverty in order to avoid paying a greater amount. News that Krantz was sitting on that kind of cash would certainly cause the cold-blooded killers to take action, and Chico knew it.

Word on the street was that Bulger and Flemmi were going after Chico and his two million, if he were to beat the charges against him. A money laundering case against Krantz was turned over to the United States Attorney's Office. Fred Wyshak now had his first crack at Bulger and Flemmi. He and a few trusted prosecutors would work on Krantz. Chico would be given a choice; either work with the government prosecutors, or do some serious prison time. Wyshak was as good, if not better, at getting an individual to roll, as was John Connolly before him.

Fearful of a long prison sentence along with the forfeiture of two million in cash, it didn't take long for Chico to cave in. He agreed to become a witness against Bulger and Flemmi. He also began to direct prosecutors to others who had been paying Bulger and Flemmi "rent." The ball was now rolling, heading straight to Bulger and Flemmi. Other bookmakers were falling in line with Krantz and agreed to become key witnesses against Bulger and Flemmi. A grand jury was hearing the evidence, and talk of federal indictments against Bulger and Flemmi was emerging. However, prosecutors were troubled with reports that Bulger and Flemmi were informants. They began asking for confirmation that Bulger was an informant and for an opportunity to review his file. The prosecutors were denied their request. They were told that pursuant to the Attorney General's guidelines and Bureau policy, the FBI would not confirm or deny Bulger's status.

All through the Bulger-Connolly reign, the guidelines had been ignored and violated. Only now, when it suited them, would the FBI deem the Attorney General's guidelines appropriate. Despite repeated attempts by the U.S. Attorney's Office, requests for information with regard to Bulger's relationship with the FBI were rebuffed.

Meanwhile, although no longer employed by the Bureau, John Connolly was able to keep his childhood friend Whitey Bulger abreast of the grand jury investigation. Connolly knew that Bulger and Flemmi were targets of the grand jury probe; he was able to monitor the progress of the case through a few still loyal to him. Mike Buckley, a close friend and colleague of Connolly's, was suspected of providing Connolly with information after his retirement. Connolly reassured his two prize informants not to be concerned. His continuing arrogance would blind him to the serious events that were about to take place.

Bulger and Flemmi were monitoring reports concerning the grand jury probe and its progress. They knew that the grand jury would, unless extended or succeeded, expire in mid-September 1994 because several witnesses who had been held in contempt and incarcerated expected to be released in mid-September.

In August of 1994, Bulger said to Flemmi, "John says the indictment will be coming down. It's time to take a vacation."

"I'm going to Montreal," replied Flemmi.

"We'll stay in touch with each other by using our beepers," Bulger added.

Bulger told Theresa Stanley, with whom he had been romantically involved for thirty years, that they would take a vacation. It was a lam rather than a vacation for Bulger, and some lam it was. Bulger and Theresa visited Graceland, the home of Elvis Presley, in Memphis, Tennessee. They also traveled to Dublin, London, Rome, and throughout the United States, including New York, New Orleans, California, and the Grand Canyon. Bulger and Theresa went in style—he had an endless supply of dirty money to burn, money that had been acquired by blood, bullets, and bodies.

From September 1994 until January 1995, the two lamsters were in frequent contact by using their beepers and pay phones.

"I'm staying on top of things," Bulger told Flemmi.

"Let me know as soon as you hear anything," Flemmi said.

"No problem; I'll keep you up to date," Bulger responded.

Bulger had been using the alias "Tom Baxter." He and Theresa Stanley stayed with the Matos family in Selden, New York, before they decided to return to Boston shortly before Christmas 1994. They remained in Boston for a few days before leaving on another trip.

In January 1995, Flemmi, too, returned to Boston. On or about January 3, 1995, Flemmi received a phone call from Bulger at his mother's house.

"There's a prosecution memorandum that was sent to Washington, recommending we be indicted," Bulger said.

"When do you think it will come?" Flemmi asked.

"From what I understand, we will be indicted in about a week, or around January 10," Bulger responded.

The information no doubt came from Connolly, who had been monitoring the grand jury investigation for his two prize informants. Connolly still had a few agents loyal to him in the Boston Bureau.

Connolly's information was on the mark. However, the cocksure and arrogant Flemmi miscalculated. He believed that he had time to wrap up some business affairs, not to mention his farewells to the many women in his life. Flemmi, however, did not realize that by not leaving promptly, he ran the risk of being arrested on a complaint before he was indicted, in the same manner that had been employed to capture Russo, Ferrara, and Carrozza. This form of arrest was used by the government due to concerns about leaks that would allow defendants to skip town before forthcoming indictments were issued.

Wyshak and his prosecutors had developed a strong case with which to charge Flemmi, Bulger, and George Kaufman, that of conspiring to extort bookmaker Burton Chico Krantz.

On January 5, 1995, Flemmi was spotted at the Quincy Market, a popular shopping center in the historical section of downtown Boston. Quincy Market was the "in place," comprised of a host of ethnic restaurants, along with endless high-end specialty stores. Flemmi had been at the Quincy Market overseeing the renovation of Schooner's, a restaurant owned by his sons. The carefree gangster was too involved with the progress of the soon-to-be-hot spot, and the glamour girl with him, to pay attention to the undercover state troopers who had been waiting for Flemmi's arrival. He was promptly arrested and brought to FBI headquarters.

Once inside headquarters, the arrogant Flemmi was confident that former Agent Connolly would take care of the problem. He could at least expect a reasonable bail then hit the road, maybe hook up with Bulger once again. He was certain that his service to the FBI would afford him some consideration. He had avoided far more serious situations thanks to Connolly and earlier, Agents Paul Rico and Dennis Condon.

When Flemmi was arrested, Bulger and Theresa Stanley were heading back to Boston. She had had enough "vacation" and wanted to go home.

Bulger agreed to drop her off, and then leave again until the heat cooled down. But while driving through Connecticut en route to Boston, they heard a news flash on the car radio—Steve Flemmi had been arrested. Bulger made a quick change of plans, and he and Stanley were on their way back to New York.

In anticipation of the imminent indictment of Bulger, the United States Attorney's Office again asked the FBI whether he was an informant, because it was anticipated that the government would have to disclose exculpatory information to Bulger and the codefendants. The Boston office of the FBI still refused to comply with the request. They were concerned that confirming Bulger's position with the FBI would open up a can of worms.

The Boston Division of the FBI expressed the view to FBI headquarters that there was no reasonable expectation that Bulger or Flemmi would raise the issue of their former informant status. Just as in the case of Sonny Mercurio, Bulger and Flemmi would be alerted to their imminent indictment, thus giving them the opportunity to flee. With the two being on the lam, as Mercurio had been, their informant status would not be raised nor would there be a legal issue involving the codefendants.

The arrogant FBI in Boston also believed that if issues of Bulger and Flemmi's relationship with the FBI were raised by the codefendants, no judge would compel disclosure of their status.

After a series of tug-o-wars between the United States Attorney's Office and the Boston FBI, Special Agent in Charge Swensen made a decision to disclose the identities of informants to the United States Attorneys. The information had to be disclosed; failure to do so could wreck the upcoming organized crime indictments scheduled to be returned on January 9 or 10, 1995.

Three representatives of the U.S. Attorney's Office met with high-level members of the Boston FBI. U.S. Attorney Donald Stern and two of his assistants were told that Bulger and Flemmi were indeed FBI informants, and requested that the information not be disclosed beyond those in the meeting. The Boston FBI felt certain that U.S. Attorney Stern would respect the FBI's position concerning disclosure.

On January 10, 1995, a superseding indictment charged Bulger, Flemmi, George Kaufman, Francis P. Salemme, Francis P. Salemme, Jr., James Martorano, and Robert DeLuca with a RICO conspiracy.

The FBI began a fugitive investigation of Whitey Bulger. Charles Gianturco was put in charge of finding Bulger. His brother Nick had earlier credited Bulger with a warning not to attend a meeting that according to Nick Gianturco saved his life while he was an undercover agent in "Operation Lobster." Nick Gianturco had dined with Bulger, Flemmi, and John Connolly. He had exchanged gifts with the two informants. Nick Gianturco's close relationship with Connolly, and to some degree with Bulger and Flemmi, led one to question the sincerity of Charles Gianturco's attempts to locate Whitey Bulger.

On January 17, 1995, a magistrate judge conducted a bail hearing concerning Steve Flemmi. Upon leaving the courtroom, Flemmi saw Agent Edward Quinn. He knew that Quinn was one of the boys who was aware of his informant status with Connolly. Flemmi, who was refused bail, began to panic. No longer was he the cocksure gangster who had always had his way with the law. He needed to get out on bail and go on the lam until his problem could be resolved.

Flemmi thought that Agent Quinn would at least do something to facilitate his bail. "How about a break on bail?" he said to Quinn. However, Assistant United States Attorney Kelly, who was with Quinn, told Flemmi that Quinn could not speak to him because Flemmi's attorney would object.

This can't be true, thought Flemmi. He had always had a way of avoiding far more serious charges, including extortion and murder. Flemmi began to gain control of his thoughts. Surely Bulger would reach out and get their problems squared away. All he had to do now was wait quietly; it would only be a matter of time.

He had been a fugitive for more than four years before Agent Paul Rico had rescued him. Flemmi thought how foolish he had been not to leave

Boston as his partner Bulger had. He had been warned in advance to flee, yet his arrogance had clouded his judgment. On or about January 23, 1995, Bulger returned to the Boston area to drop off Theresa Stanley. Theresa had had enough and wanted to return to South Boston and her family. The brazen Bulger decided to stay in South Boston for awhile to tie up some unfinished business. The defiant gangster would make brief appearances in South Boston, if only to send a message to certain individuals that he was still someone to fear, even while a fugitive. On one occasion in February of 1995, Bulger met with an associate at a Boston church. In August 1995, Stephen Rakes, who had owned the South Boston liquor mart until Bulger and his gang decided they wanted it for their own, ran into the menacing Bulger in South Boston, months after he had taken off.

Bulger had received information that Rakes had been before a grand jury that was investigating the extortion. Bulger made it quite clear to Rakes that he was keeping a close eye on the proceedings. Whitey wanted to make certain Rakes understood that although a wanted fugitive, Bulger was still a cold-blooded killer. The terrified Rakes would lie when he first appeared before the grand jury, but would later recant and admit he had been extorted by Bulger and others.

Bulger had been socializing at various locations throughout South Boston while a wanted fugitive. It was clearly evident that the bold gangster was not very concerned about being apprehended. Bulger obviously had some indication that the FBI was not searching too strenuously for him. Although Connolly had retired, chances were that he was still keeping a watchful eye over his childhood idol through information supplied by agents still loyal to him at the Boston Bureau.

After dropping off Theresa Stanley, Bulger picked up another long-time girlfriend, Catherine Greig. Together, they would flee Boston to begin a life on the lam. Unlike Bonnie and Clyde, they would assume the role of an average married couple. While a fugitive, Bulger would continue to keep in touch with Kevin Weeks, who was reporting on the circumstances in Boston. Bulger also made a call to John Morris. Morris had been promoted to Chief of the Training Administration Section of the FBI Academy in Quantico, Virginia.

"I'm calling you to remind you that you took money from me. I have witnesses. If I go to the can, you go with me. You better do something to straighten out the charges against me, you hear me, you fuck!" said Bulger.

"I hear you," replied Morris.

Bulger would continue life as a fugitive with Catherine Greig by his side.

Steve Flemmi, Frank Salemme, and Bobby DeLuca would continue to wait in their cells at the Plymouth County Correctional Facility in Massachusetts for a trial date.

On May 21, 1996, the government obtained a third superseding indict-ment, including charges against John Martorano, Bulger, and Flemmi's favorite hit man. Martorano had fled Boston in 1978, just ahead of the race-fixing indictment. He had enjoyed life on the lam, relocating in Boca Raton, Florida. For years, the FBI in Boston had information that Martorano was liv-ing in Florida. This information was given to Connolly by Bulger and Flemmi; however, no action had been taken to arrest the hit man.

Martorano's attorney's (Weinberg) desperate plea for bail for the fugi-tive hit man was a long shot. As expected, Judge Wolf declined the argument made by the very capable Weinberg. However, the judge did find a bit of humor in denying the bail request, saying, "With regard to the defendant, it seems that he took an arrogant delight in his fugitive status." When Martorano was arrested, he had a Florida driver's license in the name of Vincent Joseph "Rancourt," as in "ran from court."

Most of the Winter Hill gangsters had inherited their arrogance from Bulger and Flemmi, their role models. However, it was easy for Bulger and Flemmi to flaunt their arrogance; after all, they had enjoyed the protection of John Connolly and the FBI.

Chapter 15

THE BEGINNING OF THE END

The defense would now obtain discovery from the government. In every criminal case, the defense must receive from the government evidence it intends to use against the accused. The defendant's attorney is given time to study the material and listen to the countless hours of tape recordings in order to prepare for trial. If it can be proven that the evidence was obtained illegally, a judge may be convinced to throw out a part of, or in some instances, the entire case. Steve Flemmi could have cared less about reading the many pages of discovery, or listening to any government tapes. He had faith that John Connolly and Whitey Bulger would come through and get his problem squared away.

However, Cadillac Frank Salemme and Bobby DeLuca had no expectations of being rescued by anyone. Salemme had spent nearly seventeen years in prison for the Fitzgerald car bombing, thanks to the treachery of Steve Flemmi. After only a few brief years of freedom, he was now facing another long prison term if convicted, thanks again to Flemmi. He needed desperately to beat the government's case against him. He would begin to carefully listen to every tape given to him by his attorney, Anthony Cardinale.

DeLuca and Salemme would begin the arduous task of listening to the many tapes from their cells at the Plymouth County Correctional Facility. One tape of particular interest was a conversation taped at the Logan Airport Hilton between Salemme, New York mob boss Natale "Big Chris" Richichi, and porn king Kenny Guarino. The three had met to discuss mob business. Richichi and Guarino had to report to Salemme, who was then the appointed head of the Boston LCN. Both Richichi and Guarino were heavily involved in the porn business, a profession Salemme detested.

Guarino had made arrangements for the room at the Hilton where the meeting had taken place. DeLuca and Anthony The Saint St. Laurent had been waiting in the coffee shop for the meeting to end. Being only "soldiers," they were not permitted to sit in with Richichi and Salemme.

While listening to the tape, DeLuca detected faint voices whispering in the background. He and Salemme were puzzled: Why were the voices of strangers on that tape? After countless times of replaying that one section of the tape, the two men were convinced something wasn't right. A call was made to Attorney Cardinale explaining the weird events. The tape was cleaned of static and the quality enhanced. The tape revealed the voices saying, "The Saint should have had Kenny ask detailed questions, not all this other crap. We could, you know, narrow the topic."

It became obvious to Cardinale that the voices on his client's tape were those belonging to FBI agents. They had been listening from the room next door and the powerful roving bug had picked up their conversation as well as that of their subjects. Tony Cardinale quickly concluded there had been a bit of skullduggery by the FBI. This was his chance to break the case against his client wide open. He also concluded that Kenny Guarino and Anthony St. Laurent were FBI informants and had tipped FBI agents off in advance of the meeting's location.

Attorney Cardinale was certain FBI agents had used a roving bug at the Hilton Hotel to intercept his client Salemme. Cardinale concluded that agents had used the powerful device rather than a conventional bug in order to protect the identity of their informants. The government had requested authorization for a roving bug by lying to the issuing judge, saying they had no advance knowledge of the location to be bugged. If Guarino and St. Laurent were indeed informants, then agents must have known the location of the meeting in advance and therefore, there was no need for the use of a roving wiretap. If St. Laurent and/or Guarino were informants working to set up Salemme, then agents knew the hotel and room number.

The judge who had issued the warrants was never told by FBI agents that some of those present during the intercepted conversation were in fact informants. Had the judge known, the warrants for a roving bug might not have been issued because the information could have been obtained through the informants. It was obvious to the defense attorney that the government wanted to protect its sources. Cardinale rightfully concluded that agents, using the extremely powerful roving bug, did not realize their voices, as well as those belonging to the subjects of their investigation, were being intercepted.

Cardinale was ecstatic. It was the break he had been looking for. He began to file new motions with Judge Mark Wolf, asking for a hearing to look into possible FBI misconduct. He would ask for an evidentiary hearing to determine whether evidence the government intended to use against his client should be suppressed on grounds that a roving bug would not have been authorized had prosecutors not concealed names and positions of government informants from the issuing judge. The attorney began to zero in on the tapes. He believed that the government, far too often, knew in advance where certain mob meetings were going to be held.

The defense attorney concluded that in all of those meetings, a roving bug was used to protect FBI informants' identities. Cardinale determined that if he could prove that government prosecutors had lied to the issuing judge, then he had a shot to have some, if not all, of the evidence against his client thrown out. The heart of his motion was that FBI agents knew where mob boss Richichi was to meet with Cadillac Frank Salemme yet lied to the judge in order to protect their informants.

All through 1996, Cardinale and the government prosecutor, Fred Wyshak, battled over the issue of government misconduct. Wyshak didn't want Cardinale to go any further. He knew that the FBI had for years violated the law when seeking authority to use the roving bug in an effort to protect their sources, and not solely in the Hilton case. He was concerned that Cardinale was getting too close and could open up a can of worms. Wyshak and his gang of government prosecutors would battle Cardinale's every move, claiming the defense attorney was on a fishing expedition. But the relentless Cardinale would not back off. His argument to the sitting judge, Mark L. Wolf, was that a special hearing was needed to get some answers to the question of government cover-up.

Cardinale and the government prosecutors continued to swap blows. The attorney was now broadening the scope of his attempt to expose government informants to include others and not only Guarino and St. Laurent. Cardinale was fully aware of the story given to *The Boston Globe* by Supervisor John Morris indicating that Whitey Bulger had been an informant for the FBI. Not only did *The Globe's* article on Bulger stir interest in Bulger, but Cardinale's client Salemme had long suspected that Bulger could be a double agent. The extremely street-smart Salemme heard talk on the street regarding Whitey Bulger and began putting the pieces together. Much earlier, Steve Flemmi knew that Salemme was very capable of uncovering his treachery and his role as an informant. Flemmi's fear of exposure by Cadillac Frank had prompted him to desperately try to eliminate Salemme with the help of Agent Connolly. Salemme didn't need a building to fall on him to encourage Cardinale to press the issue on Bulger. The Hilton Hotel tape would be the government's Achilles' heel.

On March 21, 1997, the defendants moved for evidentiary hearings on their motions to suppress certain electronic surveillance evidence. All of the defendants named in the racketeering indictments, with the significant exception of Steve Flemmi, moved for disclosure of whether Bulger, and now Mercurio and certain others, were FBI informants.

Sonny Mercurio had been arrested in Georgia with a load of marijuana after fleeing Boston. At times, Mercurio would sneak in to visit with his brother and some close friends. On one such visit, John Connolly had discovered that Salemme had information of Mercurio's role in the bugging of the Mafia induction ceremony. Connolly would send word through an associate of Mercurio that Salemme knew he was an informant, and that Mercurio should leave town immediately.

Meanwhile, Fred Wyshak and the other prosecutors battled furiously with Judge Wolf over the issue of revealing FBI informants. Attorney Cardinale and the other defense lawyers needed to be stopped. Wyshak argued that Cardinale's motion for disclosure was without merit and irrelevant to the charges in the indictment. The prosecutor warned the court that having to reveal the identity of informants would have a lasting effect on the future of the Witness Protection Program.

Judge Wolf didn't buy the prosecutor's plea. He ruled that if a codefendant in the case was an FBI informant, then it constituted exculpatory evidence, which had to, by law, be turned over to the defense. Failure to do so could destroy the entire case for the government. Cardinale and the other defense attorneys also moved for evidentiary hearings on their motions to suppress certain electronic surveillance, including the FBI's recording of the 1989 Mafia induction ceremony at 34 Guild Street. If Judge Wolf could be convinced that those tapes were obtained illegally, it could open the door for many other Mafia figures to appeal their convictions as well.

The taping of the induction ceremony was proof of the existence of the Mafia. Were Judge Wolf to rule in favor of the defense, agreeing that the wiretap of the ceremony was illegal, it would mean freedom for many convicted members of the Boston LCN, and others across the nation, including Godfather John Gotti. Without the tapes of the induction ceremony, there would be no proof of the existence of the "secret society." The tape had been played at trials involving other suspected Mafia members nationwide, and no doubt played a key role in their convictions. In fact, many of those incarcerated felt so positive about their changes for a new trial and possible freedom that some began asking for the upcoming dates of Frank Sinatra appearances.

During the process of addressing the electronic surveillance motions, Judge Wolf learned for the first time that Bulger and Flemmi were FBI informants. He knew that Attorney Cardinale's motion for disclosure of informants' identities would blow the case wide open. He also understood why government prosecutors were dead-set against disclosure. Attorney Cardinale was about to get lucky.

On March 21, 1997, Agents Nick Gianturco and Walter Steffens interviewed John Connolly as part of the Bulger fugitive investigation. Connolly, no doubt, was under no pressure during the interview. Nick Gianturco was a friend and a colleague of Connolly. During the passive interview, Connolly said that he had not seen or heard from Bulger. "I have not seen or heard from Bulger since December of 1989," was the quote by Connolly in Gianturco's 302 reports. There is, however, some question as to the truthfulness of this reported statement. In any event, Connolly also told the two interviewing agents that he had known Bulger since they were both boys and Bulger had bought him an ice cream cone at a local shop in South Boston. Connolly added that he "hoped Bulger was never caught." Connolly also spoke of an incident during a dinner party at the home of John Morris. Morris was "in his cups," and told Bulger and Flemmi that "they were so good, he could get them off of anything short of murder." However, it is clearly evident that the two cold-blooded killers had indeed gotten away with murder.

Connolly also informed Gianturco and Steffens that he knew that Bulger had phoned Morris since becoming a fugitive. Agent Steffens was startled by Connolly's statement that he hoped Bulger would not be caught. Yet, it was not included in the 302 report that Gianturco belatedly prepared on May 7, 1997, and which Steffens received. The 302 report was not filed until nearly six weeks after the interview, and it was largely inaccurate and omissive.

On May 22, 1997, the court ordered the government to disclose whether Bulger, Mercurio, and/or Robert Donati were informants. The decision was temporarily sealed to permit the government to decide whether to obtain the authorization of the Acting Deputy Attorney General, Seth Waxam, to comply with the order, or to decide instead to either dismiss the case or be held in civil contempt. If the case was not dismissed by the government, then Flemmi's role as an informant would be disclosed, along with others.

On May 30, 1997, *The Boston Globe* reported that the FBI was offering a $250,000 reward for the capture of James Whitey Bulger. At a press conference announcing the reward, Special Agent in Charge Barry Mawn reportedly stated that he "was very satisfied that there was an all-out effort by the Boston FBI to find Whitey Bulger," and that he "wanted to clear up any perception that may exist that the FBI is not aggressively pursuing him."

Many believed that the FBI was not keen on finding the fugitive gangster. For one thing, if Bulger was apprehended and decided to talk, his revelations could further embarrass the Bureau. Others hypothesized that Bulger was already dead, slain by agents, thus guaranteeing his silence forever. Some believed Bulger was on the lam, living a low-profile life-style with hoards of $100 bills stashed in safety deposit boxes around the country, along with a variety of false identity papers.

Attorney Cardinale continued to press the issue of disclosure as to whether Bulger, Guarino, St. Laurent, Mercurio, and others were government informants. Up until then, there had been no mention of Steve Flemmi, who was thought of as an alright guy. In fact, for years the Mafia had tried to convince Flemmi to become a "made member" of the LCN. His history as a ruthless gangster made him a prime candidate for induction.

The talk and rumors were about Bulger, not Steve The Rifleman Flemmi. It was far too unbelievable to even consider him as a rat. However, Cardinale and Salemme began to think the unthinkable. The attorney and client began weighing the facts. Bulger and Flemmi had been inseparable twins during their nearly three decades of crime. Salemme and Cardinale concluded that Bulger had not been acting alone, and that Flemmi had to have been a part of the unholy alliance with the FBI.

However, the attorney had to tread lightly. If the assumption was incorrect, then it could have a devastating effect on the racketeering case for everyone involved. It could prompt Flemmi to turn on Salemme and become a government witness against the defendant.

Cardinale wanted Salemme's take on pressing the issue of Flemmi's possible role as an informant. Salemme didn't hesitate in agreeing with Cardinale in their suspicion of Flemmi's possible role. He instructed the attorney to go forward with disclosure on all, including Flemmi. He had no concerns that Flemmi could give damaging testimony because he had been serving time during most of the Bulger and Flemmi crime spree. It was "go for broke" time for Cardinale.

The defense attorney would ask the court to not only expose Bulger, Guarino, and St. Laurent as possible informants, but any others in the case as well. Cardinale's motion for disclosure on all involved would prompt Judge Wolf to speak to Flemmi privately. Wolf wanted to get Flemmi's take on disclosure before exposing him and Bulger as government informants.

With his attorney's approval, Flemmi agreed to meet with Judge Wolf alone. Wolf was uncertain whether Flemmi had told his attorney, Kenneth Fishman, of his role as an informant and how much the attorney knew. The judge would begin by informing Flemmi that he was leaning toward ruling for the defense on the issue of informants, and if he did so, what was Flemmi's position concerning being exposed? Flemmi must have felt that this could not be real—a bad dream could be the only explanation for what was happening. He had served the FBI for three decades, and had dined and exchanged gifts with a number of agents and a supervisor. He had been an arch criminal his entire life—a gangster who had killed anyone who would stand in the way of his rise to the top of the heap.

Flemmi quickly began to gather his thoughts. He had been told by the FBI, and in particular Supervisor John Morris, that he and Bulger could do anything they wanted as long as they didn't "clip" anyone. That's it, he thought; I was given permission to commit crimes, short of murder, as a reward for being an FBI informant. Flemmi decided to reveal his thirty years of service as proof that he had immunity. Flemmi's argument would be that he and Bulger had been authorized to commit crimes by none other than John Morris.

During a dinner at the home of Morris in 1985, he and Bulger had expressed concerns that they had been picked up on the Anguilo tapes at

98 Prince Street. It was at that dinner that Morris had assured both him and Bulger that they would be protected as long as they didn't murder anyone. Flemmi immediately decided to disclose to his attorney, Fishman, that he had been an FBI informant for nearly three decades. The attorney no doubt was shocked by Flemmi's revelation. Most criminal defense attorneys would not represent informants. It was an unwritten rule; most would refuse to get involved with rats. The good defense lawyers did not care to be a part of their defense, no matter how high the fee. Renowned criminal defense attorney Oscar Goodman from Las Vegas openly admitted that he had turned down millions of dollars from those who had cooperated with the government and were subsequently seeking his representation.

Attorney Fishman knew that playing the immunity defense was a big gamble for Flemmi. He would now have to rat on the FBI, just as he had done for decades on rival mobsters. True to his character, Flemmi would give up anyone to save himself, but for some unexplained reason, he would remain loyal to John Connolly.

However, Paul Coffey of the Justice Department had a different angle for Flemmi. Coffey's offer to Flemmi was to plead guilty to the racketeering charges, testify for the government, and enroll in the federal Witness Protection Program after serving a short sentence. Coffey expressed to Flemmi that he wanted to help him, and that his cooperation in the case with the government was important.

"If I was so valuable to you, what am I doing being indicted?" Flemmi asked. Flemmi had kept silent since his arrest in early 1995. It could be that Flemmi was of the notion that Bulger and John Connolly would work some type of magic, as Agents Paul Rico and Dennis Condon had performed in the past. Yet, it was now becoming apparent to him that he had been left twisting in the wind. Flemmi was going to make his move to save himself. He could not envision himself behind bars. It may have been appropriate for others to do time, but not him. The big-time gangster was about to roll the dice in the biggest crap shoot of his life.

For decades, he had enjoyed a charmed life. He had committed murder, extortion, and had participated in the overseeing of a large drug trade without suffering any consequences. But now his big gamble would fail. Instead of accepting a guilty plea and serving perhaps ten years or less, Flemmi decided to go all the way with his immunity defense. He was now ready to reveal his thirty-year relationship with the FBI in order to show justification for the crimes he had committed. He had miscalculated. He did not take into account to what degree his disclosure would affect others. Flemmi would now be in no-man's-land. He had both G-Men and gangsters angry at him. He and his attorney began preparing papers detailing his long career with the FBI and the promises the Bureau had made to him.

In response to the judge's order, the government confirmed that Bulger had been an informant. However, the Department of Justice arrogantly declined to obey the order to confirm or deny whether Mercurio and/or Robert Donati were informants in connection with the electronic surveillance of the induction ceremony. Instead, the Justice Department requested the judge to reconsider the order. The reason the Justice Department was fighting over the issue of disclosure of the other informants was to prevent the defense from uncovering the misconduct that had been carried out by the government in the case.

Judge Wolf denied the government's motion for reconsideration. He ordered Mercurio to appear in court to answer whether or not he had been an informant during the Mafia induction ceremony. Mercurio was being held in Georgia on state charges. He had been apprehended while attempting to smuggle a load of marijuana and additionally, he had been charged with shoplifting.

On June 18, 1997, the aging, obese gangster sat in the witness chair and informed the court that he was an FBI informant when he attended the induction ceremony. Previous supporters of Mercurio in the tight-knit Italian North End community of Boston were shocked at the revelation. They had openly defended Sonny while rumors were being spread that he was an informant. He could no longer be part of the community, and had lost his circle of lifelong friends.

Mercurio was quickly whisked away to continue to serve a brief prison sentence for all his criminal charges. After a short stretch in protective custody, Mercurio would receive a new identity and relocation. The relocation was not limited to him alone. His family would also be enrolled in the protection program, including a generous cash allowance for all. One source close to the proceedings claimed that Mercurio received the outrageous sum of $400,000 in taxpayers' money from the government.

In response to a new court order, the Acting Deputy Attorney General cleared Robert Donati as an informant, one of the few who was not a rat. On June 26, 1997, the court ordered government prosecutors to produce documents to defense attorneys that were relevant to their motions to suppress, and to Flemmi's claim that he had received immunity. The FBI's alliance with Bulger and Flemmi was now beginning to unfold. Flemmi continued to gamble on his claim that he had been authorized to participate in a host of crimes as a reward for his services as an informant. The government's prosecutor objected to the volume of discovery that had been ordered turned over to the defense. Federal Prosecutor Wyshak and Judge Wolf began to battle over the enormity of secret FBI files required.

Wyshak was concerned about the amount of corruption that would surface. The prosecutor's effort to limit the scope of discovery would fail. Thousands of transcripts and FBI documents were now admitted into evidence. The defense would now call to the stand a host of FBI agents along with former government prosecutors. The list of witnesses included three FBI supervisors as well. The secret FBI reports revealing Flemmi's role as an informant showed the depth of his treachery. The Flemmi and Bulger files revealed that the two had ratted on a number of fellow gangsters, including Flemmi's lifelong friend, Cadillac Frank Salemme; Howie Winter; and their favorite and often-used hit man, John Martorano. Revelations detailing the depth of Flemmi's double life stunned his codefendants. Salemme in particular was devastated. He was now fully aware that Flemmi had been responsible for his arrest in New York.

Hit man Martorano sat silently, showing no emotion. However, his thoughts were quickly focusing on his line of defense. He knew he could easily bury Flemmi and Bulger with his testimony detailing murders he had committed at their behest. It was now payback time. He would come out swinging, getting in his blows. His plan was to cut as good a deal as he could for himself.

While hearings continued, Flemmi, DeLuca, Salemme, and Martorano would spend the remaining part of 1997 commuting between the courthouse and the Plymouth County Correctional Facility. During that period, the defense attorneys also filed a motion to dismiss charges against the defendants. Attorney Cardinale's motion to dismiss included the contention that the government had engaged in systematic, outrageous misconduct. The attorney's affidavit charged that FBI Agent Connolly had attempted to foment violence by telling him in 1989 that Salemme was planning to kill his then-client Vincent The Animal Ferrara. Also, Steve Flemmi filed a notice that as part of his defense, he would assert that he was authorized by the FBI to engage in the acts now charged as crimes.

The government responded with a motion opposing the defendants' claims. Their motion stated that the defendants were not entitled to a pretrial hearing to dismiss, and that their claims would be proven to be without merit at trial. Over the remaining months of 1997, the court held a series of hearings regarding motions to dismiss and other matters.

In June of 1997, the Attorney General established a task force of Department of Justice and FBI personnel to investigate the allegations of misconduct raised by Flemmi, among other issues. After additional hearings, on December 18 and 23, 1997, the court granted Flemmi's motion for an evidentiary hearing on his motion to dismiss based on immunity. Flemmi's claim of immunity would prove to have catastrophic consequences for him. He had forfeited an opportunity to cut a deal that he could have lived with; he could have pled guilty, served a few years in prison, and then enrolled in the Witness Protection Program. He could have seen daylight at some point in time. Instead, Flemmi's claim that he had been authorized to commit crimes allowed the opening of secret FBI informant files.

Those secret files revealed a host of government misconduct and prompted the Attorney General to investigate the Bureau in Boston. Had Flemmi accepted the government's offer to plead guilty, none of the murders he committed would have been exposed and all the bodies would have remained buried. The court, however, did not grant the defendants' request for an evidentiary hearing on their motion to dismiss. With that, it was time for John Martorano to make his own move. Flemmi's revelation had caused his one-time friend to turn on him and cooperate with government prosecutors.

–*Chapter 16*–

JOHNNY ON THE SPOT

In January of 1998, the court began evidentiary hearings to address Flemmi's claim of immunity and other matters. The hearings continued at a slow pace, often interrupted by numerous recesses. Months went by without any meaningful developments until July of that year, when hit man John Martorano made his move and took aim.

He had been transferred out of the Plymouth County Correctional Facility during the early morning hours to an undisclosed location. Martorano had heard enough. In particular, he had learned how Bulger and Flemmi had avoided indictment in the 1979 horse race-fixing case, compliments of John Connolly and others. He had been forced to go on the lam for his role in the race-fixing case, while Bulger and Flemmi had escaped the charges and later informed the FBI of his location.

It was now, "Here's Johnny!" The loyal gangster was ready to tell government prosecutors everything. He would confess to twenty murders, many on orders from Bulger and Flemmi. The handsome, powerfully-built gangster was now willing to testify against the two mob bosses. Testifying against his former associates in crime would be the most difficult thing a loyal gangster could do.

For Mercurio, Bulger, Flemmi, and others, ratting came easy. It would come easy for men without honor or principles. Deep down, most authorities who receive information from informants have no respect for them. Most authorities secretly despise them for their role as informants. Those who inform on others in order to receive some monetary compensation for their treachery are considered similar to dogs. Although they may not eat another dog's feces, they smell it.

Martorano was furious. He had been loyal to Bulger and Flemmi. He had been forced to leave Boston and start a new life in Florida, abandoning his wife Carolyn and their two children. Meanwhile, Bulger and Flemmi had remained in town to reap the rewards of their new, uninterrupted criminal activities. He was also bitter that his younger brother Jimmy had gone to prison for his part in the race-fixing case.

Martorano confessed to twenty murders, including the killings of Roger Wheeler and John Callahan. In exchange for his cooperation, he would receive a twelve-and-one-half-year sentence. The hit man was able to receive the light sentence for the twenty murders because he could give extremely valuable testimony to government prosecutors. They were especially interested in the murders of Roger Wheeler and John Callahan. Those two hits in particular, carried out by Martorano on orders from Bulger and Flemmi, would lead to charges that could carry the death penalty for the South Boston gangsters. Martorano would also appear before a Tulsa grand jury. During his testimony there, the hit man revealed how H. Paul Rico allegedly used John Callahan to provide him with a note detailing World Jai Alai owner Roger Wheeler's work habits and a description of the intended victim. Later, Tulsa police would call for murder charges against former Agent Rico.

Early on, a judge found that Rico had suborned perjury and committed perjury in a Rhode Island trial. When Rico was brought out of retirement to assist in the government's investigation of then-Judge Alcee Hastings, his perjurious testimony was never questioned by the Justice Department.

Martorano confessed to killing the Tulsa Oklahoma millionaire Roger Wheeler in 1981. He would also confess to the 1982 murder of John Callahan, the former president of Wheeler's World Jai Alai in Miami. Both Florida and Oklahoma are states that allow the death penalty for murder convictions. Martorano's plea agreement would exclude him from any capital punishment, but not so for Bulger or Flemmi.

News of Martorano's agreement would reach all the way to Washington. House Majority Leader Dick Army of Texas was upset with the deal, prompting him to issue a letter to then-Attorney General Janet Reno. "What signal does this Administration send when it allows dangerous predators like Mr. Martorano to receive a token slap on the wrist after a life of crime?" Army wrote. Army's letter also included complaints made by Boston's black leaders who alleged that Martorano had targeted blacks. The Republican House Leader was "alarmed to hear that Mr. Martorano may have sought out in particular black citizens as his victims," the letter said. Army urged the Department of Justice to reconsider the deal.

However, U.S. Attorney Donald Stern did not agree with Army, saying his office had no evidence that Martorano's killings were racially motivated. According to Stern, top level officials of the Department of Justice were aware of the deal prior to an agreement. "Whether the Attorney General intends to do anything at this point is wholly up to her," Stern told *The Boston Herald*. "My strong view is that this agreement, however distasteful it is to me and others, is in the interests of justice."

In another statement defending the Martorano deal, U.S. Attorney Stern said, "The reality is that the way you prosecute organized crime cases, and the way you catch murderers, is with the benefit, however distasteful it is, of insiders who were in a position to know. And he [Martorano] is an insider in a position to know, we believe, a great deal."

On September 9, 1999, the government filed a plea agreement with Martorano, which provided for his cooperation in the upcoming trials. John Martorano's younger brother, James, would follow in his brother's footsteps. He also agreed to provide evidence that could connect Bulger and Flemmi to more than a dozen murders, dating back four decades. Martorano would also reveal to federal prosecutors that former FBI Agent Paul Rico was in on the plan to kill Roger Wheeler. He had corroborated Brian Halloran's story earlier as to Rico's role in the murder. Halloran's revelations on events concerning Wheeler and his World Jai Alai had prompted the South Boston gangsters to silence him.

The hit man's plea to killing Roger Wheeler came as part of a controversial deal with federal prosecutors and would lead investigators to begin focusing on former Agent H. Paul Rico's involvement in the murder, along with that of Bulger and Flemmi.

Cutting ties with Bulger and Flemmi was an easy call for Martorano, especially after learning of their role as informants. However, Martorano wasn't satisfied. He wanted Flemmi's handler and former Agent H. Paul Rico, and Bulger's overseer, John Connolly. The hit man was now ready to go all the way. However loyal John Martorano had once been, it was now ancient history.

"Fuck that sense of loyalty shit," said a gangster in the know, describing the relationship between Martorano, Bulger, and Flemmi. For those two bosses, "there was more fear than loyalty. For all their fucking bravado, we're still talking about a couple of punks."

Chapter 17

BIG GAMBLE, BIG LOSS

In late August 1998, Steve Flemmi took the witness stand to answer questions regarding his claim of immunity. Federal Prosecutor Fred Wyshak would fire off question after question at the gangster. Flemmi's theme was that he had been promised protection and that he would not be prosecuted for any crimes, with the exception of murder, in exchange for his service as an informant. Flemmi told Prosecutor Wyshak that he and Bulger were promised protection by then-Supervisor John Morris while attending a dinner at Morris' home. Flemmi claimed that he and Bulger "had done a number" on the Mafia; that he would not have done so without protection. However, when the gangster was asked questions about his role in the drug trade, Flemmi asserted his Fifth Amendment privilege. Additionally, when asked about Stephen Rakes, the former owner of the South Boston liquor mart who had been forced to sell out to him and Bulger, Flemmi again asserted the Fifth. The battle of wits between Flemmi and the Chief Prosecutor would continue for over a week.

Finally, the song and dance routine by Flemmi would come to a dramatic conclusion when asked if he and Bulger had been warned to flee before their indictment in 1995. This was the moment everyone had been waiting for. This would be when John Connolly would be implicated. But instead of uttering Connolly's name, Flemmi responded, "Yes, we were warned by John Morris." Flemmi was still trying to protect the real tipster, still clinging to the hope that Connolly would rescue him and back his claim of immunity. Flemmi had falsely pointed the finger at Morris as the one who had warned the two gangsters of their impending indictment, and thus obstructed justice. However, no one was convinced by Flemmi's assertion, least of all his codefendant, Frank Salemme, who was furious. He had managed to control himself from attacking the informant during the course of their incarceration, but the Morris story would be the final straw. Cadillac Frank had had enough. Flemmi's continuing mission to protect Connolly was hurting the case for all the defendants.

During a recess break, the capable Salemme went after Flemmi with rage in his eyes. However, the informant refused to tangle, instead retreating to a corner like the rat he was. After shouting some threats, Salemme managed to control himself. Flemmi would keep his distance, avoiding any further contact with Cadillac Frank.

The court proceedings continued. A host of FBI agents would take the stand and deny any violations of FBI guidelines for handling informants. One key witness to testify was former Supervisor John Morris. He had been part of the government misconduct and cover-up early on. He had cut a deal for immunity with government prosecutors, and agreed to tell all. One revelation was Morris' confession of accepting bribes from Bulger and Flemmi through John Connolly. Morris told the court that he and other agents, including Connolly, had often gotten together for dinner with the two informants.

He admitted that between 1980 and 1988 he met socially with Bulger and Flemmi, and accepted cash and gifts. Morris admitted taking the bribes delivered by John Connolly. He also admitted that he had approved Connolly's approach on how to use Bulger and Flemmi, and went along with the cover-ups. He also confessed to obstruction of justice by tipping off the two gangsters about investigations. Although Morris accepted responsibility for his role in the unholy alliance, he placed most of the blame on John Connolly. Under the pretense of furthering the war against the Mafia, Morris had been easily manipulated by the slick G-man/con man from South Boston. He also attributed his failed career in the FBI to Connolly's policy of using Bulger and Flemmi without supervision or control.

Morris was in fear of Connolly's influence. He was also keenly aware of Connolly's powerful political connections, and wanted to remain close and in agreement with him. Defense attorneys for Flemmi began to relentlessly pressure Morris to admit that he had promised the gangster immunity. Morris would take blow after blow from the defense and although bloodied, he remained standing.

Next, Morris would tell the same story of governmental misconduct on the part of Connolly to a federal grand jury. Following Morris to the witness stand would be the former Debbie Noseworthy, who had worked for Morris at the Boston office, and had now become Mrs. Debbie Morris. She had stood by her man through it all. She would corroborate Morris' claim that Connolly had given her the necessary funds for her plane fare to visit Morris years earlier.

Details concerning the court proceedings and confessions made front page news. John Connolly would publicly condemn Morris. He would remind the press that he had brought down the LCN and was responsible for the incarceration of numerous "stone cold killers." He openly denied Morris' revelations, proclaiming he would take the witness stand and rebuff the accusations.

Upon hearing of Connolly's boast, defense attorneys decided to call the con man's bluff. However, when called to the witness chair and asked to confirm his previous public statements, Connolly invoked his Fifth Amendment right. Connolly still didn't get it. Even after his bluff had been called, he continued to make public statements defending his actions as an FBI agent. One statement in particular was his claim that "the FBI knew what Bulger and Flemmi were. They didn't have a paper route when the FBI first met them. All Top Echelon Informants are murderers. The government put me in business with murderers," Connolly said.

The rogue agent who still didn't get it would continue his public relations blitz.

Steve Flemmi's big gamble on the issue of immunity would fail. The court ruled that the FBI had promised Flemmi protection in exchange for his services as an informant and reasoned that Flemmi had in fact received that protection in the form of being warned of pending investigations and wiretaps. He and Bulger had been tipped to certain informants, and been told whom to stay away from as well. But the court held that Flemmi had *not* been promised immunity from prosecution and that the term "immunity" had never been used in conversation with him.

During questioning by defense attorneys who were desperately trying to have Morris admit he had promised Bulger and Flemmi immunity, the former supervisor stood firm in his denial. Morris told the court he didn't have the power to grant the gangsters immunity. He understood granting immunity was a legal process requiring records, and there was nothing written or recorded to substantiate Flemmi's claim.

Flemmi expected the FBI would overlook some of his criminal activity, provide him with information concerning any investigations that were being conducted which might affect his activities, and warn him of any imminent charges against him. The court concluded the FBI had held to its part of the bargain. It further stated that the FBI's protection had permitted Flemmi and Bulger to survive repeated efforts by various law enforcement agencies to investigate their activities, and had allowed them to profit as a result of their contribution to the FBI's campaign to destroy the Italian Mafia.

"He [Flemmi] was promised protection, and that protection was provided until January of 1995. Thus, Flemmi's motion to dismiss based on an alleged promise of immunity generally is being denied," said Judge Mark Wolf. Flemmi's big gamble had backfired on him. His claim of immunity had exposed his role as an informant, causing many of his associates to turn on him.

On September 15, 1999, Judge Wolf issued a factual finding. The 661 pages did not sit well with Connolly. Wolf's ruling placed most of the FBI corruption and evil-doings on Connolly's shoulders. Wolf pointed the finger at Connolly as the person who had tipped Bulger and Flemmi of the January 10, 1995 indictment. According to Wolf, the mobsters were not as bad as the handful of rogue agents, led by Connolly. Wolf's findings were clearly focused on the enormity of misconduct on the part of Connolly. "When members of the Organized Crime Squad received reliable information about criminal activity in which Bulger and Flemmi were engaged, they regularly consulted Connolly and then did not pursue any investigations," wrote Wolf. Among those who participated in the process of consulting Connolly and subsequently deferred to the commitment he had made to protect Bulger and Flemmi were "Acting Special Agent in Charge Larry Potts, Supervisory Special Agent Bruce Ellavsky, Rod Kennedy, John Newton, James Blackburn, and James Lavin." Retired FBI Agents Paul Rico and Dennis Condon were also a focus of an ongoing investigation into corruption and cover-ups.

Wolf's findings would expose the corruption in the Boston Bureau, prompting then-Attorney General Janet Reno to take action. She would appoint a Connecticut Federal Prosecutor, John Durham, to investigate the wrongdoing that had taken place in the Boston FBI. The Boston Bureau would become the most heavily investigated in the history of the FBI. Durham would personally select a team of investigators, none of whom was affiliated with the politics of Boston. Connolly, Paul Rico, Dennis Condon, and other former agents would be targets of a federal grand jury probe into corruption at the Boston FBI office.

Although different from the mobsters who were connected with the Mafia, Connolly had his own gang. He had powerful connections with the "who's who" of the Boston political arena. One of his biggest supporters was the then-Senate President Billy Bulger, Whitey's younger brother. It was rumored that Billy Bulger had used his clout to secure a high-paying position with Boston Edison for Connolly after retirement. There was also a secret society of FBI agents called "The Club." Those belonging to "The Club" made certain that no outsiders would cause any problems for the members. It was rumored that they had their own team of assassins who would go into action if needed. The arrogant Connolly had even accepted an interview with the NBC program "Dateline" to pitch the good he had achieved during his career, and to promote his innocence.

The news media began battering Connolly, labeling him a rogue agent. The former agent who had taken an oath to uphold the law would fail in his sworn duty. Instead, his loyalty was to his beloved Southie, and Whitey Bulger. Connolly's sole interest was protecting Bulger, under the pretense of destroying the Mafia. Connolly had gone to his hands and knees and allowed him to be covered in sludge while joining Bulger in the underworld sewer of waste matter. Under the pretense of following the Bureau's mandate to take down the Italian Mafia, the South Boston G-Man had involved himself in criminal activity with his childhood neighbor. Connolly had a sick and perverted admiration for Whitey Bulger. Eventually, his fondness would come into criticism and, in the end, his own destruction.

The cocksure G-Man was always a man about town. The Prince of the City could be found at his oft-frequented Tecce's restaurant in the Italian North End section of Boston. Dressed to the nines, waiting for his favorite entrée, "Steak Mafia," to be served, Connolly would vocally defend his reputation.

"There was no moral justification, because it was never a moral decision," Connolly said. "This was a business decision. This is a business we're in, the business of eradicating crime. And to do that, you need criminal informants. This day, this very moment, law enforcement agents all over the country are making deals with criminals."

Once again, Connolly just didn't get it. He was correct in his assessment of the use of informants by other law enforcement agencies. However, most of those agents had not crossed over the line, as had Connolly. They did not exchange gifts, drink each other's expensive wine, or dine together. They did not obstruct justice or protect their informants by tipping them to investigations nor warn them to flee in order to avoid arrest. And they most certainly did not instigate the murder of those who posed a threat to their unholy alliance.

The arrogant Connolly was still playing the part. It was difficult to distinguish the flamboyant Connolly from the mobsters he had pursued throughout his career.

Chapter 18

TWO WEEKS

Other events—all bad—began to unfold for Bulger, Flemmi, and John Connolly.

In November of 1999, Kevin Weeks and Kevin O'Neil were arrested and charged with racketeering, extortion, and money laundering. The forty-three-year-old Weeks, a top deputy of Bulger's, was often referred to as Whitey's surrogate son. Weeks had the responsibility of carrying messages between Steve Flemmi and John Connolly, conveying the former agent's regret for Flemmi's troubles. Connolly no doubt had deep concerns with regard to Flemmi's loyalty to him. The gangster could "roll" at any time. Should Flemmi decide to make an about-face and reveal all, it would have had dire consequences for the former agent.

Weeks would also meet with Bulger on several occasions since Whitey had become a fugitive. He would keep Bulger updated on events and supply the fugitive gangster with his much-needed heart medication.

The fifty-one-year-old O'Neil, also a top lieutenant for Bulger, was mainly responsible for handling the gang's money. He had purchased the South Boston liquor mart from Bulger, which had earlier been extorted from the Rakes. O'Neil also owned "the bucket of blood" Triple O's bar where Bulger would often hold court. O'Neil was held without bail. There were concerns that while Bulger was on the lam, he and Kevin Weeks could continue to run the gang. At first, Weeks would voice his loyalty to Bulger. But he had never faced serious charges such as racketeering, extortion, and money laundering. Soon his knees began to buckle. The residents of South Boston were becoming aware of the change in the once cocksure gangster. The joke in the neighborhood was how long it would be before he would cut a deal and testify. The opinion of many was "two weeks." Weeks would subsequently be known as Kevin "Two Weeks."

More and more information would surface revealing the depth of Bulger and Flemmi's treachery as informants. It was becoming difficult for Weeks to continue to support Bulger openly. He was constantly harassed. "How does it feel, Kevin, knowing your boss Bulger and Steve Flemmi are rats?" Weeks would often be asked. It didn't take long for Weeks to give in. He soon realized that Bulger was no longer what he had appeared to be, a stand-up tough guy. Weeks felt abandoned by Bulger. He was ready to make a deal, but first he had to prove he had bona fide information in return for a lenient sentence.

−*Chapter 19*−
ROGUE AGENT

In December of 1999, the former boss of the Boston LCN, Cadillac Frank Salemme, decided to throw in the towel. He had grown weary of fighting the case. He was tired of getting up at four A.M. from his cell at the Plymouth County Correctional Facility and of the two-hour ride that followed to the federal court in Boston. Most important of all, he could no longer put up with sitting next to the recently revealed informant, Steve Flemmi.

The long-time stand-up guy pled guilty to racketeering charges and received an eleven year, four month sentence. As part of his plea agreement, he was not required to testify. Yet, he agreed to go against the grain and appear before the Connolly grand jury.

After his retirement, Connolly had met with Salemme and told him he would warn Bulger and Flemmi to flee in order to avoid arrest in their upcoming indictment, a clear admission of obstruction of justice. Once again the arrogant Connolly didn't get it. He had arrested Salemme in New York back in 1972 due to the skullduggery of Flemmi, Agent Dennis Condon, and himself. Connolly was also suspected of instigating the attempted murder of Salemme by rival gangsters. For Connolly to now seek out Salemme, and pal-him out in order to stay on his good side is astonishing. Connolly needed allies, especially those who could testify against him. The "I was only doing my job and no hard feelings" approach with the honorable Salemme would not work.

Cadillac Frank did not buy into the former agent clarification. He was going to do what was right in his heart.

However, it was still a difficult call for the ultimate stand-up guy to make. The Mafia oath of Omerta applied to all, not just mobsters. He was torn between the code, which he had always respected and abided by, and letting the rogue agent slide. The statute of limitations was about to run out on the charges against Connolly. Salemme would not receive any consideration for his testimony against the former FBI agent. In fact, his eleven-year-four-month sentence was the high end of the federal sentencing guideline. He was willing to accept the scorn of other LCN members for his position as well. Yet, Frank Salemme knew his character; he knew he had always been a man of honor. He could have cared less what others thought about his decision to testify.

Most LCN mob leaders agreed with Salemme, saying, "He did the right thing in getting that Irish hard-on. He [Connolly] put a lot of good people away." Connolly had been responsible for the incarceration of many Italian-American Mafia members. But most importantly, Salemme wanted the former agent and Steve Flemmi to be brought to justice for all the evil and hurt they had inflicted on others. The wise and street-smart gangster was much too clever not to begin to sort events out. All the rumors and various sets of circumstances began to unravel. He began to put the pieces together.

Salemme knew instinctively that certain murders pointed to Bulger and Flemmi and might have even been facilitated by John Connolly. He was deeply troubled by the murders of the two young girls, Debbie Davis and Deborah Hussey. Salemme knew it was no coincidence that both these young beauties had vanished while being romantically involved with Steve Flemmi. He had known Deborah Hussey ever since she was a toddler and had a deep fondness for her. Moreover, words and strong rumors from various criminals in the know would reach Salemme regarding the disappearance of the expert safecracker, Bucky Barrett. Barrett had been a close friend of Cadillac Frank. It wasn't revenge he was after; he could live with being set up for murder and ratted out. He wanted the evil cowards brought to justice.

Cadillac Frank received one concession from Federal Prosecutor John Durham for his willingness to testify against Connolly. The quid pro quo was not for his benefit, but in the interest of justice. However, Salemme bargained with Special Prosecutor Durham to look into the case of Peter Limone and Joseph Salvati. Salemme told Durham that the men had been framed for the 1968 murder of Edward "Teddy" Deegan by FBI agents and the chief witness, contract killer Joseph Barboza. Barboza's handlers at the time were Agents Paul Rico and Dennis Condon. Salemme's plea for the two innocent men who had been incarcerated for thirty-two years convinced Prosecutor Durham to dig into the facts of their case.

All in all, it was a courageous move by Salemme. He was well aware of the danger in testifying against a former FBI agent. His testimony in front of a grand jury would help secure the indictment of John Connolly.

In December 1999, a federal grand jury unsealed indictments based on the evidence presented by a special federal investigative strike force led by Assistant U.S. Attorney John Durham. The grand jury had been sitting for over a year, listening to the testimony of key witnesses. The targets of the probe were Connolly, Paul Rico, and other former agents.

On December 22, 1999, the arrogant Connolly was arrested by FBI agents at his home in Lynnfield, Massachusetts, an exclusive suburb of Boston. The former agent was not given any special treatment or professional consideration. Instead, he was treated as a common criminal and cuffed. Although FBI policy requires that suspects be handcuffed while being arrested, there are some exceptions made. It was not the case with Connolly. The flamboyant ex-agent pleaded not guilty in federal court to a five-count indictment and posted a $200,000 bailment that same day.

Magistrate Judge Marianne Bowler ordered Connolly to maintain or seek employment, abide by travel restrictions, maintain a residence, and promise to appear at all proceedings. He was also required to surrender firearms and ammunition to the local police department in Lynnfield, Massachusetts, and to have no contact with potential witnesses. It is possible those restrictions somehow helped Connolly to finally "get it." Once labeled a star in the

Boston FBI, Connolly was now subjected to the same restrictions as the criminals he once pursued while building his celebrated reputation.

Also charged in the indictment were Steve Flemmi and fugitive Whitey Bulger. All were charged with five counts of racketeering, conspiracy, and obstruction of justice. "This indictment does not allege sloppy bookkeeping or the failure to write the perfect FBI report," said U.S. Attorney Donald K. Stern. Connolly had violated the trust that the people placed in him when he took his oath of office.

Special Agent in Charge of the New England FBI Barry W. Mawn added his own regrets, saying, "I have apologized to law enforcement for these activities, and I extend that apology to the public." No doubt, Mawn was referring to other law enforcement agencies that had been frustrated in their investigations of Bulger and Flemmi.

The indictment charged Connolly with aiding the two gangsters in criminal acts of extortion, loan sharking and bribery, as well as warning the two informants of wiretaps and manipulating FBI reports. He was also charged with protecting Bulger and Flemmi by not reporting crimes with which they were involved, and by tipping them as to upcoming indictments in order that they might avoid arrest and flee.

The bribery charges in the indictment accused Connolly of delivering $7,000 in cash in three payments, along with expensive wine, to his former supervisor, John Morris, compliments of Bulger and Flemmi. Morris admitted taking the bribes, and agreed to testify, under a grant of immunity, against Connolly.

The extortion charges stemmed from the takeover of the South Boston liquor mart by Bulger and Flemmi in which Connolly failed to intervene.

South Boston was a difficult place to earn a decent living. Many residents sought employment at the nearby Gillette Safety Razor company. Others either became police officers or took low-paying jobs at City Hall. Few choices were available to most. For the Rakes, owning their own business was the exception, rather than the rule. Yet, when South Boston gangsters demanded they turn the liquor mart over to them, the South

Boston G-Man failed to intercede on behalf of the young couple's dream of financial independence.

"John Connolly is being made a scapegoat because the FBI is embarrassed by their policies and, as a result, they are looking for someone to isolate and use as a vehicle for blame," said his attorney, R. Robert Popeo. The attorney added that Connolly's arrest at home and the timing of the indictment, coming three days before Christmas, had "a tinge of mean-spiritedness."

Later, during a pretrial hearing, Connolly's co-attorney, Tracy A. Miner, told a federal magistrate judge, "The government alleges that Mr. Connolly somehow treated these informants differently and crossed over some line into criminality. It's our contention he treated these informants the way he treated all other Top Echelon Informants. Our defense is direct; it is clear that Mr. Connolly was authorized to commit all of the acts he committed with respect to informants. He was authorized to tell them to continue to commit crimes. He was authorized to look the other way. He was authorized not to press them for information about their criminal conduct."

There had been some talk of praise for Connolly's knack in cultivating informants and allowing them to participate in criminal acts in order to bring down the Mafia. However, Bulger and Flemmi were treated unlike other informants by Connolly. In particular, Bulger, who was of the same ethnic heritage, had grown up in the same South Boston housing project. Whitey was a neighbor; he, like Connolly, was from Southie, where people stuck together. Connolly worshipped and idolized Bulger, who was often referred to as the "Robin Hood of Southie." Bulger was Connolly's "good" bad guy. Unlike the other informants, Connolly would be accused of leaking confidential information to Bulger that would cause the slaying of witnesses who could be a problem for them. There is no doubt that Connolly did treat Bulger and Flemmi differently.

Chapter 20

DISAPPEARANCES UNEARTHED

In early January of 2000, Kevin Weeks was ready to tell all. After testifying before the Connolly grand jury, he began revealing to authorities locations of graves containing the bodies of John McIntyre, Deborah Hussey, and Arthur Bucky Barrett. On January 14, workers began digging in a field by Interstate 93 in Dorchester, a suburb of Boston. Bitter cold was about to settle in, making the digging more difficult.

TV camera crews and news reporters gathered in the cold, expecting a long wait for any discovery. However, Weeks' information was so good that investigators knew exactly where to dig for remains of the three victims. In fact, the information was so on the mark workers had little difficulty finding the first body. All three bodies would be quickly located. The decomposed remains had been reduced to a pile of bones.

Through DNA testing, forensic examiners made positive identifications of Arthur Bucky Barrett, John McIntyre, and Deborah Hussey. Barrett, who had broken into the Depositors Trust Bank in 1980 and stolen $1.5 million, had disappeared in 1983. He had been tortured and killed by Bulger and Flemmi after paying them his share of the cash and jewelry. McIntyre had disappeared in 1984 after telling authorities about his role in smuggling weapons to the IRA. He was ready to implicate Bulger in the gun-running operation, as well as marijuana shipments destined for Bulger's gang. Hussey, the stepdaughter of Flemmi, had been romantically involved with the gangster at an early age. She had vanished after planning to reveal to her mother, Marion, details of her affair with Flemmi. According to Kevin

Weeks, Deborah Hussey was strangled into unconsciousness by Whitey Bulger. Then Steve Flemmi finished the gruesome task with a rope and a stick. All three bodies had later been exhumed by the gangsters, in October of 1985, and reburied to the present location.

After being brutally tortured, Barrett had been forced to make phone calls to friends in an effort to raise money and satisfy the pitiless gangsters' demands. Barrett was a high-class thief. He was also generous to those close to him; he would freely give financial assistance. When word on the street revealed he had made a "score," he became a willing "touch" for almost anyone who knew him.

One of the first relatives of the murder victims to file a lawsuit was John McIntyre's mother, Emily. A motion filed by her attorneys, Steven Gordon and Lucy Karl, sought information from FBI files to determine whether her son was murdered due to information that McIntyre had been cooperating with authorities. "John's mother is seventy-two years old and in failing health," wrote the family's lawyers. "She deserves to know what happened to her son, why, and to seek redress against the persons responsible."

The files the family was seeking could expose who was responsible for the murder. There was strong speculation that former Agent Connolly had tipped Bulger and Flemmi that McIntyre had been cooperating and therefore posed a serious threat for them. "We're certainly intending to file a lawsuit relatively soon," said Jeffrey Denner, one of the family's lawyers. "There will be a variety of defendants. We haven't made a final determination, but as you can imagine we feel the FBI and certain members of organized crime were in an enterprise that resulted in the death of John McIntyre," he said.

"Despite clear statutory authority to do so, the FBI failed or refused to investigate the circumstances of McIntyre's death. The FBI did not wish to undertake any action that would unhinge its unholy alliance with Bulger and Flemmi," said one of the attorneys for McIntyre. "McIntyre was treated as a non-person, stripped of all Constitutional protection and rights, someone to be buried and forgotten."

One family member was quoted as saying, "This is just too brutal to put into words," referring to Weeks' admission. "He kills them and he buries them and he digs them up and he buries them again. Can you imagine the horror they went through that day?"

Steve Flemmi had long been a suspect in Deborah Hussey's disappearance. She had often referred to Flemmi as her father. "Everybody called her Steve's daughter," said a friend who had known Deborah for decades. "She kept to herself, but was very pleasant and nice. She always had her books with her and was studying all the time."

The remains of Bucky Barrett, an expert safecracker, were also identified. Barrett's wife, Elaine, declined to comment. "I'm sorry," she said, "I don't have anything to say."

Emily McIntyre was visibly upset at the gruesome manner in which her son's body was disposed. "I wish to God I never found out about it all," she said. "What really gives us mental and physical illness is how John was killed. It's getting to me mentally. I'm getting sick in my heart."

The families of McIntyre, Hussey, and Barrett had received some bit of closure. Justice would be forthcoming.

Weeks not only continued to provide information to authorities on Bulger and Flemmi, he was also offering evidence against John Connolly. While Flemmi was being held in the Plymouth County Jail, Weeks was the messenger between Connolly and the gangster. Weeks also pled guilty to his role in aiding Bulger, Flemmi, and others in the murders of Brian Halloran and Michael Donahue. He had served as the lookout during the shooting and disposed of the guns used.

Weeks agreed to plead guilty to racketeering, extortion, drug conspiracy, and money laundering. In exchange for his cooperation, government prosecutors agreed to recommend a prison term ranging from five to fifteen years. He would also admit to aiding Bulger, Flemmi, and others in the murders of McIntyre, Hussey, and Barrett.

More information was now being presented to the federal grand jury probing FBI corruption. New charges were added to the original racketeering indictment against John Connolly. A nine-count superseding indictment charged Connolly with leaking confidential information to Bulger and Flemmi, which instigated the slaying of Richard Castucci in 1976 and the murders of Brian Halloran and John Callahan in 1982.

In early September of 2000, investigators began to dig for the remains of Debra Davis, Paul Paulie McGonagle, and Thomas King. The dig would be focused along the shore of the Neponset River on Teneau Beach, often referred to as "Tin Can Beach" by locals. Once again, the search was prompted by information supplied by Kevin Weeks.

A backhoe began the excavation at the edge of the beach. The dig would uncover the remains of McGonagle, a Bulger rival from the past. The decomposed body of Thomas King was quickly unearthed as well. King had disappeared in 1975 after committing the unpardonable act of getting the best of Whitey Bulger in a bar fight. Hit man John Martorano confessed to killing King and implicated Steve Flemmi in the murder. Three feet from King, searchers found the remains of Debbie Davis. The then-twenty-six-year-old beauty had disappeared after planning to "dump" Flemmi for another man.

Olga Davis wanted to know if the FBI had played a role in her daughter's disappearance. The Davis family had been questioned about Debra's disappearance by agents. However, they had simply been going through the motions, rather than sincerely attempting to find out what had happened to the young beauty. Four months after the discovery of the body, Olga Davis filed a $30 million wrongful death lawsuit against Steve Flemmi and Whitey Bulger. The lawsuit also named as defendants members of Flemmi and Bulger's families, and the State Lottery Commission. Whitey was still collecting on his share of winnings from the Megabucks Lottery. Kevin Weeks and Kevin O'Neil were also named in the lawsuit.

Life has not been kind to Olga Davis. She has lost three of her children under tragic circumstances. Ronnie Davis was stabbed to death at the age of twenty-nine while incarcerated. Sandra Davis was thirty-eight when struck and killed by a car. Yet, the longest period of suffering for Olga has been the nineteen years that Debra was missing. The Davis family said FBI did more than look the other way when Debra Davis disappeared. "It was a conflict of interest for the FBI to be involved in the investigation of Debbie's disappearance when Flemmi was their main snitch," said her brother Victor.

After nearly twenty years, the Davis family was finally able to obtain some closure.

−Chapter 21−
JUSTICE

Troubles for the Boston FBI office were just beginning. The Beantown Bureau would soon become the most investigated in history. Word coming out of Washington was that many former and current agents and supervisors were under intense scrutiny for past deeds, and could be targets of the current grand jury being presented evidence by Special Prosecutor John Durham.

Although Whitey Bulger, one of the principle contributors to the erosion of the Boston Bureau, was still on the lam, the city was reeling from the stench of corruption. Kevin Weeks had given investigators a great deal of information on the criminal activities of Bulger and his gang. Weeks was providing information on former Agent John Connolly as well. In return for his cooperation, his attorney, Dennis Kelly, was preparing to ask the court to sentence Weeks to less than five years in prison.

The Suffolk County District Attorney's office would not seek to prosecute Weeks for his role in the slayings of Bucky Barrett, John McIntyre, Deborah Hussey, Brian Halloran, or Michael Donahue. Weeks' plea agreement would not be binding until after testifying at the upcoming trials. He had the goods on Bulger and Flemmi's cold-blooded pact with former Agent John Connolly.

Kevin O'Neil would follow on the heels of Weeks. O'Neil, who had been charged with racketeering and extortion, had decided to cooperate and tell all. The two Kevins had been Bulger's top men. They, along with Bulger and Flemmi, were the enforcers in a host of extortion plots.

O'Neil had been a key player in the extortion of realtor Raymond Slinger. He would later purchase the South Boston liquor mart from Bulger, renaming it Columbia Wine and Spirits. Bulger was still receiving nearly $5,000 a month in mortgage payments pursuant to the sale.

Back in August 1999, U.S. District Judge Mark Wolf had issued a restraining order preventing Kevin O'Neil and Gordon McIntyre, the trustees of Columbia Wine and Spirits, from selling the store, or reducing its equity. When federal prosecutors discovered that the gangsters were planning to siphon off the value of the store and file bankruptcy, they asked Judge Wolf to intercede.

"There is a substantial risk that the asset will be transferred, encumbered, dissipated, or otherwise made unavailable for forfeiture upon Bulger's conviction if the requested order is not entered at this time," wrote Assistant United States Attorneys Richard Hoffman and James Herbert. The Bulger gang had then laundered money from racketeering, extortion, and drug dealing through the liquor store. Stephen Rakes told a grand jury that he had willingly and voluntarily sold the store to Kevin Weeks, a top Bulger gang member. Two weeks after his initial grand jury appearance, Rakes was confronted by the gangster Bulger. "I'm watching you," was the message he imparted to a horrified Rakes.

Rakes had lost everything in the takeover, including his marriage. After being charged with perjury, Stephen Rakes would ultimately tell authorities the truth of the extortion. In April, 2000, Julie Dammers, the former Julie Rakes, filed a lawsuit, Civil Action No. 00-1598, in Suffolk County Superior Court. The civil suit detailed circumstances of the extortion and asked the court to rescind the 1984 takeover by Bulger, Flemmi, and Weeks. She had decided to step forward and claim her half of the store which had been extorted from her and her former husband.

Sixteen years previously, the struggling couple had been forced to make a choice: turn over the property to the gangsters or their children would lose their parents. "It's what I refer to as my recurring nightmare," Julie said. "And what made it all the more horrible was that everyone knew.

Everyone in Southie knew what happened to us. By everyone, yes, I mean the cops. They knew from the beginning. All the people who sent us flowers and cards when we opened the store," she continued, "just stopped talking to us. Even when we moved out of Southie and my daughter was making her First Communion, who walks into the church and sits right in back of me—Kevin Weeks and his whole family. His son happened to be in the same group.

"On what should have been the happiest day of my daughter's life, I was sick to my stomach. I remember thinking, 'They took away our business; they invaded our lives, now they're invading my church.' I used to pray I'd wake up to find we still owned our store."

Often, the only residents of Southie that she would run into were friends and supporters of Bulger and his gang. "'Oh, you're Stippo's wife. Yeah, you sold the store, huh? A legitimate business deal, right?' That was the big laugh. A legitimate business deal. We were told that's what we had to say if anyone asked."

Her marriage had been destroyed by the extortion scheme. Her husband, who had been threatened by Bulger into committing perjury, was later found guilty of giving false testimony regarding the extortion. "You talk about life lessons," Julie sighed. "There I was, trying to explain to my kids why it was so important to tell the truth. Meanwhile, they can't understand why their daddy's in court and their mommy's testifying against him."

After her husband was found guilty of perjury, they were still fearful that Bulger, although a fugitive, could turn up any time.

"Yes, I knew that Whitey could turn up at any time dressed as anything," Julie said, "because I did see him once dressed as a nun. Honest to God." However, she was not going to let Bulger destroy what was left of her. "It's a way to close the wounds, to right a wrong, a way for my kids to understand what really happened, a way for me to finally get some justice."

Prosecutors would also seize Bulger's $1.9 million in Mass Millions winnings. Bulger's sister, Jean Holland, would begin to challenge prosecutors for the money. However, prosecutors claimed that Bulger hadn't purchased the winning ticket. Instead, he had paid Michael Linsky, the true winner, $700,000 in dirty money for a share of the jackpot. Some of those in the know in Southie believe that Whitey gave Michael Linsky an offer he couldn't refuse. Attorneys argued that the money should go to the families of Bulger's victims.

In October 2000, after a long battle with prosecutors, Jean Holland decided to drop her bid to claim Whitey's lottery winnings. Her about-face was due to a new federal law prohibiting fugitives from using others to challenge government seizures of their property.

However, the arrogant and defiant Bulgers would boldly refuse to give in. Whitey's younger brother, John "Jackie" Bulger, a magistrate of Boston Juvenile Court, began to challenge federal prosecutors for the return of his brother's money to the Bulger family. At some point between 1988 and 1990, Whitey had asked his brother to be a cosigner with him on a bank account that he was going to open. John Bulger agreed, and the account was opened at South Boston Savings Bank in the names of James J. Bulger and John P. Bulger. Whitey's share of the lottery money would be deposited into the joint checking account he held with his brother John.

John Bulger testified before a grand jury that Whitey Bulger had opened the original South Boston Savings Bank account on his own initiative with funds in Whitey Bulger's exclusive possession, and that he had a legal right to the funds. However, the government moved to dismiss John Bulger's claim, arguing that he had no actual ownership interest in Whitey's property.

During a hearing in U.S. District Court, government prosecutors argued that Whitey Bulger, together with others, had been involved in criminal activity for a period of some thirty years. The government was also seeking forfeiture of approximately $200,000, which it claimed was derived from Whitey Bulger's illegal extortion, racketeering, and money laundering enterprises. In particular, prosecutors referred to Whitey Bulger's extortionate purchase and subsequent sale of the South Boston liquor mart, and its property, along with Whitey's questionable role as a shareholder in the Massachusetts State Lottery.

When questioned in a *rem action* brought by the government in seeking forfeiture of funds derived from Whitey's illegal extortion, racketeering, and money laundering activities, John Bulger did not fare too well. When asked to explain details of the joint account, John Bulger said:

A: My brother just came to me and asked me to sign some cards, and he was opening an account, I guess, and I put my name, my social security number, and my address on there, on the little white cards.

Q: Your brother, James Bulger, came to you and asked you to . . .

A: Yes.

Q: - put your name on an . . .

A: Yeah.

Q: - account?

A: Yeah. He was . . . opening an account and he asked me if I would go on it.

John Bulger denied any knowledge of the source of the deposits made into the account, said he didn't know how deposits had been made into the account, nor how they had been made after Whitey Bulger had become a fugitive. John Bulger explained that he had withdrawn money from the account in August of 1995 after he'd learned that the government had confiscated James' lottery proceeds. "I took it out of the South Boston Savings Bank because of . . . I felt . . . I took it upon myself . . . if . . . it belongs to my brother, and I took it out, and I felt that the government, after they confiscated his lottery, I felt that they were going to confiscate the money, and I was just looking out . . . ."

After Whitey Bulger became a fugitive, John Bulger claimed that he made several transactions involving funds in the joint account without Whitey Bulger's explicit direction. He gave a wedding present of $25,000 to Nancy Stanley. John Bulger stated: "I just thought that my brother would . . . where he wasn't around, would just . . . he told me a long time ago, he was going to have a wedding for Nancy Stanley, and he didn't. And I just took it upon myself . . . I just . . . I . . . I gave it to her."

Nancy Stanley was the daughter of Theresa Stanley, one of two long-time Whitey Bulger girlfriends. Theresa had traveled with Whitey when he'd received word of his upcoming indictment. She had tired of being on the lam with Whitey even though the two had traveled to Ireland, London, Venice, and parts of the southwestern United States. She missed her children, and Whitey had taken her back to South Boston. He'd then picked up Catherine Greig, who would become his sidekick, riding shotgun while Whitey continued his travels on the lam.

John Bulger continued to explain how he'd used money from the joint account to travel, making trips to Florida and Bermuda. The government inquired about the source of the funds for the trips during John Bulger's grand jury testimony.

Q: You said you borrowed money from the account?

A: Well, I . . . I took the money from the account and . . .

Q: You took the money from the account?

A: I took the money. My brother would let me take that money.

John Bulger also stated that he'd withdrawn money from the account belonging to Whitey Bulger, approximately $13,000, to buy a car. He continued to give confusing statements as to whether the money taken from the joint account had been a loan, and if it had been a loan, how the money was to be repaid.

Q: But just so that the record is clear on these vacation trips here, is it your testimony that you have actually paid the money back to the account since those trips, back to the joint account?

A: I think so, yes. I owe him some money, but I just took some money, and I was going to pay him back, you know, when I see him and that's, I've taken some money from time to time.

John Bulger continued his song and dance routine, but it was obvious that he was being less than truthful with his answers. Eventually, the government reached a settlement with him over the joint bank account he held with his fugitive brother, Whitey. However, prosecutors would continue to seek seizure of Whitey's yearly lottery winnings, and later, a federal judge would approve the forfeiture of Whitey Bulger's $1.9 million share of the Mass Millions Lottery jackpot, claiming it was part of a money laundering scheme.

On Friday, November 9, 2001, John Bulger was arrested by FBI agents at his South Boston home. The agents cuffed the recently retired sixty-three-year-old John Bulger during his arrest, just as they would any other common criminal. The four-count indictment against him charged John Bulger with committing two counts of perjury and two counts of obstruction of justice. The swagger had not left the unfazed Jackie Bulger, who was released on $10,000 bail by U.S. Magistrate Judge Charles B. Swartwood. The arrogant Bulger pled not guilty to charges that called for a maximum thirty-year sentence. During a grand jury appearance, John Bulger was asked by a federal prosecutor, "At any time in the last three years, has anyone given you any message to the effect that your brother Jim's still alive?"

"Never," Bulger replied, according to the indictment. The smartass, cocksure Jackie, along with all the Bulgers and for that matter, other South Boston politicians, had a "fuck you" attitude about him. The whiskey-nosed gang of corrupt politicians, in their supreme arrogance, felt they were untouchable. They ran the show; they were the ringmasters in the political arena of Boston.

But Jackie Bulger had been set up. Prosecutors had information provided by Whitey Bulger's girlfriend's twin sister, Margaret McCusker, that Jackie had received news of his brother. "An acquaintance of John P. Bulger received telephone calls from James J. Bulger on or about August 1996, and thereafter told John P. Bulger about certain contents of the acquaintance's conversations," the indictment read. After lying to a federal grand jury with regard to receiving Whitey's phone calls, Margaret McCusker ultimately told the truth. She received a six-month house arrest sentence. John Bulger also claimed he had no knowledge about any safe deposit box belonging to his brother. However, government prosecutors contended that he had paid the rent for the box that had been opened by Whitey Bulger and his longtime girlfriend, Theresa Stanley, in Clearwater, Florida.

Instead of doing the right thing and showing even some small remorse for the families of Whitey's victims, John Bulger would battle with them in court over who should get the killer's yearly lottery winnings, a genuine class guy.

Federal prosecutors did a bit of the right thing. As part of the indictment for money laundering and racketeering back in 1997, prosecutors had seized $14 million in cash and property belonging to Steve Flemmi and Whitey Bulger. One piece of real estate claimed was the home of Flemmi's former live-in girlfriend, Marion Hussey. Prosecutors told a judge that they did not believe it "in the interest of justice" to take the Pleasant Street condominium that Flemmi allegedly bought for Hussey, noting that her daughter was allegedly killed by Bulger and Flemmi.

However, U.S. Attorney Donald K. Stern said the government would not drop its claim to Bulger's lottery winnings because the money could end up back in Bulger's hands or go to his brother John, who had filed a claim for it. Stern made a point to inform the victims' families that if the government were to win the case against the two gangsters they, the families, could then file for a portion of the money. The families of victims John McIntyre and Michael Donahue had filed multimillion-dollar suits against the FBI and former agents. The families of Deborah Hussey and Debra Davis would file a wrongful death suit against Bulger and Flemmi for millions, including Bulger's lottery winnings. The family of Michael Milano, who had been mistakenly killed, also filed wrongful death suits, including one for $14 million against Whitey Bulger.

Milano was only thirty years old when he was slain while sitting in his car at a Boston traffic light in 1973. Hit man John Martorano confessed to killing Milano, who had been mistaken for a rival gangster. It is alleged that Bulger was with Martorano at the time and ordered the hit on the undeserving Milano, who was driving a car similar to that owned by the intended victim of the murderous gangsters.

Cadillac Frank Salemme would also receive a token bit of justice. In April 1997, fifteen people were charged with conspiring to kill Salemme in an attempt to take over control of the New England Mafia. All but two of the defendants pled guilty. Vincent M. Gigi Portalla Marino and John J. Patti contested the charges. Both men were found guilty at a second trial, the first having resulted in a hung jury.

On May 24, 2000, John Patti was sentenced to thirty years in prison. Earlier, Marino had received a thirty-five-year sentence. Codefendants Robert F. Bobby Russo Carrozza, the half-brother of Joseph J.R. Russo and a captain of the Russo-Ferrara faction of the Boston Mafia, received a two-year sentence. U.S. Attorney Donald Stern alleged the men lined up behind Carrozza in an attempt to seize control of gambling, drugs, and extortion from the Mafia faction loyal to Salemme. However, Sonny Mercurio, Steve Flemmi, and John Connolly should also have been charged in the conspiracy to murder Salemme. Mercurio had set up Salemme for an ambush. At Flemmi's urging, Connolly had allegedly instigated an attempt on Salemme's life by informing the press of Cadillac Frank's appointment as the new mob boss. "It appears that the leak to *The Boston Herald* may have had the foreseeable effect, if not purpose, of provoking the attempt to murder Salemme," Judge Wolf wrote.

Cadillac Frank had without question paid his dues. He had been a loyal soldier for decades and had earned a shot at the top spot. Instead, all he received was a long prison term and later, a murder attempt against his life. It was not the type of reward the faithful and trusting Salemme deserved. In time, Cadillac Frank would get his revenge, even if served up cold.

Kevin Weeks continued to give federal prosecutors information on Bulger, Flemmi, and others. Weeks also reported that he had talked to Bulger at least once a month while Bulger was on the lam. Later, when Bulger became more concerned about ongoing events, the calls became much more frequent. During one early conversation, Bulger told Weeks he was considering hiring an attorney to challenge the forfeiture of his lottery winnings.

There were those who questioned the effort being made by the FBI to apprehend Bulger. Some suspected that if Bulger were caught, and decided to talk, he could have caused even more problems for the Boston FBI.

Some were even suggesting that the FBI had more agents assigned to damage control than they did to finding Bulger. There were reports that Bulger and Catherine Greig had been spotted in New York, Louisiana, Wyoming, Iowa, and Mississippi. The last sighting had placed the two in Fountain Valley, California, where Greig had gone into a beauty salon for a shampoo and blow dry, while a man believed to be Bulger waited outside in their parked car.

On September 28, 2000, a superseding indictment added multiple charges of murder to Bulger and Flemmi's growing list of criminal activities. The new charges were added to existing racketeering cases against the two gangsters and also included additional charges of extortion, money laundering, and shaking down drug dealers and bookmakers. Bulger was charged with the murder of sixteen men and two women. Flemmi was charged in ten of those murders.

"The victims include strangers who happened to be in the wrong place, longtime criminal associates, friends, and others whom they believed might provide information to law enforcement or could otherwise threaten their organization," said U.S. Attorney Donald K. Stern. The indictment also charged Flemmi with lying when he testified that former FBI Supervisor John Morris had tipped him and Bulger to the 1995 indictment against them in order to protect John Connolly, who was the actual person responsible for the tip to flee. The new indictment came as a result of testimony provided by hit man John Martorano and Kevin Weeks. According to information supplied by Weeks and Martorano, the killings spanned a period beginning in 1973 through 1985.

On October 11, 2000, former FBI Agent John Connolly was charged in a superseding indictment with leaking information to Bulger and Flemmi, which prompted them to kill two FBI informants and a potential witness against them. The indictment alleged that Connolly had told Bulger and Flemmi that Brian Halloran was an FBI informant, and was about to supply information implicating the two gangsters in the Roger Wheeler murder. The tip by Connolly caused them to murder Halloran in May of

1982, along with Michael Donahue. Donahue was an innocent victim who happened to be in the wrong place at the wrong time.

Connolly was also accused of warning his two prize informants that John Callahan was being sought as a link in the Wheeler murder. Connolly's alleged tip provoked Bulger and Flemmi to take action, hiring their favorite hit man, Martorano, to murder Callahan in August of 1982. Connolly was also charged with obstruction of justice for allegedly trying to "dupe" the court by writing an anonymous letter to Judge Wolf about former Boston Police Detective Frank Dewan. The indictment alleged that Connolly was behind a letter sent to Judge Wolf, who was presiding over the racketeering case against Bulger and Flemmi.

The foolish plan by the arrogant Connolly, who still didn't get it, was an attempt to lead the judge off in a different direction. The letter had been written on Boston Police stationery and signed by three officers, alleging that Dewan was corrupt and had "privately alluded to planting both information and evidence in order to get Bulger and Flemmi." Dewan, an honest cop, had been a thorn in Bulger's side for many years. The good cop could not be bought by Bulger. He had made a choice to go after the ruthless killer and his gang, and in doing so, became subjected to the wrath of Connolly and other Bulger allies. The pressure on Dewan, who had stood alone in his battle against the connected Bulger, became too great. The frustrated detective quietly resigned from a job he had loved, and accepted defeat.

But justice and vindication, although tardy, would come to Dewan through Connolly's own arrogance. "I'm down here in Florida enjoying life and he's up there worrying about going to jail for the rest of his life," said Dewan. "I knew there were lies and rumors being spread and now the public knows." During a raid of the liquor store that Bulger and his gang had extorted from Stippo and Julie Rakes, investigators found a $205 receipt for liquor sold to FBI Agent Dick Baker, along with a written memo: "Dick Baker, friend of John Connolly." Not only had the Boston FBI failed to protect the struggling young couple from being extorted by the gangsters who took their store, they willingly accepted the huge liquor discounts provided by Bulger and Flemmi. The liquor was given as gifts at the FBI's Christmas party.

Later, Connolly would publicly accuse Dewan of planting the slip of paper with his name on it, saying, "He tried to frame me." However, once again, the arrogant Connolly was shooting from the hip. The foolish agent with his cavalier attitude toward the truth would have to wipe the egg off his face.

Detective Kenneth Beers, who had participated in the liquor store raid, called Connolly's statement "baloney." "Frank [Dewan] wasn't there when we found the liquor slip," Beers said. "Frank did it the right way, and he was incorruptible and maybe it bothered people." Always playing by the rules, Dewan had gone after Bulger the right way.

Leonard Henson, a former prosecutor who worked with Dewan, compared the detective to Frank Serpico, who had also encountered problems with a group of corrupt New York City police officers. As was the case with Serpico, Dewan had few willing supporters. Even after retirement, the cop who wouldn't play ball with those protecting Bulger would have his reputation called into question. Connolly's alleged letter to Judge Wolf characterized Dewan as corrupt, with a vendetta against Bulger.

William Johnson, a retired Boston police deputy superintendent, said the police department had failed Dewan. "Every time he pointed his finger at corruption, instead of going after the people he pointed at, they went after him." Dewan spent most of his career working on organized crime in South Boston, Whitey Bulger's home turf.

John J. Coleman, a former Special Agent in Charge of the DEA's Boston office said Dewan "wasn't comfortable at the time working in his own department because working in Southie and working on organized crime just wasn't a popular thing for any cop to be doing in Boston. It was a career-ender for a lot of cops, unless you were on the right side of the Bulger gang."

The guess was that Bulger's childhood friend, John Connolly, had enormous influence on the protection that the gangster had received, while exerting his wrath on those who tried to go after Whitey. "He became

Diogenes, the lone Boston police officer walking through the dark with a lantern of truth," said Sergeant Detective Paul Barnicle, referring to the Greek philosopher who searched for an honest man.

However, some of those who had chosen to go with the flow in protecting Bulger and Flemmi would not escape unscathed. A few in law enforcement had allied themselves with the gangsters for the money. Others did it for the association; they secretly worshipped and admired the gangsters and their flamboyant life-style. Then there were those who did not want to pursue Whitey because of concerns for the possible repercussions from William Bulger, the well-connected, slick and powerful politician.

While Whitey had not lost his two brothers' love and support, Flemmi enjoyed his own as well. The Rifleman's younger brother, Michael, had retired after serving thirty-two years as a Boston police officer. He was ready to support and help his older brother, and would answer the call if needed. On November 3, 2000, Michael Flemmi was charged with moving an arsenal of guns, including seventy high-powered weapons and silencers. The indictment alleged that Michael moved then stored the weapons cache at the request of Steve Flemmi.

The tip had come from Steve Flemmi's son, William Hussey, also known as William St. Croix. Hussey and his Uncle Michael moved the guns before agents arrived with a search warrant on January 13, 2000. The weapons had been moved from the East Third Street home belonging to Steve Flemmi's mother, to a new location in Somerville, Massachusetts. William Hussey had at first supported his father, until strong evidence indicated that his half-sister Deborah Hussey had been murdered by Flemmi and Bulger. Kevin Weeks, who had led investigators to Hussey's burial site, was ready to testify to Steve Flemmi's involvement in her death. Later, forensic examiners would identify Deborah's remains. William Hussey also told investigators that Steve Flemmi was planning an escape from the Plymouth County Correctional Facility where he had been held since his arrest in January 1995. Flemmi informed William Hussey that he had approached a guard with a $50,000 offer to assist in the escape attempt.

Hussey's revelation prompted authorities to quickly transfer the stunned gangster to a protective custody cell at an undisclosed prison in New York. Investigators were also made aware by his vengeful son of Flemmi's boast of secret bank accounts containing huge amounts of cash in the Caribbean.

Steve Flemmi filed a motion addressing the conditions of his new location. The five years of confinement had not been kind to the once "buffed" gangster. He and Bulger had, in the past, worked out feverishly and had taken the necessary steps to stay in excellent physical condition. The now pale and thin Flemmi took the stand to voice his complaints.

When Assistant U.S. Attorney Brian T. Kelly questioned the gangster about the Caribbean bank accounts, Flemmi said that he had opened one in the Cayman Islands over a decade earlier with a small deposit. However, William Hussey had informed prosecutors that Flemmi had revealed he had a great deal of cash in banks all throughout the Caribbean. When asked about the reported $50,000 offer he had made to a guard at the jail, Flemmi shot back, saying, "If I had $50,000, I'd hire more attorneys."

"Isn't it true you're pretending to be indigent and are perpetrating a fraud on this court?" Kelly asked.

"I take the Fifth," Flemmi said.

"Did you give your son $20,000 for chemotherapy treatments for cancer?" Kelly asked.

"I take the Fifth," Flemmi again responded.

Prosecutor Kelly stated the reason Flemmi had filed a motion for his return to the Plymouth jail was that he had received special treatment from a guard he had befriended. Although Flemmi was by all accounts a ruthless killer, he was also a charmer. Many a victim had been taken in by Flemmi's soft-spoken words and genteel manner.

"I didn't get special treatment," Flemmi responded.

"Didn't you once slip out of your handcuffs during a trip to court? That's what your codefendants Frank Salemme, Robert DeLuca, and John Martorano reported."

"I think they're all testifying against me because they're getting consideration from the government, and it's definitely not true," said Flemmi.

The revelation by Salemme, DeLuca, and Martorano was a token bit of payback, in particular for Salemme and Martorano. They had been loyal to Flemmi for decades. During the proceedings, Flemmi complained to his attorney, Kenneth Fishman, about his inability to receive the necessary government discovery in order to organize his defense. He also made reference to his limited access to telephone calls, and that he'd lost his ability to focus. "My concentration has been reduced," said Flemmi, adding that he was kept awake until dawn by the screams of other inmates, and had lost his ability to concentrate and therefore to properly prepare his defense. "I'm being isolated. Whip me down mentally so I can't focus on my case. That's what it's all about," complained Flemmi.

Prosecutor Kelly took issue with the gangster, saying, "Is there anything else giving you problems?"

"Yes, this indictment I'm under. It's my mental stability for all these charges, and not being able to defend myself," added Flemmi.

Earlier, Flemmi had developed a nervous twitch, which had now become more pronounced. The facial muscular contractions were apparent to Cadillac Frank Salemme. "It's the devil eating his body," commented Cadillac Frank.

The twitch-ridden Flemmi continued, saying, "I'm rattled from being kept in isolation for so long."

In truth, in all probability, the underlying factors for Flemmi's inability to focus or sleep had more to do with recurring nightmares. The ghosts of Deborah Hussey and Debbie Davis, with whom he had made love for years, must have had a haunting effect on the beaten gangster. The thought of the once young and beautiful women, whose decaying bodies had been reduced to piles of bones, would have weighed heavy on even the most hardened of criminals. Being isolated made it easy for the ghosts of Flemmi's many murder victims to revisit him. "Do you feel you're suffering from some kind of delusion? Do you know where you are today?" asked Prosecutor Kelly.

"I know where I am today," said Flemmi. "I'm not insane yet." It's possible the screams of Bucky Barrett, who had been tortured before finally being murdered, hadn't yet surfaced in Flemmi's nightmares.

While the mediocre attempt to find Whitey Bulger continued, the FBI had begun tracking telephone calls of those they suspected might be relaying messages for the fugitive gangster. Investigators placed a "pen register" on the telephone at Tecce's restaurant. The restaurant was a popular eatery in the predominantly Italian section of Boston's North End where anyone who was anyone, including John Connolly, could be seen ordering their favorite Italian cuisine.

Tecce's was located directly opposite Francisco's restaurant. It was at Francisco's that Connolly and other agents had arrested Jerry Anguilo. While approaching Tecce's, there is no doubt that Connolly had to have gazed at Francisco's, recalling the arrest and crowning achievements of an era when he was Prince of the City. Connolly was a regular at Tecce's, so much so that when the head chef was told of Connolly's arrival, he would begin preparing the former agent's favorite dish, "Steak Mafia," before the waiter placed the order. The popular entrée comprised tender beef slices, large potato wedges, with peppers and mushrooms sautéed in a light tomato sauce.

Investigators had placed the pen register at Tecce's restaurant hoping the cocksure Connolly, who used the house phone often, would be relaying information relating to the fugitive Bulger. The pen register tap would supply investigators with phone numbers of outgoing calls. Authorities suspected that Bulger was in contact with friends by calling places he knew they frequented, and Whitey knew that Connolly was a regular at Tecce's.

During his frequent appearances at the restaurant, Connolly had gained many supporters. He would pitch his side of the story, proclaiming no wrongdoing, over glasses of Chianti wine. To those who were unaware of Connolly's evil and wickedness, he was a good guy who was undeserving of the wrath directed at him.

In late 1999, the FBI had begun tracking telephone calls out of the homes of William and John Bulger. However, the pen registers had been in place for only a few days before being discovered. On November 16, 2000, a two-count federal indictment charged Richard Schneiderhan, a retired former State Police lieutenant, with conspiracy to obstruct justice and obstruction of justice. Also charged were his brother-in-law, Edward Duff, and Duff's daughter, Linda Reardon. Reardon, who worked for Bell Atlantic, was accused of telling her father about the pen registers. Duff then passed the information to Schneiderhan.

The indictment charged Schneiderhan with informing Kevin Weeks about the pen registers. Weeks told investigators that Schneiderhan had delivered a note to Weeks warning that the Bulger brothers' phone calls were being tracked. He had picked up the note left by the retired trooper at the South Boston Rotary Variety Store. Weeks then delivered the information to the Bulger brothers.

The indictment alleged that Schneiderhan had a personal friendship with Steve Flemmi. The two had grown up in Roxbury. The indictment also stated that the former officer was friendly with Bulger and Flemmi's favorite hit man, John Martorano. The FBI had hoped that the calls could aid investigators in their halfhearted attempts to locate the fugitive Bulger. However, in reality, no one could actually believe that the street-smart "arch criminal" Bulger would have his brothers use their home phones to deliver any messages for him.

Weeks also told investigators that the former State Police officer had tipped the gangsters about a bug that had been secretly installed at the Lancaster Street garage in 1980. The garage had been the center of mob activities. After the bugging had been confirmed by John Connolly, Bulger and Flemmi avoided the garage. Hit man John Martorano, a leading member of the Winter Hill Gang, also "pointed the finger" at Schneiderhan, telling investigators that the Winter Hill gangsters had him in their pocket. According to Martorano, Schneiderhan received cash from the gang to help pay medical expenses for a heart condition.

During a search, investigators recovered three letters from Schneiderhan's home. One letter, addressed to "Paul," a code name for Flemmi, "provided shocking insight into Schneiderhan's apparent unconscionable relationship with both Flemmi and John Martorano," a report stated. The letter clearly indicated how some in law enforcement had been taken in by the life-style of the flamboyant mobsters.

Two of the letters retrieved were addressed to Schneiderhan's son, Eric. In one letter in particular, Schneiderhan revealed his faith in Flemmi. "He [Flemmi] has never let me down and I don't think he will ever let you down," he wrote. In the other letter, Schneiderhan tells his son about "a green plastic bag up over the chairs in the shed." The letter does not reveal the contents of the bag; however, he instructs his son, "Do not tell anyone about what is there. Use it as best you can to complete your education and keep ahead."

State Police Colonel John DiFava was shocked when learning of the charges, calling Schneiderhan a "great investigator." "I think there's a lesson here that anyone, regardless of whether they currently, or have carried a badge, if they step over the line, they have to pay the price," he commented.

In July 2001, Linda Reardon pled guilty to obstruction of justice and received probation. Her father, Edward Duff, admitted he had told his brother-in-law, Richard Schneiderhan, about the pen register tap after receiving the information from his daughter. Duff also received probation.

However, Schneiderhan was determined to fight the charges against him. He would display a similar position to that of John Connolly before him. Each man refused to accept responsibility for their alliance with the gangsters, believing they had done no wrong. Although both men had failed in their oath to uphold the law, neither one was willing to admit their mistakes. Schneiderhan's attorney, James Duggan, contended his client had committed no crime by telling the Bulger brothers to "remain law abiding." However, there is compelling evidence to suggest that Schneiderhan had compromised the Lancaster Street garage investigation back in 1980.

The location had served as a headquarters for Bulger and Flemmi, where the "who's who" of the greater Boston underworld would often be seen meeting with the two gangsters. The State Police had managed to secretly install several listening devices in the garage. The investigation quickly fizzled when it became apparent the gangsters had been tipped to the presence of the bugs. Kevin Weeks claimed the tip had come from Schneiderhan. The cozy relationship the gangsters maintained with a few corrupt law enforcement officials explained why the Boston Police were never able to convict Bulger or Flemmi.

Special Federal Prosecutor John Durham offered not to bring charges against Schneiderhan's son, Eric, if he would plead guilty to obstruction of justice charges and serve prison time. Schneiderhan refused to plead guilty and Durham made good on his threat. Eric Schneiderhan was charged with lying to a grand jury in August of 2001. The indictment claimed that the young career Army officer had lied when he denied that his father had ever referred to Stephen Flemmi by the code name "Paul" in letters. Federal prosecutors contended that "Paul" was Flemmi. One letter found during a search of the ex-trooper's home included a reference to his son. "When you talk to him, his name is 'Paul' and your name is 'Lefty.' Never use anybody's real name," he said in the letter, which began, "Eric, if you are reading this, then the worst has happened."

Duggan would begin to ask the court to dismiss charges of obstruction of justice against his client because the search for fugitive Bulger was a "sham." There had been persistent rumors that if the fugitive gangster was caught and decided to talk, his revelations could result in further embarrassment for the FBI. For that reason, there were those who questioned attempts to find the elusive Whitey Bulger.

Bulger and Flemmi had managed to corrupt some personnel in all three branches of law enforcement: local, state, and federal. There is an obvious need to monitor law enforcement officers with local and ethnic roots. There is a great temptation to ignore their sworn oaths and "go native" when it comes to one of their own. John Connolly, a son of South Boston, had admired Bulger's swagger and tenacity as a youth. He continued to worship Whitey Bulger even into adulthood. Former State Police Lieutenant Richard Schneiderhan and Steve Flemmi had grown up together in Roxbury, Massachusetts, and remained close friends.

The FBI had formed a "deadly pact" with Bulger and Flemmi in their quest to infiltrate the Italian Mafia, and to gain information on the secret society. However, the scales of justice would eventually tilt in the wrong direction, and it would be Bulger and Flemmi who would infiltrate the FBI. Soon information had begun to move the other way, and the gangsters had put that information to deadly use.

–*Chapter 22*–

EXONERATION

On November 29, 2000, at press conferences in Boston and Southern California, the FBI announced it was raising the reward for James Whitey Bulger's capture from the current $250,000 to $1,000,000. The higher reward was due in part to ward off criticism of their feeble attempts to find the fugitive gangster. "It's our expectation that this extraordinary sum will induce individuals with information about Bulger's whereabouts to come forward," said Special Agent in Charge Charles Prouty of the Boston office of the FBI. The crafty Bulger had avoided arrest since his January 1995 indictment. The only fugitive on the FBI's Ten Most Wanted List with a higher reward was Osama bin Laden, from $5,000,000 to the current $25,000,000.

Posters of Bulger and his companion, longtime girlfriend Catherine Greig, were being circulated along the Mexican border. It was believed that Bulger would often cross over into Mexico to acquire the medication he needed to treat a heart condition. The medication could be purchased in Mexico without a prescription.

Nearly five years after Bulger had become a fugitive, the FBI would finally get its act together. Bulger's face would appear in federal buildings and post offices across the nation, a move the Feds should have taken long before. His picture would also be shown on the television program "America's Most Wanted." Still, there were many who believed that the FBI was not really interested in apprehending its former star informant. The tardy effort by the government only strengthened those beliefs.

In early October 2000, John Durham, head of the Special Task Force investigating corruption in the Boston FBI office, would keep the promise he had made to Frank Salemme. Durham had begun digging into the 1968 murder convictions of Peter Limone, Joseph Salvati, Henry Tamelo, and Louis Greco. The four men had been found guilty by a Suffolk County jury in the slaying of gangster Edward Teddy Deegan. The chief witness against the innocent men had been Joseph Barboza.

However, hit-man-turned-witness John Martorano told Peter Limone's attorney, John Cavicchi, that Barboza had told him that he had killed Teddy Deegan and was framing Limone and the others because the Mafia "screwed me, and now I'm going to screw as many of them as possible."

Barboza had lied concerning the true identities of Deegan's killers. Both the FBI and Suffolk County prosecutors knew that Barboza had done the hit with the help of Jimmy The Bear Flemmi and others. Barboza's FBI handlers at that time were H. Paul Rico and Dennis Condon. Limone and his attorney, Cavicchi, alleged that the FBI gave its blessing to Barboza's lies in order to gain convictions against the Boston Mafia and to curry favor with Jimmy Flemmi's brother, Steve, who was Agent Paul Rico's valuable informant. Agents Rico and Condon needed Steve Flemmi in their effort to bring down the Italian Mafia.

The destruction of the LCN was Washington's top priority. Agents who were successful in "doing a number" on the Mafia could receive promotions, along with other benefits. Steve Flemmi was Condon and Rico's inside man; he could infiltrate the secret society. He had been given the O.K. to commit any crime, which included protection for his brother, the prolific and ruthless killer, Jimmy The Bear Flemmi.

Limone and three others were originally sentenced to death in the electric chair at the Walpole State Prison in Massachusetts. For the actual killers of Deegan to feel no remorse was one thing; they had lived by murder and mayhem. However, that those who had sworn to uphold the law joined in the conspiracy to frame innocent men, and were willing to see them fry, is shameful. Agent Paul Rico would not have shed any tears had the executions taken place. Fortunately for Limone and the others, their lives would be spared when Massachusetts abolished the death penalty in 1974. Their sentences were changed to life in prison. However, Henry Tamelo and Louis Greco would eventually die behind bars. They could not outlive the opportunity for possible exoneration. Agent Paul Rico did not lose any sleep over the two innocent men who had died in prison, nor for their families.

Three years earlier, in 1997, Joseph Joe the Horse Salvati had a stroke of luck. Because of his continued reports regarding the evidence of Salvati's innocence, newsman Dan Rea of WBZ-TV in Boston, had won Salvati his freedom. Then-Governor William Weld commuted Salvati's sentence, and he was released from prison after having served thirty years behind bars.

Federal Prosecutor Edward Harrington was Barboza's overseer. Harrington had built a successful career as a federal prosecutor by turning many a mobster into a government witness in order to gain convictions on scores of LCN members. He had given special attention to his prize informant, Joe Barboza. Harrington was responsible for getting Barboza the best deal possible for his testimony, which included cash payments and relocation after testifying. He would work closely with State Prosecutor Jack Zalkind to help secure a conviction in the Teddy Deegan case.

It was alleged that Harrington also withheld evidence that Barboza may have been lying. An informant's report, which would have been available to him within a week of the murder but was withheld from defense attorneys, named a far different set of participants than did Barboza.

"In other words, it would have shown the complete testimony of Barboza at the trial implicating Greco, Tamelo, and Limone to be a complete and utter falsehood," said Limone's attorney, John Cavicchi. Harrington had a reputation as a hard-nosed prosecutor. He, like John Connolly, had a knack for turning mobsters into cooperating witnesses in his war against the Mafia.

One of the defendants in the Deegan trial said he was nowhere near the murder scene and subsequently passed a polygraph test. Yet Harrington never subjected Barboza to a polygraph. When Barboza told his attorney, F. Lee Bailey, he wanted to admit his lies at trial, Bailey arranged a polygraph. Barboza was being held at Walpole State Prison and was having second thoughts about testifying against the mob. Bailey later suggested that Harrington had prevented the polygraph. "Mr. Harrington went to Walpole and somehow the polygraph test went away. The FBI said, 'Fire Bailey, or you are here forever.'"

Harrington would relish his successes, and would use his convictions as a stepping stone to advance his career. He would join up with Robert Kennedy's Justice Department, where anything underhanded was acceptable in the war against the Italian Mafia. Kennedy made no bones of his hatred of the Mafia; he despised them with a passion. Later in his career, Harrington would be given a federal judgeship by Ronald Reagan.

A few years later, Joseph Barboza would detail his life as a hired gun for the mob in a book. The ruthless killer would pay homage to his friend by dedicating the work, "To Edward F. Harrington, with respect."

In December 2000, a special FBI task force headed by John Durham dug up old documents at FBI headquarters in Washington, D.C., revealing the wrongful convictions of Limone and three other men. The secret hidden documents shed light on the actual killers of Edward Teddy Deegan. The reports showed that then-FBI Agent Paul Rico had received information on the Deegan slaying the day after it had occurred. Rico had received the information from an informant whose identity was redacted—blacked out—of the report. The informant told Rico he had spoken with Jimmy Flemmi, who had admitted his part in killing Deegan and revealed the names of four other men who were involved with him. The informant provided Rico with a detailed account of the Deegan murder, and gave him the names of five men who allegedly carried it out: Jimmy The Bear Flemmi, Joseph Barboza, Ronald Cassesso, Wilford Roy French, and Romeo Martin.

Peter Limone's attorney filed a motion for a hearing to investigate the new evidence supporting Limone's claim that he had been framed for the Deegan murder. Judge Margaret Hinkle of the Middlesex Superior Court in

Cambridge agreed with attorney Cavicchi's request for hearings on the new evidence. She ordered then-Suffolk Assistant District Attorney Mark Lee to turn over the sealed documents to defense attorney Cavicchi.

The irate judge asked Prosecutor Lee, "Why is there such a volume of things that were not turned over to Mr. Limone?"

"I honestly cannot answer that right now," Lee responded.

The scores of Limone's relatives who had packed the courtroom felt some degree of optimism at Judge Hinkle's bewilderment. They had known all along that Peter was innocent, and had supported him throughout his nearly thirty-three years of imprisonment.

But attorney Cavicchi was impatient. He had watched his previous client, Louis Greco, an innocent man, die in prison. The silver-haired, sixty-six-year-old Limone was thirty-three when he'd been sentenced to death in the electric chair. But Peter would find strength in his wife, Olympia ("Olly"), and their four children. Not only had Olly had the difficult task of raising four children alone, but she'd managed to visit Peter religiously while doing it.

Peter had grown up on Chamber Street in the West End of Boston; Olly on Hale, a few blocks away. They were neighborhood sweethearts. The West End was mostly comprised of Italian-Americans who looked out for one another. Youngsters playing stickball on the cobblestone streets would be interrupted by the call for supper from family members leaning out tenement building windows. Those who failed to heed the supper call would be sternly reminded by concerned neighbors. The evening meal was most often a feast of Old World recipes, which had been handed down for generations and created from scratch.

While serving his life sentence, Peter dedicated countless hours counseling suicidal inmates who had lost all hope. Limone was readily accepted by those who were lost. In avoiding death in the electric chair, he brought credibility to many seeking his help. He was a prime example to those in need to never give up. Giving comfort to others was something Peter had learned while growing up in the Italian West End community of Boston, where members of the ethnic group of people took a special interest in one another.

Peter also organized a boycott of prison phones when a policy of eaves-dropping on phone conversations with family members was enacted at the facility. The boycott failed when some inmates began to make outgoing calls in spite of the listening devices. Peter had principles. He believed that the state had infringed on his right to private family conversations. He would never again use the phones to communicate with loved ones. "He hasn't called this house since," said his wife.

On December 12, 2000, in Middlesex District Court, both the defense and the Suffolk County District Attorney's office began arguing their positions on the issue of the admissability of newly-found key documents. The government had become reluctant to undo the wrong that had occurred. They were well aware of the house of horrors the new documents would reveal. The District Attorney argued against producing the once-hidden documents on the grounds that Limone "has made no showing that these documents were not previously available." But Limone's attorney said information had only recently appeared in files on the case and should have been available to defense attorneys when Limone had originally gone to trial. "They couldn't have prosecuted the case if this information was known to the police," attorney Cavicchi said.

The District Attorney also objected to an affidavit from criminal defense attorney Joseph J. Balliro, Sr., who said he had information that Limone and others were innocent. One of his clients, Jimmy Flemmi, had told him the details of who had killed Deegan, and affirmed it in an affidavit.

Attorney Balliro had at times represented Jimmy The Bear Flemmi. He had no knowledge that his brother Steve Flemmi was an FBI informant. Balliro could not come forward with the information he had received from The Bear during Limone's trial due to attorney/client privilege. However, the District Attorney's office would disagree. "Balliro's duty of confidentiality to his client was no more binding at the time of the defendant's previous motions than it is now," Assistant District Attorney Mark Lee and Paul B. Linn argued in a motion.

On the following day, both sides would continue to battle in court over the issue of admissibility of the newly-discovered secret documents. The defense would also be seeking a new trial, based on the new evidence.

Attorney Cavicchi began by informing Judge Margaret Hinkle that he had spoken to John Durham of the FBI's special task force. "He indicated what he had seen was highly relevant," the attorney said.

Suffolk County Prosecutor Mark Lee countered, saying, "While evidence shows Barboza was not a savory individual and lied, inconsistencies in his testimony are not enough to warrant a new trial."

Attorney Cavicchi responded, "The government's entire case was built on Barboza's revenge antics. If Barboza's testimony is false in any particular, it destroys his credibility everywhere."

The courtroom was once again packed with family and friends of Limone. They would be given some ray of hope by Judge Hinkle's statement when saying, "The evidence in front of me tends to show there should have been more stringent cross-examination of Mr. Barboza." However, the supporters of Limone had been disappointed far too many times during his thirty-two years of incarceration. They had been expecting the best, only to suffer defeat after defeat in getting Limone's case overturned. They had pleaded Limone's case to governors and high-ranking politicians, all to no avail.

Attorney Cavicchi closed by telling the court that, "The government concealed from Limone's original defense team information that would have bolstered his innocence. They perpetrated fraud upon the Commonwealth."

Judge Hinkle responded, "I don't want accusatory language. I want facts."

She then informed both defense and prosecution that she wanted a copy of the 7,000-page transcript from the original trial, and was preparing to thoroughly review Barboza's testimony. She also indicated that she would discuss John Durham's newly-discovered evidence as well. January 5, 2001, was the date set for another hearing.

On December 19, 2000, the secret reports that John Durham had discovered during the Justice Department's probe of FBI corruption were
turned over to Limone's attorney and Suffolk County District Attorney
Ralph Martin. In a cover letter to Cavicchi, Limone's attorney, which
accompanied the FBI reports, Durham and U.S. Attorney Donald K. Stern
wrote that the Justice Task Force, the U.S. Attorney's Office, the Boston
FBI, and FBI headquarters "understand the potential significance of the
enclosures to Mr. Limone and Mr. Salvati. These documents are being
made available to you with the concurrence and encouragement of the
Boston FBI and FBI headquarters."

Although Joseph Salvati's sentence had been commuted in 1997, after
serving nearly three decades behind bars, he now wanted justice and total
exoneration.

The reports discovered by Durham clearly showed that the Bureau not
only knew the wrong men had been convicted of the Deegan slaying, but
agents had also been aware of the murder plot two days before it happened
and had not interceded to prevent it.

"This is a disgrace. If it weren't so tragic, it would be laughable," said
Cavicchi. The mind-set then was to convict any Mafia member or associates, whether guilty or not.

The explosive FBI reports showed that then-FBI Agent Paul Rico had
received details on the Deegan murder the day after it happened. Rico then
wrote a report two days following, to then-FBI Special Agent in Charge in
Boston, James L. Handley, who four days subsequent wrote his own report
about the Deegan murder and sent it to Hoover at FBI headquarters in
Washington, D.C. The reports revealed top FBI officials, including then-
Director J. Edgar Hoover, may have hidden information that could have
prevented Limone, Salvati, Greco, and Tamelo from being convicted of the
Deegan hit.

They also revealed that then-FBI Agent Paul Rico had received, from
an informant, names of the five men who had actually carried out the murder. Shortly after the men were wrongly convicted, word spread quickly

throughout the underworld that Jimmy The Bear Flemmi, Joe Barboza, Ronnie Cassesso, Roy French, and Romeo Martin were responsible for the Deegan murder.

It didn't take long for the names of those who had actually been involved in the Deegan murder to surface in the Italian-American community in Boston. Friends of the wrongfully accused men from the neighborhood decided to protest outside Suffolk County Courthouse. The protestors, who had been interviewed by local newsmen, claimed that then-Suffolk County District Attorney Garrett Byrne, whose prosecutors were working closely on the case with Paul Rico and the FBI, was engaged in a conspiracy to frame innocent men because they were of Italian descent. The protest would, however, fail. The ones with political clout were mostly of Irish descent or "wasps"—none would "come to bat" and seek redress.

Boston lawyer Victor Garo, who was representing Limone's codefendant, Joseph Joe the Horse Salvati, went as far as telling WBZ-TV in Boston that the prosecution was an FBI "murder conspiracy" because punishment for murder at the time was death in the electric chair. Four of the defendants received death sentences back then.

Attorney Garo had, in the 1980s and then again in the 1990s, unearthed new evidence suggesting Barboza had implicated innocent men, including Garo's client, Salvati, but his motion for a new trial was opposed by the Suffolk County D.A.'s office and later denied by the Massachusetts Supreme Judicial Court.

"It's my opinion that the federal and state governments conspired to murder Joe Salvati and the murder weapon was the indictment," Garo said in an interview. "The coverup started in 1965, and continues in the year 2000. When does it end?

"I find all of this outrageous. This is an organization (the FBI) that we the people are supposed to be protected by and they are breaking laws whenever they want to," said the frustrated Garo. He said it was no secret that the Bureau's war against the Mafia was of the highest priority, with no concerns for the consequences. "Sensationalism and good press became more important than human rights and human decency," Garo said.

Although new documents that had been made available to Suffolk County D.A. Ralph Martin by Durham were extremely significant, Martin nevertheless would oppose Limone's motion for a new trial, and refused to be interviewed about the FBI reports.

"I am stunned," Zalkind said. "I have never seen any FBI reports that were signed by Paul Rico, and I was the prosecutor."

A key witness in the Deegan murder case, Anthony "Stats" Stathopoulas, would also come forward with a shocking revelation. Stathopoulas' testimony during the Deegan murder trial corroborated the key government witness in the case, Joseph Barboza's account of what took place the night of the slaying.

While seated in the witness chair, Stathopoulas had pointed the finger at Louis Greco, saying he looked like the man he saw leaving the alley where Deegan had been killed, shortly after the "hit."

Stats, however, was now singing a different tune. Stathopoulas said that it was former Boston Police Homicide Detective John Doyle who had identified Greco as the shooter for him. A member of then-Suffolk County District Attorney Garrett Byrne's office staff, whose name Stathopoulas could not remember, had then told him where Greco would be sitting at the defense table, he said.

"They told me the seating arrangement in advance," Stathopoulas said.

Garrett Byrne and John Doyle were dead; however, the chief prosecutor, Jack Zalkind, denied ever coaching Stathopoulas, or anyone else.

Now a prestigious attorney in Boston, Zalkind said, "I treated this case as professionally as any prosecutor could."

Defense attorney John Cavicchi strongly disagreed. Cavicchi said Stathopoulas' affidavit had been kept in the Suffolk County District Attorney's files and was only recently turned over to him. Only after the court ordered the affidavit turned over to the defense as discovery in Limone's motion for a new trial, was the document made available. The affidavit should have been turned over much earlier to the defense attorneys in their efforts to secure a new trial.

The then-Suffolk County District Attorney's office displayed the same arrogance as the FBI had done. They were all birds of a feather when it came to getting a conviction, most notability in alliance against those of Italian descent.

"If I did something like that, I would be disbarred and put in prison," Cavicchi said.

Attorney Cavicchi said he would investigate events in the Stathopoulas matter. He wanted the names of the people who had been involved in the Greco frame-up, and who had coached Stathopoulas to implicate an innocent man. He also planned to get answers as to why prosecutors had failed to come forward with this information. Instead, they had hidden this important fact from the defense for thirty years.

On Friday, December 22, 2000, Judge Margaret Hinkle called a hearing after receiving the newly-discovered records. Friends and family members of Limone had completely overwhelmed the Middlesex County courtroom, hoping once again for the best.

"It's just a travesty of justice," said Janine Limone, who was one year old when her father went to prison. "Thirty-three years is such a long time."

Also present in the courtroom was Roberta Greco, Louis Greco's wife of seventeen years. Louis Greco had died in prison, an innocent man, while hoping for the truth to one day be revealed. "He was innocent. He never did it. I've been saying it for years, and no one would listen," said Roberta. She had been in her twenties when her former husband had gone to prison. "You have no idea when men are sent to prison, what happens to their families," she said. "People stare at you; you're the wife of a murderer."

To add to her grief, she had lost her oldest son, who took his own life on December 27, 1997, at the age of forty-two. He was just thirteen years old when his father had been sent to prison. "He walked into prison to see his father one day, and Louis' leg had been amputated," Roberta recalled. "That was one of the worst times." Louis Greco suffered from diabetes.

It wasn't only the men who went through hell while wasting away in prison. Nearly every family member would suffer as well. Olly Limone had raised four children alone. For years she had taken her kids on buses and trains to see their father in prison, including the seven years he spent on death row. She took her sons to hockey practice and had gone to graduations without her husband at her side.

Aside from the issue of a new trial for Limone, attorney Cavicchi was preparing to ask Judge Hinkle to grant bail for his client.

"We're hoping they let him out on bail for Christmas," said Janine Limone. She had hopes that her father would be able to walk her down the aisle at her April wedding.

Yet Suffolk County District Attorney Ralph Martin's office remained opposed to Limone's bid for a new trial.

"The D.A. won't own up to this," responded Limone's attorney. "The D.A. is still in denial."

Also voicing his objection to the District Attorney's position for a new trial was Joseph Joe the Horse Salvati's attorney, Victor Garo. Garo had fought the charges against his client since 1976. Through Garo's hard work and persistence, he had been able to get Salvati's sentence commuted in 1997. However, that was not enough; he was still working to have Salvati's name cleared once and for all. "It is time for the government, with all of these amounts of evidence, they should dismiss the charges against Joe Salvati," Garo said. "The time has come."

When asked to comment on the hidden reports, then-chief prosecutor in the case Jack Zalkind said, "If there were reports in this case which had exculpatory evidence in them, they should have been turned over to me."

When told that new information alleged that FBI agents in the case knew Barboza had lied on the witness stand, Zalkind responded, saying, "I thought Paul Rico and Dennis Condon were absolutely good guys. If they were holding back on me, oh my God." Whether Zalkind was being candid, or should have received an Oscar for "Best Actor," one could only guess. He was aware that then-Agents Rico and Condon were the forces

who had convinced Barboza to "flip." He was also well aware of the direc-
tives coming out of Washington to bring down the Mafia at any cost.

During the hearing on Limone's bid for a new trial, Middlesex Superior
Court Judge Margaret Hinkle released Attorney Joseph Balliro, Sr., of his
lawyer-client privilege. Balliro requested the release in order to divulge
information he had been told decades earlier regarding the slaying of Teddy
Deegan, from his then-client Jimmy The Bear Flemmi. Attorney Balliro
had submitted an affidavit stating his client had confessed to the Deegan
murder in the 1960s, before The Bear passed away. Attorney Balliro's affidavit also stated that Flemmi, the brother of Steve Flemmi, had informed
him that Limone, Joseph Salvati, Henry Tamelo, and Louis Greco had
played no part in Deegan's murder. Balliro had known some of the wrongly
accused men since childhood. He had been raised in the same Italian-
American community of Boston's North End. He had been prevented by
the attorney-client privilege from exposing true facts in the Deegan murder case. He would painfully watch in silence as one by one the men would
begin to waste away in their prison cells.

However, Balliro would now be permitted to reveal confidential information he had received from Jimmy The Bear Flemmi.

In 1998, the Rules of Professional Conduct, a code governing the conduct of lawyers in Massachusetts, were changed. The lawyers were now
allowed to come forward and talk, if they learned from a client that innocent people had been wrongfully convicted of a crime.

A second criminal defense attorney was also willing to come forward
with testimony that could help Limone in his effort to obtain a new trial.
Legendary Boston attorney Ronald J. Chisolm said in an interview with
The Boston Herald that he had received information in 1976 from his
client, Ronald Cassesso, who had been indicted with five other men for the
Deegan murder. "They were innocent men being charged, I knew that,"
Chisolm said. The attorney was corroborating the hidden FBI reports indi-
cating that four of the six men convicted, Joseph Salvati, Peter Limone,
Henry Tamelo, and Louis Greco, were innocent. At a 1967 meeting at

Walpole State Prison, he and his client, Ronald Cassesso, had discussed the murder case. "I asked him who was involved in the Deegan murder and he told me. He said he was involved.

"Barboza was involved; The Bear, Jimmy Flemmi, was involved; and Roy French was involved. He said Salvata, Tamelo, Greco, and Limone definitely were not involved. He also told me Agent Rico had been to see him and wanted him to corroborate Barboza's story, and if he did, he wouldn't do any time for the Deegan killing," Chisolm reported. "At some point, Rico said, 'We can get you together with Barboza and get your stories straightened out.'"

Cassesso turned down Rico's proposal. It was a generous offer. Those who decided to play ball and follow a proscribed script could expect huge rewards for their testimony. In addition to relocation, a new identity, and a large "cash bonus," a cooperating witness would also receive a *minuscule* prison sentence. However, all those who decided to "roll," thereby hurting others while accepting generous rewards for their false testimony along with a very short prison sentence, lived thereafter a lifetime of guilt and regret. Ronald Cassesso would die in prison in 1991.

When asked how he felt concerning the practice of prosecuting innocent men for first degree murder, which called for execution, Chisolm said, "You know the realities of life, they're going to frame them and they don't care." The fabrication of evidence in organized crime was the rule rather than the exception. "This was not the first case where the Feds were out of line," Chisolm added. "If you deal with this and you've seen it a lot, you just fight your own battles."

The fabrication of evidence in organized crime cases proved to be extremely successful. The ease with which convictions were achieved became apparent, causing the government to expand the practice to other criminal cases as well. It would now become a common occurrence. One only has to recall the scandal that surfaced suggesting that the FBI crime lab was routinely fabricating evidence in order to assist prosecutors in making their cases.

Gaining convictions on members of organized crime was an *obsession* of Agents Paul Rico and Dennis Condon. However, in the Deegan case, measures had to be taken to placate Steve Flemmi. It was well-known that Jimmy Flemmi was not only a participant, but one of the shooters that night. Agents Rico and Condon could not seek a murder charge against Jimmy, the younger of the Flemmi brothers; Steve would never have allowed it.

When Chisolm learned that the code governing the conduct of lawyers in Massachusetts had been changed, he decided to contact Victor Garo, the attorney for Joseph Salvati. "This is just more evidence in a mountain of evidence that shows Joe Salvati and Peter Limone to be innocent," Garo said. "It is about time that the Suffolk County District Attorney's office does the right thing and dismisses all charges."

In 1995, the Suffolk County District Attorney's office opposed Salvati's motion for a new trial, which was denied by the Massachusetts Supreme Court as well. District Attorney Ralph Martin continued to oppose Peter Limone's motion for a new trial.

At the time that prosecutors from the Suffolk County District Attorney's office returned murder indictments in the Deegan case, some in local law enforcement had been convinced that four of the men indicted were innocent. When learning that secret documents might have suppressed evidence on the Deegan hit, one local law enforcement investigator said it confirmed his belief that not all of those charged had been participants in the murder.

"It's a sad thing when you have to frame people to set them up," said the investigator. "I'm not saying these people didn't do something in their past, but they were not involved in the Deegan murder."

Limone had one conviction, and that was for running a local dice game.

Just hours after the body of Deegan was discovered, local investigators were receiving tips from informants revealing the names of those involved in the hit.

"I got a tip the night of the murder that the guys who did it were driving a red Cadillac with a black roof and that they had gone to the Ebb Tide (a nightclub in Revere Beach) on the Boulevard," the North Shore investigator said. "I took a look in the parking lot, and sure enough, there's the Caddy. We went in, identified a few guys, and they were taken to Chelsea P.D. to be interrogated. I remember it as clear as day and I know I didn't see Joe Salvati, Henry Tamelo, Limone, or Greco there that night. When you get 'em, you got to get 'em right," he said. "I used to tell those wise guys, 'If I get you, I'm going to get you right, and when I do, I don't want to hear no crying about it.'"

It was obvious that the investigator was not as sophisticated as the elite FBI Agents Paul Rico and Dennis Condon. He didn't have the machine that the FBI possessed. He was simply a hard-working, blue-collar type investigator. Yet, he truly believed that the only way to make a case against someone was by the book, and not with the use of skullduggery.

On December 22, 2000, Middlesex Superior Court Judge Margaret Hinkle, in considering Limone's bid for a new trial, agreed to allow attorney Joseph Balliro's affidavit into evidence, revealing his then-client Jimmy The Bear Flemmi's confession to his role in the Deegan murder.

Balliro's affidavit also stated that Flemmi had told him that Limone, Henry Tamelo, Joseph Salvati, and Louis Greco had been wrongfully accused, and had played no role in the crime.

Amid the avalanche of mounting evidence, Judge Hinkle declined to rule on Limone's request for bail, or on the motion for a new trial. Instead, she called for yet another hearing the following week.

Hinkle's decision to continue the hearing was a huge disappointment to the many friends and family members who had packed the courtroom in anticipation of Limone's release for the holidays.

"They're engaged in a continuing obstruction of justice and a conspiracy to violate Mr. Limone's civil rights," said his frustrated attorney, Cavicchi.

However, Limone's son, Peter, was more upbeat. He had never given up hope of winning his loving father's freedom. "We're moving along and hopefully he'll be home soon," he said.

"I don't know how they sleep at night—Rico and Condon—knowing what they did," said Limone's feisty wife, Olly. She had painfully experienced years of frustration and setbacks as court after court had refused to review the case. Olly knew her husband had been framed. This was the most promising opportunity yet to win his freedom, and she was not going to let it go. A call had been made to the then-governor of the state, Paul Cellucci, asking him to issue a pardon for Mr. Limone.

"I'm going to try to do anything I can because it is a miscarriage of justice," said Kelly A. Timilty, a member of the governor's counsel. "If we have a man sitting in prison for thirty years for something he didn't do, we have to correct that." Timilty promised to do whatever was necessary to secure Limone's release from the maximum security correctional institution in Norfolk, Massachusetts. "I want to see if we can get a pardon hearing as quickly as we can," Timilty said. "These men might not be here today if the death penalty had not been abolished, and that frightens me."

There are those who believe that the then-governor, Italian-American Paul Cellucci, was ready to grant a pardon for Limone, had Judge Hinkle refused to order a new trial. There are those who also believed that Cellucci had experienced his own anti-Italian prejudices while struggling to achieve in the predominantly Irish political arena of Boston. Whether the governor's office position was a cause for action, or someone had begun to believe in the facts revealed in long-hidden FBI documents, one can only speculate. Calls for exoneration in the case were becoming more frequent and more emotional.

"I don't understand why he's still in jail," Limone's attorney, John Cavicchi, said. "This case is a disgrace."

The calls for justice by Limone's family members were relentless. He had spent yet another Christmas behind bars.

In response to the criticism of Suffolk County District Attorney Ralph Martin's opposition to releasing Limone on bail while the newly-discovered documents were being reviewed by Judge Hinkle, a spokesman for Martin issued a statement: "We have no interest in keeping an innocent man in prison, but we have no interest in making a rush judgment either," said James Borghesani.

However, attorney Cavicchi was not impressed with the statement from the District Attorney's office. The State of Massachusetts was looking for a way out of the mess they were in. Conceding that innocent men had been framed, and that the State had been a participant, would have serious repercussions on its judicial process. The embarrassing position in which the Commonwealth of Massachusetts now found itself had its beginnings in 1965, when it had decided to form an alliance with rogue agents Paul Rico and Dennis Condon, and accept their lies and concoctions.

Cavicchi's motion was simple and direct. He wanted Judge Hinkle to throw out Limone's conviction based on a 1957 United States Supreme Court decision requiring informants' accounts be supplied to defendants. "I expect the judge to obey the law," said Cavicchi. The brilliant attorney, who had been fighting for Limone's freedom for over twenty years, had a solid argument. The long-hidden explosive documents showed that not only had top FBI officials suppressed credible evidence, but that then-Director J. Edgar Hoover had been deeply involved in the process as well.

On Thursday, January 4, 2001, Suffolk County District Attorney Ralph Martin announced that he was preparing to ask for new trials for Limone and Salvati in the Deegan murder case. Martin's abrupt reversal came amid the enormous volume of evidence affirming Limone and Salvati's non-involvement in the Deegan murder case. The District Attorney's office was expected to support Limone's motion for a new trial, a highly unusual turn of events.

The mountains of evidence, in particular the discovery of the hidden secret documents, were paramount in their decision to support a new trial. "The documents painted a very compelling picture. What happened here was wrong enough for us to come into court and say that this mandates a new trial," said Assistant District Attorney Mark Lee.

If Judge Hinkle were to grant the request for a new trial for both Limone and Salvati, odds were that the District Attorney's office was not expected to prosecute the case. It would mean immediate release for Limone, who had spent nearly thirty-three years in prison. Overwhelming new evidence had forced District Attorney Martin to back-off his tenacious defense of the Deegan murder convictions.

On Friday, January 5, 2001, Peter Limone's attorney, John Cavicchi, was ready to argue for a new trial before Judge Margaret R. Hinkle. Once again, the courtroom was packed with friends and family members who had spent tortuous weeks in anticipation of Limone's bid for exoneration and freedom.

After a brief moment of formality, Judge Hinkle ruled to vacate the conviction against Limone. She had harsh words for the FBI, criticizing the Bureau for withholding information that could have led to Limone's acquittal, saying the Agency had been "tarnished."

"It is now time to move on," Hinkle said. "Mr. Limone's long wait is over."

Limone's many supporters broke out into applause when the judge announced her decision. It was the moment they had hoped and prayed for.

"I'm very, very happy, and so relieved," said Limone's son, Paul. "It's been a nerve-racking three or four weeks. I'm just happy he's coming home. It was very difficult when I was younger," added Paul. "But we always knew he was innocent, and we always fought for his freedom."

Judge Hinkle granted the motion for a new trial filed by defense attorneys and Suffolk County District Attorney Ralph Martin. Limone's life sentence had been vacated, and he was freed without bail.

The District Attorney's office chose not to pursue the case against Limone. There would be no new trial. The secret-hidden documents revealed not only that four men had been framed, but also clearly showed that FBI agents knew that Deegan was going to be murdered, yet had done nothing to prevent it.

Outside the courthouse, flanked by his tearful wife, family, and supporters, Limone had bitter words for the Bureau, in particular, for former Agent Paul Rico, who had played a key role in the wrongful convictions. "He framed me. He knew what he was doing," Limone said, referring to Rico. "He's scum. He set it all up."

Family members and close friends embraced one another; even strangers in the crowd offered their congratulations.

"I just give thanks for the good people I have been involved with," Limone said, while placing his hand on attorney Cavicchi's shoulder. "Prison," Limone continued, "was very hard, every day in there, knowing I was innocent. I'm just happy I still have my family. Every day you look at it, and every day you know you're innocent, but you wait for this day."

When asked if he was bitter, the sixty-six-year-old Limone responded, "Of course you harbor bitterness. You have to, how can you not! It's a shame that Henry Tamelo and Louis Greco had to die in jail for nothing," Limone added. "This is one of those if we can't get somebody on what we know they did, we fabricate another case to get them. That sounds to me like anarchy," he said.

After thirty-three years, the first day home surely seemed unreal for Peter and Olly Limone. He was finally home. The father of four and grandfather of eight was preparing to enjoy one of many Sicilian dishes he'd longed for all those years.

One of the many participants in the celebration was former Prison Superintendent Abu Hanifabdal-Khallaq. Although they were of different ethnicities, Peter being of Italian descent and Abu a black man, the two had hit it off during the early days of Limone's incarceration. "He's tough," said the former Superintendent, "but very sensitive." The two men, although from different backgrounds, had great respect for one another. "He's white and that made me hold back, and I'm black and I think that made him hold back. But we put that baggage down."

During the festivities, Peter was presented with a bottle of scotch from his sister, Rose. He had given the bottle to her shortly before he was incarcerated. "I told him I'd open it when he came home," said Rose. "Today, we opened it."

While family members looked on, Peter and Abu toasted to Peter's freedom, sharing a drink of the decades-old scotch.

One way Peter had found to cope with the boredom of prison was to involve himself with the stock market. He would spend a good portion of each day with make-believe market participation. "My sister brought me *The Wall Street Journal*, and I used to buy and sell stocks in my head," said Peter.

Peter Limone had had thirty-three years taken from him and his family by a few corrupt law enforcement individuals. It would soon be payback time. The recently received, secret, hidden FBI reports would provide the basis for a civil suit.

"I want them to pay for what they did," said Limone. "The only way they understand is when you expose them in public and they have to pay. They've lived at home for thirty-three years. They had their families around them. They enjoyed life. I didn't."

Normal events that other families enjoy and take for granted such as weddings, graduations, or simply watching their children grow up had all passed Limone by. One of the many sad events that occurred during Peter's incarceration was the death of his brother, Mally, who had been a loyal supporter of Peter's innocence, and would faithfully visit Peter during his long years of incarceration. Mally's only desire in life had been to witness his brother's exoneration.

"We are going to sue everybody," said Limone's attorney.

Cavicchi was not naive about the nation's long history of Italian-American discrimination. He had studied the events that had occurred back in 1927, when Nicola Sacco and Bartolomeo Vanzetti had been executed for a crime they had not committed. Evidence that would prove the two had been victims of discrimination at the hands of the government would come too late. Limone would have suffered the same fate as Sacco and Vanzetti had the death penalty not been abolished in the State of Massachusetts.

Sarah Ehrman, the widow of Herbert Ehrman, who had represented Sacco and Vanzetti, made known her beliefs to attorney Cavicchi and others, that the two men had been falsely accused and convicted due to prejudice and a polluted justice system. Historians who have studied the case of Sacco and Vanzetti have come to the same conclusion.

On July 24, 2001, attorneys for Peter Limone, Henry Tamelo (who had died in prison in 1985), and Louis Greco (who had also died behind bars in

1995), filed a $375 million suit against the FBI. The suit claimed the FBI had hidden key evidence that would have cleared the men in the Deegan murder.

Attorney William Koski's suit sought compensation for the suffering the families had endured throughout the frame-up. "The FBI as an agency knew this, allowed this to happen, and perhaps fostered its happening," said Koski.

Limone's suit also accused the government agents of pressuring members of the parole board against granting him a commutation. Each time it seemed certain the votes were there in favor of commutation, the Feds would step in with a knockout blow. The agents would *falsely* inform the board members that they had information indicating Limone was antici- pating his return to the LCN. That information was completely untrue, yet the board members did not want to challenge the powerful FBI.

"I was just destroyed every time he was turned down," said Olly Limone. "Eventually, you just give up," she said, adding that her husband's exoner- ation was "a miracle."

"One thing we want to do in the civil action is find out who knew what, when, and whether there was any steering of Barboza's testimony," said attorney Koski.

Joseph Salvati's attorney would wait to file his suit against the FBI. Attorney Victor Garo said the government should do the right thing, come forward to right the wrong, pay Salvati for his years of suffering, and not subject him and his family to a protracted trial.

Adding his voice to condemning the evils committed by Paul Rico and other G-Men was Bill Bennett, Jr. He accused Rico of conspiring with his prized informant, Steve Flemmi, in the murder of his two uncles, Edward Wimpy Bennett and Walter; and his father, William. Federal prosecutors had leveled charges against Steve Flemmi for their alleged roles in the Bennett murders earlier. However, those charges would later be thrown out by Judge Wolf, who ruled that prosecutors had used the grand jury improp- erly to gain evidence against the two men.

Joe the Horse Salvati was bitter over the frame-up and began to voice his contempt for those responsible. "There's no way those two guys [Agents

Rico and Condon] could have acted the way they did for all those years without lots of other people knowing about it," he said. "That's great, fellas. You got to have guys going along with it. When they finally get to the bottom of all this, if they ever do, I'd be interested to see how many other guys they hook for all the crap that went down. I hope they nail a bunch. I know you're gonna think this is probably a funny thing, coming from someone like me, but there's some decent people working for the government right now. I really think they deal straight up, and they'll take this thing wherever it goes. Still, I worry. Different people have different agendas, if you know what I mean. You're never sure just who you can really trust."

Salvati was no doubt referring to Special Prosecutor John Durham as one of the "decent people" working for the government. Durham's efforts had been the key factor in unearthing the hidden documents. However, when it came to former Agents Rico and Connolly, Salvati didn't pull any punches.

"You want to know where Whitey is?! Ask Rico; ask John Connolly. With all the millions they helped Bulger make, my guess is they know or they have a real goddamned good idea. Like Stevie's [Flemmi] brother running those offshore accounts, there's just too much money for those two guys to stay indifferent."

"Preposterous," responded former Agent John Connolly to Salvati's accusations. However, many still believe that Connolly was in communication with the fugitive Bulger. Their roots were too deep, their ethnic and neighborhood ties too strong to believe otherwise.

On January 18, 2001, Judge Margaret Hinkle threw out the 1965 murder conviction against Joseph Salvati. She repeated once again the words she had spoken earlier to Limone, "Your long wait is over."

Yet again, Hinkle had harsh words for those involved in the murder conviction, saying, "The conduct of certain agents of the Bureau stains the legacy of the FBI."

Friends and family members of Salvati who had filled the courtroom broke out in applause. Although he had received a commutation in 1997 from then-Governor Weld, Salvati wanted total exoneration. Outside the courtroom, Salvati expressed mixed emotions to the judge's ruling. He had hoped that his parents, along with his attorney's parents, could have witnessed this day. The parents of both men had passed away earlier. "It's a sad day because there are a few people that couldn't make it," an emotional Salvati said. "They just couldn't last."

On January 30, 2001, District Attorney Ralph Martin announced that he would not seek new trials against Limone and Salvati. For the two wrongfully convicted men, it was officially over.

But attorney Cavicchi would seek one more exoneration. He began to file a motion, asking the State of Massachusetts to clear Louis Greco's name for the sake of his family. Greco had died in prison. Although the highly-decorated World War II veteran had received a soldier's burial, he had still been branded as a convicted killer. Attorney Cavicchi insisted that the State wipe away the stain on Greco's name.

And one of the men who had pled guilty to the Deegan murder would gain his freedom as well. On December 19, 2001, exactly one year from the day that the District Attorney's office had received the hidden documents, Wilford Roy French would be set free. The seventy-two-year-old French, who had spent thirty-four years in prison for his role in the Deegan murder, was granted release by Judge Hinkle.

In granting the frail and in-poor-health French his freedom, Judge Hinkle had words of praise for the actions taken by the prosecutors. "I want to compliment District Attorney Ralph Martin. This is a courageous step for his office to take," she said.

Although French had acknowledged his role in the Deegan murder, he should have been given access to the hidden documents prior to his guilty plea. Had his attorney been aware of the documents that could have challenged the key government witness, Joseph Barboza, French might not have pled guilty to his part in the slaying.

Upon leaving the courtroom, French was immediately whisked away by family members who offered no comment. However, the soft-spoken Roy French did pause long enough to say "Merry Christmas" with a gentle smile.

It was no secret to those in the underworld that French had been an unwilling participant in the Deegan murder. He had been ordered by the two notorious hit men, Joe Barboza and Jimmy The Bear Flemmi, to lure his friend Deegan into the execution. Barboza and Flemmi were aware that Deegan had trust in French and would not have suspected his friend as a part of any setup. Had French refused, it would have been interpreted as a sign of weakness by Barboza and Flemmi, and surely would have led to French's murder as well.

French was subsequently offered a deal to lie and testify against the four innocent men while corroborating Barboza's account of the Deegan murder. Had French been willing to go along with the frame-up orchestrated by Agents Paul Rico and Dennis Condon, he would have received a token prison sentence.

"He turned that down," said French's attorney, Phillip A. Tracy.

Deegan's family did not oppose French's release. However, Deegan's siblings were extremely upset with the FBI for failing to intercede to stop the murder. Agents knew prior to the slaying that Deegan was doomed for execution, yet never warned him or tried to prevent it. Members of Deegan's family prepared to file a civil lawsuit against the FBI for allowing their informants to murder Deegan, and then protecting them from prosecution for the crime by hiding key evidence that would have revealed their participation in the killing. The exposure of accounts in the Deegan murder and frame-up would spur a Congressional investigation.

The House Government Reform Committee, led by Chairman Dan Burton of Indiana, would begin requesting all records in the Deegan case. In particular, Burton wanted the FBI files relating to informants and their FBI handlers.

The Capitol Hill hearings would not be good news for the Boston FBI Bureau, or former Agent H. Paul Rico.

Chapter 23

H. PAUL RICO

In the early 1960s, Agent Paul Rico had begun developing Steve Flemmi as a Top Echelon Informant. Rico had so embraced the FBI's new campaign against the LCN that he would be inclined to look the other way and accept informants whose hands were smeared with blood. Rico knew that Flemmi had been involved in the murder of Cornelius Hughes during the Irish Gang War. When asked by Rico if Flemmi had any idea as to who had committed the murder, Flemmi reported that he had an excellent idea who committed the murder, but added "that it would be better if he didn't say anything further regarding the killing." Rico had good reason not to report accurately or completely information about Flemmi's possible involvement in the murder. Rico feared he would lose the authority to continue using Flemmi's services as an informant if FBI headquarters in Washington decided that Flemmi should be targeted for possible prosecution rather than continued as an informant.

There was also reliable information that Rico had protected Flemmi by tipping him to those who were planning to set him up for execution, and had also spread false rumors in an effort to instigate violence between rival gangsters considered enemies of Flemmi.

While serving as an informant for Paul Rico, Flemmi participated in the murders of Wimpy Bennett, his brothers Walter and William, and Richard Grasso. Even though Rico and other agents worked in tandem with state and local investigators on organized crime cases, Rico and his colleagues never contributed to any investigation of Flemmi's involvement in the murders of the Bennetts or Grasso. When Flemmi and Salemme were indicted for the William Bennett murder and the Fitzgerald bombing, it was Paul Rico who suggested that Flemmi flee in order to avoid arrest. Flemmi's successful flight, and the eventual dismissal of the charges, spared Rico and the FBI the embarrassment of exposing Flemmi's dual role as an FBI informant and a murderer. Rico was concerned as he was not permitted to open any informant unless he first clearly indicated to FBI headquarters that he was certain the informant could be used without danger or controversy to the Bureau.

There were other instances of misconduct by Rico in order to protect one of his informants. In *Lerner vs. Moran*, the Supreme Court of Rhode Island found that Rico had urged one of his informants to lie under oath. The Rhode Island court found that in the trial of organized crime figure Luigi Manocchio, Rico's informant, John Kelley, admitted that during Lerner's trial for murder, at the direction of Rico, he had testified falsely. During Lerner's trial, Kelley testified that he had personally cut down the shotgun used in the murders. However, during the Manocchio trial, Kelley stated that his associate had actually cut down the shotgun. Kelley said that Rico had directed him not to mention the associate's role in the murder. The associate was a valuable FBI informant who Rico wanted to keep on the streets. Kelley's explanation of why he had lied under oath: "Agent Rico told me that I should just do as he said, and everything would come out all right."

In the wake of the scandals that rocked the Bureau in Boston, new Justice Department guidelines were drafted to prevent the warm fellowship between G-Men and gangsters that encouraged murders, extortion, and drug dealing. No longer would the FBI be allowed to protect those involved in criminal conduct by concealing their identities from other law enforcement agencies. Nor would agents be permitted to dine or exchange gifts with gangsters, as Connolly and his cohorts had done.

The new rules call for all federal agencies, in particular the FBI and the Drug Enforcement Administration, to report crimes by informants to prosecutors. In the past, the FBI had been relied upon to monitor or supervise their relationship with the gangsters. The new guidelines would require greater accountability by the informants' handlers. They were prompted by the unholy alliance between the FBI with gangsters Bulger and Flemmi.

During an appearance before a grand jury, hit man John Martorano pointed the finger at former Agent Paul Rico as the person who had helped set up the ambush of World Jai Alai owner Roger Wheeler. According to Martorano, John Callahan had handed him a slip of paper detailing Wheeler's daily itinerary, along with his description. Callahan told Martorano that the written note had come from Paul Rico, then head of security at Wheeler's World Jai Alai.

"Mr. Rico was definitely involved in my father's murder," said Wheeler's son, David. "It's just taken the police twenty years to get through the obstacles raised by FBI corruption. You gotta ask yourself what were his intentions. What was he doing at Jai Alai? What was his real role?"

There is great speculation that Rico had acquired the position through the efforts of World Jai Alai President John Callahan, who was closely tied to Bulger and Flemmi. Martorano's revelation corroborated the claim Brian Halloran had made to FBI agents prior to his assassination in 1982. Halloran was denied enrollment in the Witness Protection Program, even though he was willing to shed light on the Wheeler murder, and on the skimming operation at World Jai Alai.

Tulsa Police Chief Ronald Palmer, in commenting on the investigation, said, "It's just unimaginable; I can't imagine a cop, somebody sworn to protect the law, turning it around like that." Affidavits filed by Tulsa investigators list former Agent Paul Rico, along with gangsters Whitey Bulger and Steve Flemmi, as those responsible for the Wheeler hit. "The affidavit we presented we think is very succinct and points directly to the people we would like to have in Tulsa to be tried," he said. "We believe through our work and what has been provided to us from the task force in Boston, that information is sufficient and the D.A. should move forward."

However, Tulsa County District Attorney Tim Harris, who had the sole authority to indict, was slow on the draw. Despite calls for him to indict Rico, Bulger, and Flemmi, he was reluctant to do so. A first degree murder conviction in Oklahoma is punishable by lethal injection.

"Is Tulsa going to protect its own?" asked Wheeler's son, Lawrence. "Or is Tulsa going to let its business leaders get gunned down by an outside hit man?"

Special Federal Prosecutor John Durham, head of the Justice Department Task Force, along with Tulsa investigators, called upon prosecutor Harris to indict Rico and the two gangsters. "I'm very concerned," said Larry Wheeler. "Tim Harris has never said anything of any substance of a concrete nature that would commit him to acting one way or another."

David Wheeler had concerns that the killers of his father could fall through the cracks and avoid indictment. Even with hit man Martorano's confession and the volume of evidence uncovered by the Justice Department Task Force, no one was yet to be charged. David was concerned that time would win over before the killers could be brought to justice. Twenty years after Roger Wheeler had been slain, the graying gangsters were dancing with the Grim Reaper.

"I am desperate," said David Wheeler. "I don't know where to turn. How am I going to get justice for my father?" The Wheeler family had concerns that the enormity of charges against Bulger and Flemmi, including multiple murder indictments in Massachusetts, along with the potential for charges in Florida, could delay the quest for justice indefinitely.

"We'll be waiting a decade before the people that have been implicated ever come to trial," said Larry Wheeler.

Although Tulsa District Attorney Tim Harris agreed to a plea deal with hit man Martorano, he was not indicating when others would be charged. "We believe this should be moved to the top of the pile," Police Chief Ron Palmer said. "There's a lot of things going on in the other states that tie into this. We have what we believe is a good strong affidavit and we would like to see it move forward."

No trial date had been set for the complex racketeering charges facing Bulger, Flemmi, and John Connolly in Boston's federal court. David Wheeler had spent years working with his own private investigators, as well as voicing his plea for justice on numerous talk shows. "It is ironic to find ourselves stopped cold by our own District Attorney," he said. "We're getting really fearful we will never see justice. We know there is a clock, and it's running out."

The family of Roger Wheeler accepted triggerman Martorano's detailed account surrounding the murder. However, their beliefs were further confirmed when events surfaced indicated Paul Rico's participation in the framing of four innocent men wrongly convicted of a gangland slaying in Chelsea. While exonerating Peter Limone and Joseph Salvati, Middlesex Superior Court Judge Margaret Hinkle had had harsh words for the conduct of the FBI for hiding important evidence that would have proved the men's innocence. Then-Agent Paul Rico was one of those accused in the frame-up; he had also been accused of withholding key evidence from the defense in the case.

"The stories about the release of FBI documents speak loads about Paul Rico and his history," said David Wheeler. "I hope he has every opportunity to answer for every one of these instances in court."

On March 14, 2001, prosecutors in Tulsa, Oklahoma, and Miami, Florida, filed murder charges against Stephen The Rifleman Flemmi and James Whitey Bulger. The two gangsters were accused of hiring triggerman John Martorano in the 1981 slaying of Tulsa millionaire Roger Wheeler and the 1982 murder of accountant John Callahan. Oklahoma and Florida are states that carry the death penalty for first degree murder convictions. Earlier, hit man Martorano had agreed to testify against Bulger and Flemmi, thus avoiding execution himself. However, H. Paul Rico was not included in the murder indictments. A frustrated David Wheeler expressed his disappointment, saying, "My family doesn't quite know what to make of it."

Paul Rico's attorney, William Cagney III of Miami, denied all assertions that his client had had any involvement in the Wheeler murder. The retired former agent was living a life of luxury outside Miami, unfazed by the current allegations. Tulsa County District Attorney Tim Harris tried to placate the Wheeler family's disapproval in Rico's omission from the indictment, saying, "Like all crime victims who have lost a loved one, they want complete closure. They are disappointed and it is a bittersweet day for them."

For twenty years, the tenacious homicide detective Michael Huff had continued on the trail to capture the fugitive Bulger. Huff, who was the first Tulsa investigator at the Wheeler murder scene, revealed a startling piece of information—the ruthless gangster Bulger was gay. "We didn't take that information lightly," said Huff. "It's very legitimate information."

Affirming Huff's discovery, FBI spokeswoman Gail Marcinkiewicz said, "There have been unsubstantiated rumors over the years that Bulger is gay." Bulger's sexual preference became the object of humor and ridicule throughout greater Boston. In particular, those in the underworld who had known Bulger personally had the biggest and longest laugh.

Tulsa authorities had been circulating "wanted" posters indicating Bulger could be frequenting nudist colonies or living in gay communities. The wanted posters also indicated that the gangster had extreme bad breath. The reports indicating that Bulger had been spotted in Southern California and Mexico were investigated by authorities. The FBI believed that Bulger had been crossing over to Mexico where he could obtain over-the-counter medication for a heart ailment. FBI spokeswoman Gail Marcinkiewicz indicated that Bulger's girlfriend, Catherine E. Greig, was with the fugitive, saying, "We have no information that tells us he is no longer traveling with Catherine. We encourage the public to be very, very vigilant and report all sightings of Whitey and Catherine, no matter where they occur."

–*Chapter 24*–

CAPITOL HILL HEARINGS

In early March of 2001, the family of J. Donahue, who had been slain along with Bulger associate Brian Halloran in 1982, would file a $36 million wrongful death suit against the FBI. Halloran had been marked for execution after the South Boston gangsters received a tip that he was an informant. The tip allegedly came from then-Agent John Connolly. Donahue happened to be in the wrong place at the wrong time, and in the company of Brian Halloran. The suit claimed that Donahue was slaughtered due to his "reckless and deliberate indifference of the FBI."

"Our mother never recovered, nor did we from the loss of our father," said Shawn Donahue. "Every day that he has been gone was an incredible struggle. I hope that the [FBI] agents who ruined our lives enjoyed their hours with their children over those same years because they borrowed all our time as their own. Now they have to pay us back for that lost time."

The suit would include as defendants former Agents John Connolly and John Morris. Lawrence Sarhatt and Robert Fitzpatrick, Special Agents in Charge of the Boston Bureau in 1981, were also named as defendants.

"When Mike left that day, I didn't know I'd never see him again," said Donahue's widow, Patricia. "He was the head of our family, and the government killed him. The thought of him being gunned down for no reason always bothered me, and now we know the answers." She continued, saying, "The lawsuit only lays the blame at the feet of the people who are responsible for his death."

Later, the family's attorney would add "The United States of America" as a defendant in the suit. "For the federal government to have known all these years and not told us that our father was killed as a result of their action is enough to make our heads spin," said Donahue's son, Michael. "When the information about Halloran was leaked by the FBI to our father's murderers, they killed our father."

The Donahue lawsuit was one of many filed by the families of victims allegedly slain by Bulger and Flemmi. In early April of 2001, Massachusetts Rep. William Delahunt, along with United States Reps. Barney Frank (D-Newton, Massachusetts) and Martin Meehan (D-Lowell, Massachusetts), began calling for Congressional hearings on the criminal conduct committed by the Boston Bureau. "If the American people do not believe that the system works, that justice in the largest sense is being done, they will have no confidence in their government," said Delahunt.

One major issue of the hearings would focus on whether the FBI had hidden key evidence, resulting in the imprisonment of four innocent men for the Teddy Deegan murder. "That's about as bad as anything I've ever heard," said U.S. Rep. Barney Frank. "If we saw that in a movie, we'd say no way. That's Oliver Stone. That didn't happen."

U.S. Rep. Dan Burton (R-Indiana), Chairman of the Government Reform Committee, planned to begin hearings regarding the allegations on May 3, 2001. "It is becoming increasingly clear that innocent men were left in prison to protect government informants and their interests," quoted a news release from Burton's office.

Although Joseph Joe the Horse Salvati and Peter Limone were exonerated after serving thirty-three years in prison for the Deegan slaying, it was time to settle the score. Their codefendants, Henry Tamelo and Louis Greco, also innocent, had died in prison. In commenting on Burton's decision to conduct hearings, Salvati's attorney, Victor Garo, said, "This will give an opportunity for the FBI to show to Congress and to the citizens of the United States their statement that they did nothing wrong in this case." Garo continued, "I, on the other hand, will also present my evidence."

Garo was responding to a statement made by Special Agent in Charge of the Boston Bureau Charles Prouty. Prouty insisted that the FBI had not concealed documents that would have proved the men innocent. Although the Attorney General's guidelines on the use of informants had clearly been violated, and informants had been protected from murder charges in the Teddy Deegan case by substituting innocent men as the alleged perpetrators, FBI arrogance continued unabated. The Office of Professional Responsibility had sent Charles Prouty to investigate any evidence of corruption on the part of FBI agents in the Boston Bureau. After Prouty reported no evidence of wrongdoing, he and another investigator, William Chase, were promoted by the FBI to the number one and two positions in the Boston Bureau.

John Connolly was later indicted by federal prosecutors who rejected the Office of Professional Responsibility's conclusions. Prouty discarded the idea that he was rewarded for finding no crimes by being made head of the FBI in Boston. Revelations from the Congressional hearings could further complicate the problems facing the wounded Bureau in Boston. It seemed unlikely to many that the FBI could police itself, even with the new Department of Justice guidelines on the use of informants. "It remains to be seen if guideline adjustments are sufficient to remedy the egregious infractions revealed by court hearings and testimony," the Congressmen wrote. "Legislative action may be necessary to assure consistent and uniform adherence to rules of conduct by agents and supervisors."

While Congressional investigators began preparing for the much-anticipated hearings, another scandal was being exposed by Robert Fitzpatrick, the second in command in Boston from 1980 to 1986. According to Fitzpatrick, the then-head of the Boston Bureau, James Greenleaf, had leaked the identity of an informant to a criminal defense attorney. During interviews with local news reporters and the 60 Minutes television program, Fitzpatrick had identified the informant as John McIntyre. McIntyre was slain in November of 1984, allegedly by members of Bulger's gang, after it was learned that he had been cooperating with law enforcement, detailing Whitey Bulger's role in gun running and drug trafficking.

"Innocent people were killed, murdered, and I hold certain agents responsible for that," Fitzpatrick said. Fitzpatrick placed most of the blame for the treachery and corruption in the Boston FBI office on former Agent John Connolly and Connolly's former boss, John Morris. According to Fitzpatrick, Thomas MacGeorge, then head of the public corruption division, told him that then-Special Agent in Charge Greenleaf had revealed the identity of the informant to criminal defense attorney Martin D. Boudreau. By some strange coincidence, Boudreau, a former federal prosecutor, had a host of marquee drug dealers as clients. At the same time, Bulger and Flemmi were extorting drug dealers for the right to do business, and offering protection as well.

Fitzpatrick was most critical of Bulger's childhood pal and South Boston neighbor, John Connolly. "Connolly turned out to be an informant," Fitzpatrick said. "Connolly let Bulger inside the FBI. When everybody was asleep, this guy [Connolly] went down and grabbed all the stuff and gave it out, anything Bulger needed, the information about criminal competitors, information about others ratting him out, information about other law enforcement agencies."

When Fitzpatrick had tried to make known the degree of corruption inside the Boston FBI, along with his continual suggestions that Bulger was unproductive and should have been closed as an informant, he became an outcast in the Boston Bureau. Fitzpatrick would be one of many called to testify before the Congressional Committee.

After thirty years of anxiety, the sons of the three slain Bennett brothers were ready and willing to reveal the Boston Bureau's snug association with gangsters. Billy Bennett had the harshest criticism for former Agent H. Paul Rico. He recalled witnessing the rogue agent threatening his father weeks before he was slain, allegedly by Steve Flemmi. Flemmi, who has been charged in the murders of Edward, Walter, and William Bennett, is scheduled to stand trial for the slaying at a later date.

Edward "Wimpy" Bennett, along with his brother Walter, disappeared in 1967. Soon after, William Bennett was found shot to death, his body tossed into a snowbank. According to Billy Bennett, Rico wanted certain documents that had been held by his two dead uncles. "If they took these people off the streets, my father would have lived," Billy said. "I want to tell them they need to police the police better."

Steve Flemmi's troubles continued to mount. Facing multiple murder charges, the ruthless gangster was finding it extremely difficult to obtain legal representation willing to participate in his defense. Top criminal defense attorneys who specialized in defending mobsters would draw the line when the potential client was an informant. Adding to his difficulties was Flemmi's claim of indigence.

Flemmi had made the mistake of remaining in Boston after having been warned to flee in the face of pending indictments. In suffering arrest, Flemmi had needed to foot the bill for his initial defense alone. Meanwhile, his partner in crime, Whitey Bulger, became a fugitive with blood money stashed in safety deposit boxes across the country. However, those who had firsthand knowledge of Flemmi's vast fortune—cash derived from three decades of being an arch-criminal—didn't buy his claim of being broke. One source who had been associated with Flemmi for decades estimated his fortune to be in the low eight figures.

A host of criminal defense attorneys from the greater Boston area would refuse requests from the Federal Public Defender's office to represent Flemmi. The $50 per hour fee offered by the Defender's office was in itself totally unacceptable by attorneys accustomed to far more compensation for their services. However, the single most important factor was not the meager fee being offered. No lawyer worth his salt was willing to sit in the courtroom next to a killer while defending him on charges of murdering his sweet young girlfriends. And there were even fewer attorneys who would be willing to represent a rat.

Flemmi did have two attorneys whom he had retained early on. Ken Fishman was the first lawyer hired by Flemmi to represent him, and continued to stay the course even when the gangster claimed he could no longer afford to pay him. Unable to acquire additional legal counsel, Flemmi desperately tried to cut a deal. However, federal prosecutors would not offer much. They were well aware that the gangster faced the possibility of execution in Tulsa, Oklahoma, for his role in the Roger Wheeler murder, and a capital murder charge for ordering the slaying of John Callahan in Florida. Although Bulger and Flemmi faced multiple murder charges in Boston, the alleged sordid slaying of the two young women romantically involved with "The Rifleman" had the public's wrath. There were many who wanted a piece of the ruthless gangster.

–Chapter 25–

NO TEARS

On May 3, 2001, appearing in an Oklahoma courtroom, hit man John Martorano pled guilty to the May 27, 1981, murder of World Jai Alai owner Roger Wheeler. Prosecutors had agreed to accept a second degree murder plea from the sixty-year-old Martorano as part of an earlier agreement. In exchange for the reduced charge, the loyal gangster had agreed to testify against Whitey Bulger and Steve Flemmi, claiming he had been directed by the two South Boston mob bosses to kill the Tulsa millionaire. The triggerman also revealed that former FBI Agent H. Paul Rico was involved in the slaying, detailing Wheeler's work habits through company president John Callahan. Members of the Wheeler family had attended Martorano's sentencing, still anxiously waiting for the former rogue agent to be charged by the Tulsa District Attorney. Earlier, Martorano had pled guilty in Miami to killing John Callahan in 1982, also on the order of Flemmi and Bulger.

Although the Tulsa judge had handed Martorano a fifteen-year prison sentence, questions remained about how much time the hit man would actually serve. His value as a key witness could be the determining factor. He most certainly would never set foot in an Oklahoma prison.

On the same day that hit man Martorano was accepting responsibility for the Wheeler slaying, former Agent Paul Rico was appearing before a House Committee on Capitol Hill. The Committee, led by Chairman Dan Burton (R-Indiana), had been investigating whether the FBI intentionally hid the fact that Joseph Salvati, Peter Limone, and two other defendants who died in prison, were framed by the ruthless hit man Joseph Barboza for

the 1965 murder of gangster Teddy Deegan. Barboza's handler during that
period was Paul Rico. The Committee was determined to unravel the scandalous events surrounding the wrongful imprisonment of the innocent
men. However, the arrogant former Agent Rico boldly refused to acknowledge any role played by him or others in the framing of the innocent men.

Connecticut Rep. Christopher Shays took issue with Rico's cavalier
attitude, accusing him of feeling no remorse for his actions in the wrongful
convictions.

"What do you want, tears?" Rico arrogantly responded to Shays' accu-
sation. "It'll be probably a nice movie or something," continued the defiant
Rico. The former agent admitted he had reliable information that members
of the underworld were plotting to kill the renegade Deegan prior to the
murder, and had failed to take action to prevent the slaying. Rico continued to deny Shays' accusations that the FBI had hidden key evidence in the
Deegan murder in order to protect the actual killers, its informants.

"You just don't give a fuck, do you?" shot back the fiery Shays.

"Is that on the record?" Rico responded.

In commenting on the cozy relationship between the FBI and gangsters,
"This whole episode is disgraceful," said Burton. "It's one of, if not the
greatest failure in the history of federal law enforcement."

In addressing the Committee, Joseph Salvati's attorney, Victor Garo,
had harsh words for the conduct of the FBI agents, who had knowingly
framed four innocent men. Garo detailed how Rico and others had worked
with Joseph Barboza in a plot to achieve guilty convictions based on false
testimony by Barboza. The conviction of the four alleged LCN members
would foretell the policy coming out of Washington to bring down the
Mafia at any cost.

The Committee planned more hearings in early fall to unravel the FBI's
decades-long relationship with gangster informants. Burton's committee
would begin requesting records from the Justice Department relating to the
use of informants for the past five decades. In particular, Burton wanted
documents pertaining to the South Boston gangsters, Whitey Bulger and

Steve Flemmi. Burton would also seek all reports on Paul Rico and his part-
ner Dennis Condon, as well as other documents relating to John Connolly,
John Morris, former FBI informant Joseph Barboza, and former New
England Organized Crime Strike Force Chief Edward Harrington.
Harrington had been a longtime Barboza supporter. The chairman also
demanded the records from the FBI wiretaps of New England Mafia chief
Raymond L.S. Patriarca and gambler Jerry Anguilo.

On May 15, 2001, Stephen The Rifleman Flemmi pled guilty to federal
charges of racketeering, extortion, and money laundering. Flemmi agreed
to accept a ten-year sentence. As part of the deal, Flemmi would not be
required to testify, yet he admitted he had been warned to flee the 1995
indictment. Earlier, Flemmi had testified that Supervising Agent John
Morris had tipped him and Bulger to the coming indictment. However,
Judge Mark Wolf did not buy Flemmi's assertion that Morris had been the
tipster, and instead found John Connolly the person responsible. Flemmi's
guilty plea required he forfeit five costly condominiums in a fashionable
section of Boston, two suburban house lots, and bank accounts. Flemmi's
guilty plea would have no effect on the ten murder charges, nor would it
have any stake in the capital murder charges facing him in Tulsa,
Oklahoma, and Miami, Florida.

It was a good move for the sixty-six-year-old Flemmi and government
prosecutors. Flemmi had already served close to six years awaiting trial, and
would only serve eight and a half years on the ten-year sentence. His sentencing date was set for August 21, 2001.

With the extortion, racketeering, and money laundering charges out of
the way, prosecutors could now zero in on the murder charges. Through it
all, Steve Flemmi had continued to protect former Agent John Connolly.
For over thirty years, Flemmi had ratted out other gangsters, many of whom
shared his ethnic heritage, without any concerns or remorse. Although
born to ethnic parents, his father being an immigrant from Italy, Flemmi
simply walked away. Though he had thus far refused to incriminate John
Connolly and other former agents, the true test of his disturbing loyalty

could come if convicted of capital murder in either Tulsa or Miami. There were indications that officials in Tulsa might be willing to bargain with Flemmi by offering life imprisonment rather than execution, if he would agree to implicate others. Flemmi's plea would clear the way for his trial on murder, gun possession, and extortion. His arraignment was scheduled for July 17, 2001.

But no defense attorney was willing to step up to the plate and take the informant's case. With that, Federal Magistrate Marianne Bowler ordered the Federal Public Defender's office to assign the gangster an attorney. The fact that Flemmi had been charged with murdering his two young girlfriends, one his stepdaughter, was not taken lightly by criminal defense lawyers. Steve Flemmi would have his work cut out for him at trial. Loyal hit man John Martorano, who had confessed to being the triggerman in the Roger Wheeler murder, was prepared to testify against his former boss. Flemmi's own son, William Hussey, rolled over, claiming his father had confessed to killing his half-sister, Deborah Hussey, with whom the gangster had been sexually involved.

On July 17, 2001, Stephen The Rifleman Flemmi pleaded innocent to charges he participated in ten murders during his three decades of crime, while at the same time serving as an FBI informant. At his arraignment, the South Boston gangster pleaded innocent to a total of seventeen charges, including the ten murders, racketeering, extortion, money laundering, obstruction of justice, perjury, evidence tampering, and a slew of firearms charges. Although the original indictment had been handed down in September of 2000, the arraignment had been delayed nearly a year because Flemmi had been unable to find an attorney willing to represent him. No date had been set for trial, which was expected to last six months. In addition to the federal charges in Boston, the pale and graying gangster was also facing state murder charges in Tulsa, Oklahoma, and Miami, Florida, states that carried the death penalty. Flemmi's notorious partner, Whitey Bulger, was the object of a nationwide manhunt by a joint task force of federal and state police agencies.

Congressional investigators began digging up records in San Francisco, where Joseph Barboza had killed a West Coast street thief over stolen securities while in the Witness Protection Program. The Committee on Government Reform, led by Chairman Dan Burton, was steamrolling ahead with its probe into corruption in the Boston FBI office. After Barboza had been charged in the murder of Ricky Clay Wilson, then-Agents Paul Rico and Dennis Condon, along with the head of the Organized Crime Strike Force, Edward Harrington, had come to Barboza's rescue. The trio had worked out a favorable deal for their star informant with California prosecutors. Barboza had originally been charged with first degree murder; however, after Rico, Condon, and Harrington interceded, Barboza pled to second degree murder and served a mere four years in prison. Congressional investigators probing the FBI's alliance with gangster informants would begin steamrolling at high speed, and nothing would be able to stop that train.

On August 21, 2001, gangster Steve Flemmi appeared in court to accept his ten-year sentence for racketeering, extortion, and money laundering. Flemmi had agreed to the guilty plea earlier in May. However, Judge Wolf reserved his harshest words for the conduct of the FBI rather than the gangster standing before him. Wolf chose his words with Flemmi cautiously because of the murder charges still pending against him. But Wolf pulled no punches when it came to addressing the conduct of the FBI. "The evidence in this and other cases indicates that the FBI's relationship with Bulger and Flemmi was not an isolated, aberrant occurrence attributable to anybody's South Boston roots," Judge Wolf said. "Rather, while hopefully extreme in degree, it may have been typical of the relationship that the FBI had with a number of its Top Echelon Informants."

Wolf was not wary in naming those responsible. "More than a dozen FBI officials in Boston and in Washington engaged in various forms of misconduct to protect Mr. Flemmi and Mr. Bulger. Those officials included Larry Potts, who later became the Deputy Director of the FBI." (Potts had resigned amidst allegations of misconduct during the Ruby Ridge investigation.)

"If Mr. Flemmi has committed any of the crimes with which he remains charged, he was able to do so because of the protection of the Federal Bureau of Investigation," Wolf said.

"I want to thank the court, Your Honor," said the frail and graying sixty-seven-year-old gangster.

The House Committee on Government Reform investigators continued to unmask the three decades-long government cover-up in the Teddy Deegan murder case, and planned to make known their findings during hearings scheduled in the fall. The Committee members were prepared to show how Paul Rico, Dennis Condon, and other agents had participated in various forms of misconduct to protect their informants. Investigators were calling for the release of documents to determine what had occurred in Boston for four decades between the FBI and their gangsters. However, the Department of Justice was not willing to comply with the Committee's request. Far too many in the Boston Bureau would be exposed to accusations of cover-ups and corruption if those memos were made public.

Although the frame-up in the Deegan case had occurred over thirty years earlier, there is no statute of limitations for suborning perjury in a capital murder case. The Committee's first order of business would be to focus on allegations that former Agents Rico and Condon, along with former Strike Force Head Ed Harrington, had aided hit man Barboza to escape a first degree murder charge in California in 1971. It was not good news for the three former law enforcement officials. They needed to stop the locomotive and its engineer, Dan Burton. They needed help from the top of the heap.

Investigators were prepared to show that Theodore Sharliss, who had set up Barboza for execution, was himself an informant. The Committee wanted to know if the FBI handlers were cognizant that Barboza had been slated for assassination, and that their own informant had orchestrated the murder plot. The Committee was seeking documents from the Boston Bureau in order to address a host of troubling events spanning decades.

The Committee was questioning why Whitey Bulger had not been prosecuted for the crimes he had committed prior to his 1995 indictment. The same question was asked apropos of Bulger's partner Stephen The Rifleman Flemmi. With regard to rogue Agent John Connolly, Bulger's childhood pal and overseer, the Committee wanted to know if the Justice Department had considered indicting him prior to his 1999 indictment, and had the Justice Department considered indicting John Morris, who had accepted cash and gifts from Bulger and Flemmi; and if not, why not? The Committee found evidence that Jimmy The Bear Flemmi had murdered a number of rival gangsters, including Teddy Deegan, yet he was never prosecuted. The Committee wanted answers as to why The Bear was granted a "pass" on the Deegan slaying, and why the FBI had allowed Joseph Joe the Horse Salvati to spend thirty years in prison for a murder that had been committed by their own informants.

The Committee also wanted answers as to why Cadillac Frank Salemme had been prosecuted for the 1968 bombing of Barboza's attorney, John Fitzgerald, yet alleged participant Steve Flemmi, had not. Burton's Committee also demanded to know why Rico, Condon, and Harrington had assisted Barboza in San Francisco, where he had killed Ricky Wilson while still in the Witness Protection Program, and why the FBI had gone along with his perjurious testimony, which had resulted in the conviction of four innocent men.

The Committee was interested in deliberations regarding decisions to prosecute Jerry Anguilo because there was a high likelihood that such deliberations would shed light on additional improper conduct by federal law enforcement officials.

In addition to former Agent Paul Rico's involvement in helping to orchestrate the testimony of Joseph Barboza in the Teddy Deegan murder trial, he was later found by a judge to have suborned perjury and to have himself committed perjury in a trial in Rhode Island. Had anyone provided advice that Rico should be prosecuted for perjury, or referred to state prosecutors to be prosecuted for perjury? When Rico had been brought out of retirement to assist in the government's investigation of then-Judge Alcee

Hastings, had his perjurious testimony been discussed or brought to the attention of Justice Department personnel?

Records regarding Robert Daddeico, who had allegedly changed his testimony a number of times against Salemme and Flemmi regarding the bombing of attorney John Fitzgerald, were also requested. Deliberative documents pertaining to the decisions regarding the proposed prosecution of Daddeico should shed light on why Flemmi had been permitted to escape prosecution for the bombing of Fitzgerald. They should also shed light on what prosecutors thought about how his stories had changed to benefit FBI informant Steve Flemmi.

What were prosecutors advising their superiors with regard to the extraordinary treatment of informant Steve Flemmi, and what were they thinking about the credibility of their cooperating witness, Robert Daddeico, who kept changing his testimony to enhance the case against Salemme and weaken the case against Flemmi? The witness against Salemme and Flemmi, who was now apparently under government protection, had even indicated at one point when he was being pressured by the government to provide additional testimony that "he might have some things to say, which the authorities would not want to hear." What were those things, and what advice had prosecutors given to their superiors about this witness? Chairman Dan Burton's Committee on Government Reform was about to open a Pandora's Box.

The Committee was after documents that would have revealed the greatest failures of federal law enforcement in the history of the United States. The conduct being investigated by the Committee had led to over one billion dollars in civil lawsuits against the government. The Justice Department had a huge problem. Dan Burton and the House Committee on Government Reform had to be stopped, but who was powerful enough to pull the plug?

—Chapter 26—
WHAT GOES AROUND, COMES AROUND

On September 3, 2001, James Whitey Bulger, the oldest fugitive on the FBI's Ten Most Wanted list, turned seventy-two. Unlike his partner in crime, Steve Flemmi, Whitey had been clever enough to heed the warning to flee Boston on the heels of the 1995 indictment against him. While Flemmi sat in his jail cell facing numerous charges of murder, extortion, and racketeering, Whitey and his girlfriend, Catherine Greig, continued to escape the grasp of the FBI Special Bulger Task Force.

Meanwhile, the FBI continued to deflect claims that the Bureau would prefer not to capture the fugitive gangster. Oklahoma authorities in Tulsa contended that the gangster with a distorted sexual craving and extremely bad breath might be found in nudist camps or gay bars. The glory days of Bulger, Flemmi, John Connolly, and the Boston FBI were now ancient history. The days when the G-Men and the gangsters ran the show had long passed. It was payback time for those who had been victimized by the unholy and corrupt alliance.

Francisco, the eighty-year-old brother of former gambling czar Jerry Anguilo, filed a motion to overturn his 1986 racketeering conviction. Francisco, also known as "Cat," had been released after serving nearly fifteen years at a federal medical facility in Fort Worth, Texas. Earlier, his brother Donato "Danny" Anguilo, had completed his prison sentence, while Jerry continued serving his forty-five-year sentence at the Fort Devens Medical Facility in Ayer, Massachusetts. "Cat" based his motion to overturn on grounds that the government had lied in its applications to bug 98 Prince Street, also known as "The Dog House," and had failed to inform attorneys that Bulger and Flemmi had been authorized to listen to the Prince Street tapes. "This honorable court should use its supervisory powers *Sua Sponte* to correct this grave miscarriage of justice on an innocent man," wrote Francisco Anguilo. If the motion filed by Francisco was granted, it could mean freedom for Jerry Anguilo as well. Francisco argued that, "Because of the FBI agents' and government misconduct established herein, I, Francisco Anguilo, was caused to be denied my right to due process of law and prejudiced by not having a fair and Constitutional trial."

The success that Connolly and others, along with all the king's horses and all the king's men, had achieved in the Anguilo case come tumbling down.

Aside from the numerous lawsuits underway attributed to corruption in the Boston Bureau, many law enforcement officials were being called upon to answer for their actions. The stunning revelations of corruption and lawless activity on the part of the FBI in protecting Bulger and Flemmi from investigations and prosecution brought forth dramatic and sweeping changes in the Justice Department's informant guidelines. The scandal in Boston could have long-lasting effects on the Bureau's reputation nationwide. The overzealous, scandalous, and corrupt actions by Irish agents teaming up with Irish gangsters to go after Italian mobsters had reaped its consequences. The end did not justify the means.

Cadillac Frank Salemme, the last of the stand-up guys, had witnessed the events unfolding within the New England Mafia with disgust. Although he had violated the code of Omerta by testifying before a grand jury about being tipped by John Connolly, he was still regarded with some degree of respect by most, but not all LCN members. Salemme was through with the Mafia. Gone were the men of honor; all that remained were betrayal and treachery. He began serving his eleven-year-four-month sentence at the federal prison in Otisville, New York.

However, Salemme was still suffering the effects of having been shot four times during the 1981 attempt on his life. Out of concern that bullet fragments might still be lodged in his body, Cadillac Frank was transferred to the federal medical facility in Lexington, Kentucky. The facility was originally built during the Depression Era as part of an economic recovery program, serving as a drug rehabilitation center. Rumor had it as the location where "One Flew Over the Cuckoo's Nest" was filmed.

The group of New York LCN members serving time at the institution, including a few high-level mob brass, respectfully welcomed Salemme. The mobsters were aware that Salemme had appeared before the Connolly grand jury; however, they also knew of his well-earned reputation. The mobsters had access to a variety of food stolen from the prison's main dining room. Cadillac Frank was always invited to the lavish Italian feasts prepared by the New York crew; yet, for the most part, he avoided socializing with them. Salemme was most respectful to the mobsters; however, he wanted nothing more to do with the Mafia. His job at the prison was seeing to the daily trash recycling, which required less than an hour's work each day. The former mob boss could then often be seen walking the track or sunning himself in the recreation yard. Although he disconnected himself from the mob element at the prison, Salemme did show compassion and respect to Louis Gatto, an eighty-six-year-old New Jersey mob chieftain suffering from cancer. Frank took it upon himself to personally attend to the sick man's daily laundry needs.

Salemme's test results showed no bullet fragments remained within his body and that he was in general good health. Yet, Cadillac Frank was still bothered by the treachery that had been inflicted upon him in Boston. In particular, he remained distressed with Steve Flemmi, and former Agents John Connolly and Paul Rico. Salemme was aware that Flemmi and Connolly were scheduled for trial and that Rico was in the cross-hairs of government prosecutors. Those who had lined up against Flemmi and Connolly were being rewarded for their willingness to testify. Salemme had already served a total of twenty-two years and counting, and he had four bullet hole scars reminding him of the treachery he had survived. He had made the same mistake as others in that he had trusted Steve Flemmi.

After some serious soul searching, Cadillac Frank was prepared to make his move. He was ready to testify against those who had betrayed him. Salemme was in no way seeking time off from the three years that remained on his current sentence. He wanted those who had escaped any conse-quences for their years of treachery and deceit brought to justice. He would cut a deal with federal prosecutors and agree to testify against Flemmi, Bulger, and the two former FBI agents who had handled them, John Connolly and Paul Rico. Prosecutors were extremely interested in infor-mation pertaining to Paul Rico, who had displayed his supreme arrogance towards the House Committee earlier.

October 31, 2001, was just another day at the federal medical center in Lexington, Kentucky, for Cadillac Frank. After completing his work of transporting a load of trash to the compactor, he decided to catch a few rays of sunshine at the recreation yard. Upon returning to his unit at two P.M., he was ordered to report to the lieutenant's office immediately. Salemme was refused permission to change from his recreational shorts to standard prison apparel. The U.S. Marshals who had been waiting at the lieutenant's office quickly placed Salemme in protective custody. A unit officer began packing up Salemme's personal property from Room 209. Curious inmates came by to witness the now unoccupied single-man room. Questions were being asked throughout the prison that Halloween night as to why Salemme had been packed out. He had been a model prisoner with no inci-dent reports. The following day, news that Room 209, a preferred single-man room, was up for grabs, circulated throughout the prison. Dozens of inmates began writing cop-outs requesting the immaculately-kept room.

After spending a few days in the hole, Cadillac Frank would be taken from the medical center at Lexington, Kentucky, to a waiting private jet. While being escorted in leg irons and wearing a bright orange prison jump suit, Frank opted to send his "good luck" message to a close friend who was positioned to witness the exit. That was the last time anyone would see Cadillac Frank. During the process of transferring Salemme to the waiting private government jet, the entire prison had been put on lock-down status. No movement was allowed until the subject being moved had left the institution safely. This precaution was only used in high-profile cases, or for those in the Witness Protection Program. It didn't take long for the LCN inmates at Lexington to conclude that Salemme had rolled. All but one viewed his decision to cooperate favorably. The eighty-six-year-old New Jersey mob chieftain, Louis Gatto, defended Salemme's action, saying, "He gave up an Irish FBI agent to free two Italians in Boston." The wise old mobster was referring to Salemme's role in the exoneration of Joseph Joe the Horse Salvati and Peter Limone.

On November 13, 2001, law enforcement authorities began digging in Hopkinton, Massachusetts, for the remains of Edward J. Wimpy Bennett and his brother, Walter. Hopkinton had for years been famous as the starting point of the world-renowned Boston Marathon. It was now a potential mob burial site. The information that led to the dig had come from Cadillac Frank. He had been relocated to the Boston area after agreeing to cooperate with authorities.

It was believed that Wimpy Bennett had not been giving Steve Flemmi his fair share of proceeds from the very profitable gambling and loan sharking rackets in which the two men were partnered. Talk that circulated throughout the Boston underworld painted a picture as to how Wimpy Bennett had been killed in 1967. The story went that Flemmi had lured Wimpy to a garage owned by Salemme, on the pretense of airing out their problems. However, Wimpy was greeted not with talk but instead, two shots through the head delivered by Steve Flemmi. An unsuspecting Salemme had reluctantly assisted his best friend in disposing of Wimpy's body. Three months later, Walter Bennett was also slain and reportedly buried next to Wimpy in the Hopkinton grave. Eight months following the second murder, William Bennett's body was discovered next to a snowbank in Dorchester, a suburb of Boston.

Although Cadillac Frank knew precisely where to lead authorities to dig, the first day ended without the recovery of any remains. The practice of reburying the remains of their victims was not an uncommon event for the gangsters. Six bodies had been exhumed in January of 2000, when Bulger's surrogate son, Kevin Weeks, had led authorities to the burial sites.

Although federal prosecutors had dismissed the Bennett brothers' murder charges against Flemmi and Cadillac Frank as part of a plea agreement, there was still the possibility of state charges against Flemmi. Salemme would receive a one-year reduction off the remaining three years of his sentence for his efforts in directing authorities to the burial site. But a second day of digging did not produce the much anticipated results.

After weeks of continuous digging proved fruitless, the hunt for the Bennett brothers' remains was called off. The changes in the landscape, currently a sportsmen's rifle shooting range, could have confused Salemme's sense of direction, but there was an assumption that Steve Flemmi had had the Bennett brothers' remains exhumed and buried in a new location without Salemme's knowledge. Salemme agreed to provide testimony against Bulger, Flemmi, and former Agent John Connolly. He was also to supply federal investigators with information on former Agent Paul Rico.

If events were not progressing badly enough for Steve Flemmi, he would have another piece of bad news that would keep him up at night. His son, William St. Croix, had not only agreed to testify against his father and uncle, Michael, he had also helped himself to a hidden horde of cash belonging to the gangster. St. Croix and his brother, Stephen Hussey, had gotten real lucky during a search of their grandmother's South Boston home. The brothers had located over $500,000 from a hideaway in the home. Steve Flemmi's two sons had a ball with the blood money, spending the entire treasure in less than one year.

The problems stemming from the Boston FBI's past alliance with Bulger and Flemmi continued to escalate. Lawsuits filed against the Boston Bureau for time-gone-by sins were at epidemic proportions, reaching nearly two billion dollars in damages. Stephen Rakes, who had been forced at gunpoint to sell his liquor store to Bulger and Flemmi when the Boston FBI had failed to respond to his and his wife's pleas for help, was only one of many lining up to file a federal lawsuit. In his civil suit, Stephen Rakes was seeking damages in excess of $100 million. Previously, the family of World Jai Alai owner Roger Wheeler, who had been murdered on orders allegedly from Bulger and Flemmi, had filed suit for nearly a billion dollars.

The family of John McIntyre was seeking $50 million in damages from the government. McIntyre had been slain after information surfaced that he had been cooperating with authorities.

The government faced scores of other lawsuits from those victimized by the partnership between the G-Men and the gangsters. They were now in a "Catch 22" situation. The evidence being produced to show corruption and cover-ups in order to gain convictions against those accused, would simultaneously further the cause of civil lawsuits.

Chapter 27

LIGHTS, CAMERA, ARROGANCE

Amidst all the controversy surrounding John Connolly, the arrogant former agent still didn't get it. Facing a nine-count indictment alleging numerous charges of racketeering, obstruction of justice, and leaking confidential information to Bulger and Flemmi; and provoking the killings of Richard Castucci, Brian Halloran, and John Callahan, Connolly continued promoting his image. The bold and conceited Connolly tried to pitch his life story to a Hollywood producer.

Earlier, retired undercover agent Joe Pistone had penned a book, *My Undercover Life in the Mafia*. The book had made the best-seller list, and later was made into a movie. However, Pistone had done it the right way. He was an agent who had followed the rules. Connolly used his association with Jimmy Flynn, a Winter Hill Gang member, to help pitch his life story to Hollywood. Flynn, a transportation coordinator and union official in the movie industry, had contacts in Hollywood who could be helpful in securing a movie deal for Connolly. Flynn had been acquitted of the 1982 slaying of Brian Halloran, who had been killed after information surfaced that he had been spilling the beans on Bulger and his gang.

Connolly had been a star in the Boston Bureau, possessing the talent to convince gangsters to rat on selected targets. However, that was then, during the glory days. Now, the party was over, yet he didn't get it. Connolly's circus act continued, appearing on radio talk shows and giving television interviews promoting his big lie. Connolly believed that by voicing his innocence loudly enough and often enough, it would be accepted as truth. However, he failed to acknowledge the mountains of evidence facing him and the incriminating accounts from a number of witnesses lining up to testify against him. Connolly's arrogance was getting the best of him.

Although Connolly had taken precautions to avoid exposing his close ties with gangster Whitey Bulger, he openly had embraced his brother Billy. In fact, Connolly's close and personal association with the Senate President had allegedly been a key factor in recruiting Whitey to become an informant. Connolly might have used his relationship with Billy Bulger to silence, and for the most part, control those who were critical of his way of doing things in the Boston FBI. Not only had the super-star Connolly allegedly warned Whitey of other informants and investigations targeting the gangster, he had also kept an eye out for Brother Billy at the same time. When Billy Bulger became a center of controversy with regard to his role in a scandal of the planned development of a skyscraper at 75 State Street in downtown Boston, the Feds came to the rescue.

In came John Morris, who was the supervisor of a division responsible for investigating public corruption, the same John Morris who had attended dinner parties with Connolly, Bulger, and Flemmi. The same Morris who had received cash and gifts from Bulger and Flemmi, now had the duty of investigating the bribery charges surrounding Billy. It was no wonder that the obligated Morris had promptly pulled the plug on the 75 State Street inquiry.

In early November of 2001, the Justice Department tried to quash a $50 million lawsuit filed against the FBI by the family of John McIntyre. McIntyre was slain in 1984 after word had surfaced of his cooperation with authorities, revealing Bulger's involvement with drug trafficking and gun running. This action by the Justice Department infuriated some Massachusetts Congressmen. Representatives Barney Frank, William Delahunt, and Martin Meehan issued a letter to United States Attorney General John Ashcroft calling the government's position an insult.

"The FBI and Justice Department should acknowledge mistakes were made, accept the consequences, and reconsider their litigation stance," said Representative Martin Meehan.

The victim's family attorney had uncovered shocking evidence in the McIntyre slaying that would reveal the FBI agents had provoked the murder. The Justice Department needed to bury the crimes committed by the corrupt G-Men in Boston.

For decades, the FBI in Boston had been marinated in bribery, corruption, and widespread cover-ups. Attorney General John Ashcroft was under enormous pressure to release Justice Department documents related to Whitey Bulger and Joe The Animal Barboza's dealings with agents in the Boston Bureau. Releasing the FBI files would open a can of worms, further revealing their dark past. Attorneys for Joseph Salvati and Peter Limone, who had been framed for the murder of Teddy Deegan, were seeking FBI documents uncovered by the Justice Department Task Force. The Special Task Force, led by prosecutor John Durham, had uncovered secret hidden memos that showed their own witness, Barboza, and the brother of Steve Flemmi had actually killed Deegan, yet they had encouraged perjured testimony convicting Salvati, Limone, Greco, and Henry Tamelo of the murder.

As a result of actions by crooked G-Men and their gangsters, the government was facing nearly one billion dollars in civil lawsuits filed by the victims' families. There were also concerns that internal documents would further reveal how the FBI had allowed serial killers to operate freely for over three decades. The stench of corruption coming out of Boston had reached all the way to the White House, prompting President Bush to take action.

On December 13, 2001, Bush invoked executive privilege, barring Congress from access to internal Justice Department records connected to Whitey Bulger and Joseph Barboza. Some of the crimes and corruption in the Boston Bureau had been previously exposed. However, Bush's decision to invoke executive privilege would put the lid on revealing more embarrassing conduct by the FBI.

In defending his action, Bush issued a memo to the Attorney General, saying, "Congress' access to the documents would be contrary to the national interest." His decision could rid the government of any responsibility.

However, House Government Reform Committee Chairman Dan Burton was quick to respond, saying, "This is not a monarchy." Later, at a hearing with Justice Department lawyers, a frustrated Burton said, "Everyone is in agreement: You guys are making a big mistake. We might be able to go to the floor and take this thing to court."

It was obvious the President was preoccupied with fighting the war on terrorism. It was the wrong time to be bashing the same FBI charged with protecting U.S. citizens from terrorist attacks. Bush and John Ashcroft wanted to shield the FBI from further embarrassment, which might have a negative effect on the nation as a whole, at a critical time in our history. At least that was the story. Yet innocent men had spent thirty-three years behind bars, and two had died in prison.

Burton and his committee were on the brink of unraveling the events surrounding the framing of Salvati and Limone in the Deegan slaying. However, Bush was set on preventing any further investigation of the evils committed by the corrupt G-Men in Boston. That was bad enough. Yet, there were more crimes committed by the FBI's gangsters that cried out for complete exposure.

While calling attention to the many charges of murder, extortion, and drug dealing attributed to Bulger and Flemmi, Chairman Burton said, "All this while being protected by FBI agents and Justice Department prosecutors, and this is the type of activity that the Administration is trying to cover up? I don't get it. It isn't right."

Justice Department officials took exception, claiming they had fully cooperated with the Task Force led by Special Prosecutor John Durham. Joseph Salvati's attorney, Victor Garo, was not satisfied. "Once again we have the government looking like they don't want to have the evidence come out to show what really happened in the Deegan murder case." There were accusations that Bush and Ashcroft were committed to burying the story, due in part to the one billion dollars in civil lawsuits pending. Attorney William Koski had filed a $375 million civil lawsuit against the

FBI on behalf of Limone and the two men who had died in prison, Louis Greco and Henry Tamelo.

"Everything was kept in the dark for thirty-five years, and finally, when things should really be looked at so the house can be cleaned, an entirely new Administration turns the lights out again," Koski said.

In spite of having been placed on the FBI's Ten Most Wanted List in 1999, there was still no hint of Whitey Bulger's whereabouts. FBI officials continued deflecting criticism to the effect they really didn't want to capture the fugitive gangster. Once again, rumors were circulating that if the now-seventy-two-year-old Bulger was captured, and then decided to talk, he could cause an even bigger problem for the Boston Bureau.

Although Bulger's image had been shown on "America's Most Wanted," along with massive publicity, not one lead on the ruthless killer had developed. Law enforcement authorities believed that Whitey was still alive and traveling with his fifty-year-old longtime girlfriend, Catherine Greig. Bulger was known to be an avid reader with an interest in history. The fugitive gangster, with a reward for information leading to his capture at $1,000,000, had been known to frequent libraries and historical sites. Bulger was also suspected of maintaining his physical fitness by working out at health clubs and walking along beaches with Greig.

The House Government Reform Committee, although frustrated by the invocation of executive privilege, continued its probe. One witness the Committee was anxious to question was former Massachusetts U.S. Attorney Edward Harrington. Now a federal judge, Harrington was suspected of helping Joseph Barboza beat a first degree murder charge in San Francisco. The Committee wanted to know why he, along with Agents Paul Rico and Dennis Condon, had journeyed to California to testify on behalf of Barboza, who had committed a murder while in the Witness Protection Program.

During the preceding year, Dan Burton and his Committee had been looking into the cozy relationship between the G-Men and the gangsters. The Committee had uncovered startling evidence indicating that the

Barboza case was not the only incident of corruption and cover-ups. Harrington, a former federal prosecutor and a protégé of Robert Kennedy, had embraced the government's war on the Italian Mafia. He and former Agents Condon and Rico had been subpoenaed to testify before the Committee on February 7, 2002.

In January, during an interview on the CBS news magazine 60 *Minutes*, Chairman Dan Burton told Mike Wallace that he would press on with his campaign, despite being denied access to FBI documents by an executive order imposed by President Bush. Burton was still fuming over the framing of Joseph Salvati, in order to protect the murderers, who were FBI informants.

"I always thought J. Edgar Hoover walked on water when I was a kid," Burton told Wallace. "But when I found out Mr. Salvati had been put in prison for a crime he didn't commit and they knew it, the FBI, for thirty-two years, and there was no remorse because of it, I said, 'Something has to be done.' That's what the evidence shows; Hoover was kept informed of Salvati's case on an almost daily basis," Burton said. "It's a shocking thing."

Burton continued to subpoena additional FBI documents, yet Attorney General John Ashcroft continued refusing to supply them.

"J. Edgar Hoover knew Mr. Salvati was innocent; that was a miscarriage of justice," said Burton. "He knew it and his name should not be emblazoned on the FBI headquarters. We ought to change the name of that building." Burton's Committee began investigating the murder of Tulsa millionaire Roger Wheeler; however, the Justice Department once again refused to turn over subpoenaed documents. The Committee was seeking information on whether FBI agents had frustrated efforts to investigate Wheeler's murder and others committed by their informants. Although first degree murder charges had been filed against Bulger and Flemmi, former Agent Paul Rico had not been charged.

During two days of hearings, the House Committee Chairman, Dan Burton, became enraged when informed by Edward Harrington that he had overlooked evidence that could have cleared Joe Salvati of the Deegan murder conviction decades previously. The Committee spent a good part of the day questioning Harrington for his role in helping hit man Barboza avoid punishment for a murder he had committed while in the Witness Protection Program, and aiding him to secure an early parole. "How many times did you go to defend these crudballs?" Burton asked.

Harrington shifted the blame for Salvati's conviction onto the defense attorneys. "You have to remember this was in the early days of a national governmental effort to root out a national scourge," said Harrington. Still in denial, Harrington defended Barboza's testimony as fact. "I am not prepared to say Barboza lied in that case," said Harrington.

The previous day, former FBI Agent Paul Rico had invoked his Fifth Amendment right against self-incrimination and refused to answer questions relating to that time period. At the conclusion of Rico's charade, a disturbed Representative Bob Barr had remarked to the crooked ex-agent, "I hope you sleep well at night."

After the hearings, Chairman Dan Burton said his staff was preparing a contempt citation against President Bush for ordering the Justice Department not to turn over internal FBI documents to the Committee.

–*Chapter 28*–
MY BROTHER'S KEEPER

United States District Judge Joseph Tauro announced May 6, 2002, as the date set for former FBI Agent John Connolly to stand trial on racketeering charges. Connolly's attorney, Tracy Miner, requested additional time; however, the judge refused her plea. The sixty-one-year-old Connolly had been indicted in 1999 and had been free since his arrest, posting a $200,000 unsecured bond. Connolly's crowning achievement had been the destruction of the Anguilo gambling organization in Boston. His successful war on the Italian Mafia was due in part to his alliance with Steve Flemmi and Whitey Bulger. However, that same relationship could now lead to his downfall. For many who had been victimized by Connolly's treachery, the day of reckoning was at hand.

On March 8, 2002, Gennaro Jerry Anguilo filed a petition asking a federal judge to take another look at his 1986 conviction. The conviction had resulted in a forty-five-year prison sentence for the eighty-two-year-old Anguilo. This was his second attempt to convince the judge to reopen his case. The first had been sent back to Anguilo and included a hint of optimism. U.S. District Court Judge William Young had encouraged him to file again using different legal issues. Jerry's new argument was that the 98 Prince Street wiretap would not have been granted had the issuing judge known of the FBI's alliance with the murderous gangsters, Whitey Bulger and Steve Flemmi. Anguilo also wrote that had his legal team known of the skullduggery of the FBI, the defense attorneys would have taken a more informed approach at trial, which would have resulted in an acquittal.

When news of Kevin Weeks' cooperation with authorities had surfaced, it allegedly had prompted the jailed gangster, Steve Flemmi, to recruit his younger brother, Michael, and son, William St. Croix, to move a cache of weapons from his mother's home in South Boston to a new location. According to prosecutors, the sixty-four-year-old retired Boston cop, Michael Flemmi, feared that Kevin Weeks would reveal to law enforcement the secret hiding place containing a variety of guns. On January 11, 2000, St. Croix, along with his uncle, Michael Flemmi, removed a multitude of guns and silencers from the East Third Street home in South Boston. A few days later, authorities armed with a warrant began searching the home, hoping to find the gangster's arsenal. They left empty-handed. The weapons had been transferred by St. Croix and Michael Flemmi to a new location.

However, Steve Flemmi's son had agreed to assist in moving the hidden weapons before he'd learned that his father was allegedly one of those responsible for the murder of his half-sister, Deborah Hussey, in 1984. Bulger gang member Kevin Weeks had led investigators to Hussey's buried remains in January of 2000, cutting his own deal with the government. Intent on seeking revenge, St. Croix agreed to become a cooperating witness and testify against his uncle, Michael Flemmi, while leading investigators to the relocated weapons stash.

Earlier, William St. Croix had been a key government witness against Boston real estate broker Michael Carucci. Carucci had been charged and convicted of investing Steve Flemmi's blood money. Not only had St. Croix been given immunity for his testimony, he had also been guaranteed a 25 percent cut of any additional funds forfeited.

It was obvious Steve Flemmi had reaped what he had sown. It was no surprise that his son would double-cross him; it was in the genes, a hereditary characteristic. Flemmi had for decades betrayed those close to him; now the tables were turned, not only by his criminal associates, but by his own flesh and blood.

On April 17, 2002, federal prosecutors were ready to try their case against Michael Flemmi. Inside the courtroom of Judge Richard Stearns, federal prosecutors displayed the cache of weapons before the jury. The ordinance contained scores of submachine guns, pistols, sawed-off shotguns, and enough ammunition to support a protracted war.

In his opening statement, Michael Flemmi's attorney, John LaChance, told the jury that the case against his client was based upon revenge by a slick scam artist, William St. Croix. The attorney conveyed to the jury that St. Croix had received immunity from the government, along with a large cash reward and moving expenses, for his testimony. LaChance said that St. Croix had fabricated the story against his uncle as a way of getting back at his father, Steve Flemmi.

William St. Croix had his own checkered past. He didn't wear any halo, a fact of which government prosecutors were well aware. In order to "steal the thunder" from the defense, prosecutors decided they themselves would expose St. Croix's criminal background. Under oath, he admitted to crimes of extorting drug dealers, arson, and gambling. St. Croix acknowledged he had used his father's reputation to scam drug dealers. "I used the Flemmi name," he admitted. He also told the jury he and his father had at one point become very close, prompting him to write a compassionate letter to a federal magistrate asking bail be granted for the jailed gangster. When asked by Assistant United States Attorney Fred Wyshak if he would write the same letter on behalf of his father today, St. Croix replied, "No, I would not."

St. Croix told the court that his father had confessed to killing his half-sister; the admission had been made during a visit between the two men at the Plymouth County Jail where Flemmi was incarcerated. "Yes, I did it, but I can explain," St. Croix claimed his father had told him shortly after his sister's remains had been unearthed, and the admission had made the younger man "angry as hell."

"I could not believe it. I was so mad. I was devastated," said St. Croix. He told the court that his uncle, Michael Flemmi, had also been present in the visiting room and delivered an emotional but disturbing account of the Hussey murder. "You know she was having sexual relations with black men and she was drug dealing," St. Croix claimed Michael Flemmi had said.

St. Croix angrily responded, "Mickey, your daughter was a stripper and had a drug problem, does that mean she should be dead, too?"

Attorney LaChance said that the notion that Steve Flemmi would confess a murder to a son with whom he had an on-again-off-again relationship was ridiculous.

During cross-examination, the forty-four-year-old St. Croix conveyed his feelings of disbelief when information surfaced to indicate his father was an informant. However, his father attempted to portray those reports as a ploy concocted by him to prop up his own defense.

"So he lied to you?" Michael Flemmi's attorney asked.

"He's been lying to me my whole life," St. Croix responded.

According to St. Croix, it was the deceit, the murders, and the sexual abuse of his sister at the hands of Steve Flemmi that had caused him to come forward and testify against his uncle. After sitting through four days of intense cross-examination, at one point being labeled a "supreme con man," St. Croix spoke with reporters in reference to his gangster father.

"I want to put an end to it, he's menaced everyone he's been in contact with," said St. Croix. He had come across smoothly and convincingly during his testimony. However, he did confess openly in court that he possessed his father's talent to con and manipulate others. His gangster father had lulled many of his intended victims with his gentle and calm demeanor. He also spoke with sympathy for his father's victims. "When I think about what he did to Frank Salemme, I feel so bad for Frank's kids. When I learned my father had put their father in prison, I was devastated," St. Croix said. He then added, "My heart goes out to Debra Davis' family." His father was suspected of killing the young woman in 1981. "I met Debra Davis. She was very nice. She was beautiful."

St. Croix also held his father responsible for the death of Stephane Hussey, his other sister, who had succumbed to drugs while being sexually abused by the much-older Flemmi. "She died on my birthday," St. Croix said. He related how his mother, Marion Hussey, and Debra Davis' mother,

Olga, suffered the same grief. "They both lost daughters to my father," St. Croix said.

In closing, government prosecutors told the jury that William St. Croix was not facing charges as a result of his agreement to testify against Michael Flemmi. The jury was also told that the former Boston police officer, Michael Flemmi, had crossed over the line and become a courier for his gangster brother. "It's not as if he's an accountant in Iowa helping his brother on the East Coast. He's a Boston cop working in the city where his brother is a notorious gangster." St. Croix also gave investigators information on his father's FBI handler, John Connolly.

Next to come forward and give testimony against Michael Flemmi was former Bulger lieutenant Kevin Weeks. Earlier, Weeks had cut a deal and led authorities to the burial site of the gang's victims. Weeks was prepared to tell the jury that he had stored the cache of weapons at the East Third Street home in South Boston. Weeks' claim would support St. Croix's earlier account that he and his uncle had transferred the weapons to a new location.

Yet, the case against the former Boston cop was weak. Other than the testimony of St. Croix, there was no evidence linking Michael Flemmi to the hidden guns and silencers. However, the jury was allowed to hear Kevin Weeks describe in chilling detail accounts of murders allegedly committed by Bulger and Flemmi.

Concerned that former Agent Connolly would face the same troubling issues at trial, his attorney would begin making preparations to question potential jurors. The defense attorney wanted to know whether the accounts of murder and mayhem committed by the gangsters would influence them against Connolly.

On May 3, 2002, Michael Flemmi was found guilty of hiding a cache of weapons for his jailed gangster brother, Steve Flemmi. A jury of nine men and three women took three days to convict Michael Flemmi on five counts, including obstruction of justice, possession of machine guns, silencers, and sawed-off shotguns. Flemmi was allowed to remain free on bail until his July 15 sentencing date. The guilty verdict was not good news for John Connolly.

Although Michael Flemmi had not been regarded a member of the Bulger gang, the verdict sent a powerful message to those who had fellowship with the gangsters. All the collateral details presented during the trial had no doubt played a pivotal role in influencing the jury's verdict.

On September 9, 2002, Michael Flemmi was sentenced to ten years in prison for moving an arsenal of weapons for his gangster brother, Steve.

Chapter 29

UNITED STATES vs. JOHN CONNOLLY

On May 6, 2002, the no-longer-cocky John Connolly would face off with government prosecutors to answer multiple racketeering charges. His defense would be simple and direct: He had been following orders. "I'm looking forward to clearing my name," Connolly said outside the courthouse.

Connolly's argument was that he had needed to enlist gangsters like Whitey Bulger and Steve Flemmi in order to bring down the Italian Mafia. "This was not John Connolly's policy. This was the policy of the entire FBI," Connolly said. "These people were guaranteed that they could run a loan sharking and gambling operation. We knew they were arch-criminals; however, neither I nor the FBI knew how deeply involved in crime they were," claimed Connolly. The sixty-one-year-old man, who had achieved a stellar career, called for "fairness."

However, the glory days were long gone for the once-celebrated agent. Now the methods used to achieve those past successes could send the ex-G-Man to prison for up to twenty years. The case before United States District Court Judge Joseph L. Tauro included the most serious charges that Connolly had supplied information to Bulger, resulting in the slaying of three men.

The three men killed were Richard Castucci, Brian Halloran, and John Callahan. Castucci and Halloran were murdered after word had leaked out regarding their cooperation with the FBI. According to hit man John Martorano, he had murdered Callahan on orders from Bulger and Flemmi. The slaying was prompted by fears that Callahan was talking about the murder of World Jai Alai owner Roger Wheeler. Connolly said he didn't know just how cruel and pitiless his star informants Bulger and Flemmi were. He claimed to be shocked by revelations concerning Bulger and Flemmi's brutality. He was referring to the strangulation killings of Deborah Hussey and Debra Davis, two of Flemmi's young girlfriends.

Opening arguments began on May 7, 2002, as prosecutors told a jury of seven men and five women that Connolly was so tight with his murderous informants, they'd nicknamed him "Zip," a word used by wise guys to describe an individual who refuses to pay for anything—zero. The government claimed that Connolly had received a two-carat diamond, appliances, a power boat, and a townhouse without coughing up a single penny.

The "who's who" in the Boston underworld would take a stand against the former agent. However, those government witnesses would also shed light on some of the deep secrets detailing what had occurred between the FBI and their informant gangsters. The government's key witnesses included Cadillac Frank Salemme; John Martorano, who had confessed to killing twenty people; Bulger's surrogate son, Kevin Weeks; and Connolly's former supervisor, John Morris.

The once arrogant and cocksure former agent seemed worried and uneasy. Judge Joseph Tauro would agree to Connolly's unprecedented request to sit with his wife and three sons among the courtroom spectators rather than in the customary seat at the defense table. Connolly still didn't get it. Thinking that the appearance of a loving family man would gain points with the jury was an obvious and desperate move.

Prosecutors opened the case by telling jurors that Connolly had given Bulger and Flemmi the authorization to do anything they wanted. During a dinner party, Connolly's supervisor, John Morris, had told Bulger and Flemmi, "You can do anything you want as long as you don't clip anyone." However, prosecutors told the jurors that Connolly had fingered two informants for Bulger and Flemmi as well as a witness who could pose a problem for them.

Oklahoma millionaire Roger Wheeler had been slain by former hit man John Martorano on orders from Bulger and Flemmi. Prosecutors claimed that Brian Halloran and a friend, Michael Donahue, had been murdered by Bulger and an associate after Halloran had been refused entry into the government Witness Protection Program. John Callahan had been killed by Martorano as a precaution, the fear being he could be a witness to the three previous murders. Prosecutors alleged that Connolly's tips to Bulger and Flemmi had resulted in the murders of Halloran and Callahan.

Prosecutors also informed the jurors that hit man Martorano would testify that he had murdered Richard Castucci at the behest of Bulger and Flemmi. The government alleged that Connolly had told Bulger that Castucci was working with the FBI. Jurors were also informed to expect to hear from Kevin Weeks. According to prosecutors, Weeks had admitted to being the lookout for Bulger while Whitey and his associate slaughtered Halloran and Donahue, and afterward had retrieved the weapons used. The government attorneys also planned to call Connolly's former supervisor, John Morris, who would testify that he had told Connolly of Brian Halloran's cooperation with the FBI, and that the information had prompted Connolly to warn Bulger of the danger Halloran posed to him.

Prosecutors continued their opening arguments by telling jurors that these witnesses had to be truthful, or they would face more prison time for lying.

Special Prosecutor John Durham told the jury that Connolly had purchased a $40,000 boat without the benefit of his paychecks, which were kept in his desk drawer, uncashed. He added that Connolly's uncontrollable spending had caused an angry Bulger to issue a warning that it would "cause too much heat."

"Do you think that's normal, for a public servant to go without pay for ten paychecks?" Durham asked. He then reported that Connolly's former secretary would testify she'd stumbled across a pile of uncashed paychecks in his desk. Durham pointed out that there was no way to explain how a low-level agent had bought a $40,000 speed boat and a $5,000 diamond ring for his wife without even cashing his paychecks.

Prosecutors would call attention to a meeting between Connolly and Salemme, in which he'd told Cadillac Frank about a grand jury investigation concerning him and Steve Flemmi. It was at this meeting that Connolly told Salemme he would warn him and Flemmi of any indictment against them stemming from the grand jury probe. The government attorney said they would present phone records showing Connolly had made a call to the FBI from his office the same day he had been warned of the indictments and advised the gangsters to skip town.

The government planned to show Connolly had sent a letter to Judge Mark Wolf that was purportedly from three police officers. The letter claimed another officer had fabricated evidence against Bulger and Flemmi, intending to throw the investigation in another direction. The government prosecutor claimed Boston police stationery was found in Connolly's office, and planned to call an expert on writing patterns. The federal prosecutor informed jurors that a key Bulger gang member would testify that he had personally given envelopes to Connolly stuffed with $5,000 for himself and $1,000 for another agent. "Bribes were paid, justice was obstructed, extortion was committed," said John Durham.

Connolly attorney Tracy Miner opened by telling the jurors that her client was following orders when he'd formed an alliance with Bulger and Flemmi, that Connolly was unaware of their murderous activities. "He was at the bottom," she said. "He took orders. He didn't give them." Attorney Miner told the jurors that Connolly had recruited the informants to assist in destroying the Mafia in Boston. "Everything Mr. Connolly did as the handler of Bulger and Flemmi was above board and done to accomplish the Bureau's number one goal, to take down the Italian Mafia in Boston. Mr. Connolly did not choose to associate with these people. He was told to associate with them to get information and that's what he did," said Miner.

The attorney described the sixty-one-year-old G-Man as a gifted agent under orders to infiltrate and recruit sources to help bring down the Boston mob. Miner continually told jurors that Connolly's task had been given the blessings of supervisors who approved the use of the gangsters to "get" the mob. "That was the FBI's decision, not Mr. Connolly's. Mr. Connolly had no authority to decide who the FBI would go after," she said.

Attorney Miner went on to add, "Mr. Connolly had a talent for developing informants. The FBI took full advantage of that strength. And it was their choice to use him for the purpose." In referencing allegations of her client's acceptance of bribes, Miner said that Bulger had fabricated a story about paying off Connolly to mask the fact that he and Flemmi were informants. Attorney Miner denied the government's assertions that Connolly had leaked information to Bulger, resulting in the murders of Brian Halloran and two other men. "The evidence will show Mr. Connolly did not participate in the murders, did not plan the murders, did not know in advance about the murders, and did not give information to Bulger," said Miner.

The attorney questioned the government's claim that Connolly had received a bribe from the gangsters in the form of a diamond ring. Miner told the jurors that her client had legally purchased a diamond, but not from the gangsters. She defended Connolly's socializing and accepting other gifts from his prize informants, however. "It was not bribery. It was the exchange of gifts to get their confidence," said Miner. In defending Connolly's actions, she told the jurors that other agents had been present and had accepted gifts as well.

Attorney Tracy Miner was attempting to put a positive spin on a desperate predicament. She would be facing an uphill battle in trying to discredit the government's key witnesses. Cadillac Frank Salemme was one witness who posed a problem for the defense. Connolly had extended an invitation to Salemme to meet with him at his office at the Prudential Center in Boston. Salemme would testify that Connolly had warned him and Flemmi to flee the 1995 indictment against them. Corroborating Salemme's testimony would be several key witnesses.

Early on, Connolly had arrested Salemme while a fugitive for his part in a car bombing decades earlier. Miner's argument would be that Connolly would never have given Salemme sensitive information. "Now think about that. He'll give information to the man he put in jail for sixteen years, and is head of La Cosa Nostra?" she asked the jurors.

On May 9, 2002, the government opened its case against John Connolly by calling their first witness, John Morris, Connolly's former supervisor. He cried on the witness stand as he admitted how he had dishonored and disgraced himself. Morris conveyed to the jury how Connolly had introduced him to Bulger and Flemmi over dinner at Connolly's home. He then confessed to having been personally corrupted by receiving cash and gifts from the South Boston gangsters.

Morris told of then being obligated to the gangsters, having accepted their bribes, and in turn, leaking information to Connolly of Brian Halloran's cooperation with the FBI. The tip had led to Halloran's murder. Morris admitted accepting the money and gifts had been a mistake, but added, "I didn't want to rock the boat. I didn't want to get on the wrong side of them. I didn't want to alert them to the fact that I placed myself in a compromising position." He acknowledged telling *The Boston Globe* that Bulger was an FBI informant, hoping those published reports would cause the Bureau to cut its ties with Bulger. Morris also told of a phone call he had received from Bulger, who'd threatened to reveal the bribes, and asserted that he had a witness who would back him up. Bulger was insistent that Morris phone the newspaper and persuade them to retract their story. Morris told Special Assistant U.S. Attorney Leonard Boyle, "In the past, I've lied to stay out of trouble, but since the immunity order, the only way I can stay out of trouble is to tell the truth."

During cross-examination, defense attorney Tracy Miner took issue with Morris, who claimed to have found religion. Miner suggested he'd found God after being granted immunity, and having agreed to testify for the government. "You got religion after the Wolf hearings," Miner said mockingly.

"I got religion in 1995, right after Bulger called me," said Morris. "I got serious religion. I prayed every night." Morris' former secretary, and new wife, told the jury that she had received $1,000 from Connolly for a plane ticket so she could join Morris in Georgia. In all, Morris testified he had accepted a total of $7,000 from the gangsters.

Federal prosecutors claimed Connolly had written false internal Bureau reports designed to protect Bulger and Flemmi, and to steer investigators away from his prized informants. The reports had allegedly been filed by Connolly to cover up murders committed by Bulger and Flemmi.

Fearing for Halloran's safety, Morris said he had recommended Halloran for the Witness Protection Program. However, his plea had fallen on deaf ears.

Next to take the witness stand was the sixty-one-year-old former hit man, John Martorano. It was the most frightening day of testimony thus far. Martorano calmly and professionally revealed to a stunned, packed courtroom how he had killed twenty people. According to Martorano, Bulger had told the gangsters that they had a friend in John Connolly. He said that Bulger had told him that Connolly was obligated to his brother for helping him go straight. "Connolly owed Billy [Bulger] a favor," said Martorano. "He went to Billy and said, 'What can I do to help you in return?'" The former Senate President had responded, "Just keep my brother out of trouble," recalled Martorano.

The confessed hit man unemotionally detailed killing rival gangsters and potential witnesses, some on orders from Bulger and Flemmi. Martorano fingered Connolly as the leak which led to three of those killings. As a result of the information allegedly supplied by Connolly, he, Bulger, Flemmi, and other Winter Hill Gang members had killed Richard Castucci in 1976, said Martorano. Martorano also implicated Connolly in the schemes to murder Brian Halloran and John Callahan. During questioning, Martorano put into place why Halloran had been killed. According to Martorano, he had been called to a meeting with Bulger and Flemmi in the early part of 1982. "At this meeting, Bulger was doing most of the talking," said Martorano to prosecutor John Durham, "and he told me that his friend Zip informed him that Halloran went up and made a statement to the FBI."

Also discussed at the meeting was what to do about John Callahan. Callahan had been involved in the plot to murder World Jai Alai president Roger Wheeler in 1981. Martorano had confessed to the murder he'd committed on orders from Bulger and Flemmi. The Beantown hit man claimed that Bulger and Flemmi told him they had talked with Connolly about the Callahan problem.

"They were trying to convince me that their friend John [Connolly] said that we're all going to go to jail for the rest of our life if something doesn't happen to John Callahan because the FBI is going to put so much pressure on him," said Martorano. Bulger and Flemmi urged Martorano to kill Callahan because he posed a threat to the gang. Martorano admitted in open court that he and Joseph MacDonald had killed Callahan in 1982. He also testified that the Winter Hill gangster had secured a stolen two-carat diamond ring for Bulger to pass on to Connolly as a gift for Connolly's wife.

Martorano also testified that former Agent Paul Rico had been involved in the plot to kill Roger Wheeler, and had provided information on Wheeler's habits.

During cross-examination, the cool and calm Martorano easily matched wits with defense attorney Tracy Miner. She had never come across the likes of an individual who had literally become accustomed to being under the gun. The defense attorney began grilling Martorano about the deal he had cut with the government in which he had confessed to twenty murders in exchange for his singing like a canary. Miner reminded Martorano he would have been facing decades of prison time had he not agreed to the government deal of a twelve- to-fifteen-year sentence.

"I want them to recommend three if they could," Martorano shot back. When Miner pointed out that his plea agreement had allowed him to escape the death penalty in Oklahoma and Florida, Martorano calmly stated, "When I shot those people, I wasn't aware. It didn't matter." When attorney Miner suggested he was often involved with hookers, an irritated Martorano replied, "I might give them money, but not for sex."

The ever-loyal gangster had been extremely upset when he'd learned that his longtime friends had been FBI informants for thirty years. "They were talking about friends of theirs," Martorano said, "not just the Mafia."

John could accept, to some degree, ratting on the LCN. After all, they were rivals for control of the rackets. "He informed on me," Martorano told defense attorney Miner.

The attorney shot back, asking, "You were furious?"

"Disgusted, furious, upset," replied Martorano. In particular, he was angry with Flemmi for telling Connolly and the FBI of his Florida location while he was a fugitive.

"You told another inmate you wanted to kill him," said attorney Miner.

"Sure," said Martorano.

"But you couldn't have killed him?"

"Oh," he said confidently, "I could have."

"There were guards around."

"I could have done it," said the hit man assuredly.

"There were no guns," said a skeptical Miner.

"That didn't matter," replied Martorano.

Attorney Miner kept grilling the hit man, asking how many murders Flemmi had been responsible for.

"You'll have to go down the list of names," responded Martorano.

"Robert Palladino?"

"Stevie told me he was informing on my brother. Or someone else," he replied. Palladino had been set to testify against his brother, Jimmy, in an earlier murder.

"John Jackson?"

"He told me, same situation."

Then attorney Miner asked about an individual named Herbert Smith.

"He gave Steve Flemmi a beating," said Martorano.

However, two teenagers who happened to be in the car with Jackson at the time had been slain as well.

"They were people I thought were guys," was the hit man's position. "I couldn't see. It was dark."

"You were a foot away," rebuked the defense attorney.

There was no response from Martorano. Attorney Miner continued hammering away at the former hit man. "Did Mr. Flemmi have anything to do with the murders of Al and Joe Notrangeli?"

"Nothing," said Martorano, "except he gave me the machine gun to begin with."

Al and Joe Notrangeli, both nicknamed "The Indian," had been killed during a war with the Winter Hill gangsters.

Attorney Miner was getting to the heart of the defense, questioning why Martorano had decided to testify against Flemmi. "He could have given you up," she said, "on any of these murders."

"And I think he would have," said Martorano.

"So you wanted to get him first?" asked Miner.

"Maybe," responded Martorano. "That was in my mind, too. Eventually, I decided to settle the problem legally and do what I'm doing now," he said.

The cross-examination conducted by defense attorney Tracy Miner displayed an obvious lack of success in discrediting Martorano. When Miner asked if it was fair to describe him as ruthless, John Martorano hesitated a brief moment, then said, "Yeah, that's fair to say."

The parade of gangsters to take the stand against former G-Man John Connolly would continue. Kevin Weeks, often referred to as Whitey Bulger's surrogate son, had a great deal of low-down on his former boss. For starters, Weeks told of a "hit car," complete with a smoke-screen and souped-up engine, used solely for special duty. "We called it the 'tow truck'," Weeks told the jury. "It was basically a hit car."

Weeks began by telling the jurors how he had been present when Bulger and Flemmi discussed the information they had received on Brian Halloran's cooperation with the FBI. Halloran was willing to shed light on the murder of Tulsa millionaire Roger Wheeler, a murder orchestrated by Bulger and Flemmi, according to the testimony of confessed hit man John Martorano.

However, due to the efforts of a few agents allegedly led by John Connolly, Halloran had been denied admission into the Bureau's Witness

Protection Program. Although warned to stay out of South Boston, the foolish gangster had failed to heed the advice.

Weeks began to lay out details of the Halloran slaying to a mesmerized jury. He told them Halloran had been spotted by a Bulger associate outside the Pier restaurant on Northern Avenue in South Boston. When Bulger received word of Halloran's appearance, he quickly took action. Bulger was next seen driving the "hit car" and wearing a wig and moustache, testified Weeks.

Bulger, in tandem with an associate "who had a ski mask on," drove to the restaurant where Halloran was last seen. Waiting nearby with a police scanner and walkie-talkie, Weeks communicated to Bulger. "I told him the balloon was in the air. We used to refer to Brian as 'balloon head'," said Weeks. "Jim Bulger leaned across the passenger seat, yelled, 'Brian!' and started shooting with a carbine," testified Weeks. Bulger made a U-turn and returned, firing off a hail of bullets into Halloran's car.

Weeks also revealed how funded money from gambling and extortion was used as Christmas payoff gifts. Weeks testified he had personally delivered two cash-stuffed envelopes to Connolly. One envelope, marked with a "Z" for "Zip," contained $5,000 for the South Boston agent. The other, marked with a picture of an orange, contained $1,000 destined for Agent John Newton, nicknamed "Agent Orange" by Bulger. Newton was a Vietnam veteran.

Bulger's former lieutenant testified other agents had been on the gang's Christmas list. Weeks claimed he'd tagged along with Bulger during the Christmas shopping trips. All the recipients were given code names. "Pipe" was Jim Ring, a supervisor of the organized crime squad. "Vino" was John Morris. "Nicky" was Agent Nicholas Gianturco. Connolly would then deliver the gifts. Weeks testified that Bulger said that "Christmas is for cops and kids. Most of the cops who'd been good to the White Man all year got cash in an envelope," said Weeks.

Under questioning by Assistant U.S. Attorney Leonard Boyle, Weeks claimed that then-retired Agent John Connolly came to him on December 23, 1994, to warn Bulger to leave town because FBI Agent Dennis

O'Callaghan had told Connolly that indictments were coming down against Bulger, Flemmi, and Cadillac Frank Salemme. Weeks testified that he and Connolly discussed the imminent indictments and arrests inside the liquor locker at Bulger's South Boston liquor mart. Weeks immediately warned Bulger of the indictments, and he quickly left town, eventually making the FBI's Ten Most Wanted List. Weeks said that Connolly told him the tip had come from then-Assistant Special Agent in Charge Dennis O'Callaghan. Steve Flemmi had foolishly procrastinated leaving town, thinking he had a few weeks ahead to wrap up some business affairs. He'd been arrested on January 5, 1995, and then all hell had broken loose.

Instead of calling into question the serious allegations brought against her client, attorney Miner decided to attack the witness' credibility and violent past. As she had done with the previous witness, John Martorano, the defense attorney would zero in on the deal the gangster had cut with government prosecutors, bargaining for the minimum amount of prison time possible.

During cross-examination, Weeks boldly responded to questions with an attitude straight from a James Cagney movie. He maintained he was telling the truth, but admitted he had once joked to the government he'd confess to killing Kennedy in exchange for immunity. When defense attorney Miner asked Weeks whether the Bulger group had sized up their victims for strengths and weaknesses before first moving in, Weeks replied, "As far as we were concerned, everybody was weaker than us."

"There wasn't a person in America you couldn't intimidate?" Miner asked incredulously.

"We weren't all over America. We were in Boston," Weeks said sarcastically.

He ridiculed the defense attorney when she asked if Bulger had told him to get a body bag during an extortion attempt in a bar with real estate broker Raymond Slinger. Weeks corrected the attorney's account of the situation, saying that Bulger had told him to get Slinger a bottle of beer, not a body bag. "I don't think every bar in Southie has body bags," Weeks added mockingly. "I'd state right out that I'd kill them. I didn't need to threaten with body bags."

The burly, impeccably-dressed gangster displayed the demeanor of a professional. Defense attorney Tracy Miner began focusing her cross-examination on the night Bulger had become a fugitive: December 23, 1994.

"It was kind of a famous date," said Weeks. "When Jim Bulger took off. It was two days before Christmas." The bold gangster testified he had paged "Jim" to tell him about Connolly's warning of the coming indictments. Bulger, along with girlfriend Theresa Stanley, picked up Weeks in South Boston, and the three drove to Copley Place in downtown Boston.

"You got to Copley Place from South Boston in fifteen minutes?" asked defense attorney Miner in disbelief. "Rush hour Christmas?" she added.

"You ever drive with Jim Bulger?" Kevin Weeks asked with a degree of smugness.

"He can't make cars disappear," said attorney Miner.

"Jim Bulger makes a lot of things magically disappear," responded Weeks. "Jim Bulger's an aggressive driver," Weeks said.

Attorney Miner asked Weeks to describe the events after entering Bulger's car. "Did you say, 'Mr. Bulger, I have some information for you'?" she asked.

"I never called him Mr. Bulger," Weeks said. He'd called him Jim. "You didn't know Mr. Bulger," Weeks added confidently. "You didn't ask him questions. You listened. He told you what he wanted you to know." Weeks took his association with Whitey Bulger as a business venture. "Every business I was involved in, he was my partner," said Weeks. However, that was as far as the former Bulger enforcer was willing to go. "I'm not going to put Jim Bulger's business out on the street."

After Bulger had become a fugitive, FBI agents asked Weeks if he was still in touch with the gangster. He had said no. "They approached me," he said. "I had nothing to hide."

"Because you were lying," said Miner.

"Correct," responded Weeks.

There were, however, incriminating telephone records that bolstered Weeks' testimony. Phone records introduced by government prosecutors indicated that Connolly had called the Boston Bureau two hours before telling Weeks of the coming indictments.

Under intense cross-examination, Weeks pointed the finger at Connolly as the person who had revealed to Bulger that one of the two men aboard the *Valhalla* fishing trawler was cooperating with investigators about a shipment of guns destined for the Irish Republican Army in 1984. According to Weeks, Bulger and his gang had corralled John McIntyre, who admitted to being the informant. Soon after, McIntyre had been killed by Bulger.

Defense attorney Tracy Miner's cross-examination of Kevin Weeks would be a disaster. When Weeks was asked about his role in the McIntyre slaying, he shot back that it had been John Connolly who'd tipped Bulger that McIntyre was spilling the beans to authorities. The gang thought about sending McIntyre to South America, but then decided against the plan.

Later, when the government prosecutor discussed Bulger and Flemmi's roles as Top Echelon Informants, Weeks disagreed with the characterization. "It was the other way around. John Connolly was giving them information."

The day after Weeks testified regarding bribes paid to a handful of corrupt agents, Special Agent John Newton was suspended by the FBI.

"The FBI has taken action deemed appropriate in light of recent trial testimony given concerning Special Agent Newton," said Boston FBI Special Agent in Charge Charles Prouty.

The next gangster-turned-government witness to take the stand against John Connolly would be Boston Mafia boss Cadillac Frank. Unaware that his partner Steve The Rifleman Flemmi had been ratting him out, Salemme had spent seventeen years behind bars due to Flemmi's treachery. Upon being appointed boss of the Boston LCN, Salemme had been set up for execution by trusted Mafia associate Sonny Mercurio in August of 1989. Salemme had been hit four times, yet had recovered from the assassination attempt, although the wounds would require constant medical attention for years to come.

He was unforgiving of the FBI for failing to warn him prior to the murder attempt, even though they had clearly received knowledge of the plot from an informant. Cadillac Frank was most critical of Steve Flemmi, a lifetime partner and childhood friend, who had betrayed him for years. "It was a breach of friendship that went back to when we were kids," said Salemme.

Cadillac Frank took the witness stand and began expressing his thoughts on today's Mafia. "It's too loose today," said the sixty-eight-year-old Salemme. In comparing the current LCN to the old men of the honored society, Salemme expressed displeasure, saying, "It's too loose today. You were pulled off the street into a basement. No one knew, there was certainly no celebration with prosciutto and figs." Salemme was mocking the infamous October 1989 induction ceremony where a government wiretap caught the baptismal ritual on tape for the first time, leading to a Mafia family's destruction.

Salemme expressed how the Mafia had degenerated, fueled by years of deadly quarreling among the crime families and the sudden rise of informants. Still trembling as a result of wounds suffered during the assassination attempt against him years before, Salemme acknowledged Connolly had leaked information to him regarding the coming indictments. He told jurors he had run into the former agent while using a pay phone at Boston's Prudential Center in Boston. And even though Connolly had arrested Salemme twenty-two years before, sending him to prison for seventeen years, he had boldly approached the gangster that day, saying, "I hope there's no hard feelings. I was just doing my job."

"Absolutely not, you had to do what you had to do," responded Salemme. He had never suspected that Connolly and Flemmi had been in cahoots, and responsible for his arrest.

Salemme told jurors it was at that chance meeting that Connolly had said, "You have an open invitation to come to my office."

Still looking fit and trim, and impeccably dressed, Salemme said he understood that Connolly was on the take. He testified that Flemmi had siphoned two payments of $5,000 each from their illegal gambling partnership for use as bribes delivered to John Connolly.

A few days following their first encounter, Salemme testified that he decided to meet with Connolly in an effort to gain some insight on the current sitting grand jury. "What did he tell you about the indictments?" prosecutor Durham asked.

"He said there were no indictments out yet and he'd let my friend Steve know," Salemme told the jury. Connolly's former secretary, Kathleen Orrick, would also testify that Salemme had met with Connolly at his office.

On January 5, 1995, Salemme said he was called to his ex-wife's home, where he received information from Steve Flemmi that indictments were coming down on January 10th.

"Who did he say the information had come from?" prosecutor Durham asked.

"John Connolly," responded Salemme.

However, the government did not wait until January 10th, deciding instead to arrest Salemme and the others on a complaint that very night, before the indictments were issued. Cadillac Frank managed to avoid arrest for several months, but was later apprehended in Florida. Steve Flemmi carelessly ignored the warning and was arrested on January 5, 1995. Whitey Bulger fled immediately and remains on the FBI's Ten Most Wanted List.

The former Mafia boss seemed genuinely wounded by Flemmi's deceit while describing his early days with Flemmi when they were both feared, up-and-coming gangsters. He began revealing shocking accounts of murders during the gang wars of the '60s. Cadillac Frank systematically laid out the slayings of Edward Wimpy Bennett and Walter Bennett in 1967. He and Steve Flemmi had worked as enforcers for the Bennetts, who controlled all of the gambling and loan sharking in Roxbury. He pointed the finger at Steve Flemmi as Wimpy's killer, firing a bullet into the side of the victim's face. "Over numbers, and there was a girl involved," explained Salemme.

Walter Bennett sought revenge for his brother's slaying. Although not part of the original problem between the two men, Salemme would stand by his friend. Together, Cadillac Frank and Steve Flemmi would strike first against the revenge-seeking Walter Bennett.

"Yes, I planned the demise of Mr. Walter Bennett," Salemme told the court.

When the third Bennett, William, posed a threat, once again the two best friends sprang into action. After being shot at close range, Billy Bennett was to be buried next to his two deceased brothers, Wimpy and Walter. However, things hadn't gone as planned, and Billy Bennett's body was found in 1967 laying next to a snowbank in the Mattapan section of Boston.

Outside the courtroom, Bill Bennett's son, Walter, said tearfully, "At least my family has a place to go. I can go to the grave and tell my father what happened here today. My cousins don't even have that much, because my uncles' bodies still haven't been found. I needed to hear it," said Walter. "It was tough, but I needed to hear him say what we knew in our hearts for all these years. He and Steve [Flemmi] killed my dad and my uncles."

Earlier attempts by investigators, spurred by information provided by Cadillac Frank, to locate the buried remains of Walter and Wimpy Bennett had failed. "I can see that there's a truth in what he's saying up there," Walter said. "Salemme makes a powerful witness, I think, because what he's trying to say is the truth. But that doesn't change how I feel about him."

Frank Salemme would continue confessing to other murders. He described how it took him several attempts to kill Punchy McLaughlin in 1965. Punchy had been one of the most feared and brutally capable killers in Boston. Oftentimes, he would dress as a woman when stalking an intended victim. It took great courage to go up against the dangerous Charlestown gangster. "It was kill or be killed. He was moving fast. I could- n't take a chance," Salemme said.

Cadillac Frank testified that Steve Flemmi had killed Frankie Benjamin, a local bookmaker, in the same bloody period of the 1960s. According to Salemme, he had walked into the Dudley Lounge in Roxbury to find his friend standing next to Benjamin's body. He'd then proceeded to help his childhood pal in disposing of the body. Once again, the loyal friend could be counted on when needed. He also fingered Flemmi as the builder of a bomb the pair had used to blow up defense attorney John Fitzgerald's car in 1968.

"John Fitzgerald was trying to play both ends and be a lawyer and a crook," Salemme said. According to Cadillac Frank, it had been Steve Flemmi's plan to plant a bomb in the car of Joe Barboza's attorney, John Fitzgerald. After enlisting Salemme's help in the bombing plot, he would orchestrate Salemme's arrest in New York by South Boston native, Special Agent John Connolly. Salemme would then spend the next seventeen years in prison, while the charges against Flemmi would be dropped. After his release, Flemmi would once again reach out for his best friend. He convinced Cadillac Frank that they had a great opportunity to advance in the criminal world because they had an FBI agent in their back pocket—John Connolly.

During cross-examination, Salemme told of becoming a "made man" in June of 1988. "I was a king's man, assigned to the head of the family," said Salemme. "The oath is to be loyal to the family at all costs," revealed Salemme. "The family is number one, even above your own family."

"You agreed to commit murder?" Connolly's defense attorney Tracy Miner asked.

"Yes," Salemme replied.

According to Salemme, he was summoned to New York by the five Mafia families whose control extended all the way to New England. Four of the five families supported his position as boss of the New England LCN.

"I didn't want the job [as boss]," he said. The Mafia commission in New York told him to take over. The testimony of imprisoned former Mafia boss Salemme was explosive. John Connolly's attorney, Tracy Miner, was unable to lay a glove on the convincing Salemme.

Not only had Whitey Bulger allegedly been protected by John Connolly and others, but he was portrayed as the protector of his beloved South Boston. There were many who promoted the Bulger myth as one who robbed from the rich and gave to the poor. There was also the fictitious tale of Bulger's anti-drug stance. However, there was one honest cop who hadn't bought into those claims. Boston Police Sergeant Frank Dewan spent a good deal of his career chasing Whitey Bulger. It was a most unpopular decision for Dewan to make, one that would cost him his job. Detective Dewan committed the unforgivable sin of heading a successful investigation against a host of drug dealers connected to Whitey Bulger. In retaliation for Dewan's pursuit of Bulger, a letter had been distributed among law enforcement authorities describing Dewan as a corrupt cop. A second letter had been sent to then-sitting Judge Mark Wolf, seeking to have the case against Steve Flemmi thrown out. The letter was intended to place the allegations of corruption on Dewan rather than the FBI agents in the Boston Bureau. John Connolly was eventually charged with being the author of those letters. Connolly's former secretary at Boston Edison testified that the type on the two anonymous letters shared the same characteristics as other documents she had typed. She also revealed having discovered Boston police stationery in Connolly's desk at the company office.

Next to take the stand was Boston Police Officer John Ford. He briefly stated, "Connolly didn't like Dewan. He said he was always chasing Mr. Bulger around."

The testimony corroborated Kevin Weeks' earlier revelations that Connolly had used Boston Police letterhead to send a forged letter to Judge Mark Wolf.

On Monday, May 20, government prosecutors rested their case against John Connolly.

THE CASE FOR THE DEFENSE

The first defense witness called to testify was Dennis O'Callaghan, the former second-in-command in the Boston Bureau. O'Callaghan asserted he had played no role in warning Bulger of the 1995 federal racketeering indictment. He further stated he had no idea why Bulger enforcer Kevin Weeks had accused him of the tip-off. O'Callaghan did admit that Connolly had often called him seeking information on the progress of a grand jury investigation that was targeting Bulger. However, O'Callaghan

strongly maintained he had never told Connolly of the pending indictment. His denial was in stark contrast to Kevin Weeks' statement that
O'Callaghan had been the source of the leak.

During cross-examination by prosecutor John Durham, O'Callaghan
was hammered for failing to investigate claims of corruption against
Connolly by drug dealer Joseph Murray in 1989. Murray had alleged that
Connolly and Special Agent John Newton had been selling wiretap information to Bulger. O'Callaghan acknowledged he had ordered two agents to
interview Murray, but they had reported to FBI headquarters that the claim
was without merit. However, under relentless questioning, O'Callaghan
was forced to admit that the 209 reports filed by the agents revealed that
they had never questioned Murray about the bribes.

"The question was never asked and the investigation was closed," said
Durham.

"Yes," responded O'Callaghan, admitting he had signed off on the
report to Washington, calling Murray's claims unsubstantiated. The report
filed by the interviewing agents indicated Murray was not asking for anything in return for his cooperation. According to the report, "Murray said
that Whitey Bulger and Steve Flemmi have a machine and that the Boston
police and the FBI have a machine and he cannot survive against these
machines. The information he furnished now will help save the life of a
friend or a loved one in the future."

Under intense grilling from Durham, O'Callaghan admitted the report
on Murray's interview made no mention of even one question about the
claim of bribery. Durham waved the 209 report in O'Callaghan's face, asking him over and over why Murray had never been asked about his
allegation that Connolly and Agent John Newton were on the take from
Bulger and Flemmi. All O'Callaghan was able to offer was a shrug, while
admitting that FBI headquarters had been informed that Murray's claim
was unsubstantiated and it was recommended the investigation be closed.
O'Callaghan was an obvious disaster for the defense. When asked if
Connolly had received any information as to when Bulger and Flemmi

were going to be indicted, O'Callaghan stood firm. "I have never discussed FBI business with John Connolly since his retirement in 1990, I don't recall him ever asking me when an indictment was coming out."

However, Durham presented the transcripts of O'Callaghan's earlier testimony before the federal grand jury that had indicted Connolly. Durham pointed out that O'Callaghan had testified that Connolly had called him often during the months leading up to the indictment of Bulger and Flemmi. Durham told the witness he had testified that Connolly wanted to know about the progress of the grand jury. O'Callaghan answered, "He would ask me if I had any knowledge of whether they were going to indict them." He tried desperately to do the right thing for his good friend John Connolly. However, in a matter of just a few minutes, O'Callaghan did a complete U-turn. He transformed from a defense witness to an unintentional witness for the prosecution.

Prosecutor Durham also told the jurors that the FBI had received information that John Connolly and others had acquired free Red Sox tickets, once belonging to a now-deceased season ticket holder who was being investigated by the Boston FBI for possible fraud. O'Callaghan acknowledged being suspended for five days for interfering with the internal investigation.

The following morning O'Callaghan was back on the witness stand with a fresh new approach. Defense attorney Tracy Miner would desperately attempt to rescue O'Callaghan's sorry testimony. He would now boldly sing a different tune, claiming that Ed Clark, one of the agents who had interviewed drug dealer Joe Murray, told him Murray had no information as to bribes offered to Connolly and Newton. According to Clark, "He [Murray] put that in there because that would make certain that they'd come out and interview him," O'Callaghan testified.

Attorney Miner had an extra bounce in her step. She called Agent Ed Quinn next. Quinn testified that Murray thought the notion of bribes being paid to Connolly and Newton was bizarre, and claimed his wife had made it up. "Mr. Murray started to laugh and he said, 'She's crazy,' and 'There's nothing to it,'" Quinn testified. However, there was a problem with the testimony of Agents Clark and Quinn. Murray was not available for questioning. He had been shot to death in 1992, allegedly by his now-deceased wife.

Miner's desperate attempt to clean up O'Callaghan's on-again-off-again testimony was an abject failure. What made it all the more devastating was that he had been heralded as the prime defense witness in a sterling cast of characters. His testimony was to have been key in rebutting Kevin Weeks' claim that Connolly had told him the indictment tip had come through O'Callaghan.

Connolly's defense would only call five witnesses, one a current sitting federal judge, Edward Harrington. The former federal prosecutor would inform the jurors of the importance of informants in destroying the Italian Mafia in the early days. Harrington said Connolly's success in infiltrating the secret society through the use of informants had been very significant. He praised Connolly for recruiting Bulger and Flemmi, who had enabled the FBI to wiretap the Anguilo headquarters at 98 Prince Street in the Italian North End of Boston.

However, Edward Harrington certainly didn't wear any halo himself. He was under intense scrutiny from the House Government Reform Committee over his role in helping hit man-turned-government-informant Joseph Barboza to beat a death penalty rap in Santa Rosa, California, in 1974. Barboza had killed a man while in the Witness Protection Program.

During cross-examination by Special Assistant U.S. Attorney John Durham, Harrington was asked about guidelines regulating gifts to FBI agents. "I would caution an agent against extravagant gifts, of course, but small gifts, who knows?" said Harrington, then added that minor tokens such as a birthday card were tolerable. "In order to have a good informant, there has to be a close working relationship," he said. He did acknowledge cash gifts and cases of wine, like the ones allegedly given to Connolly, were unacceptable.

The defense would call other former agents to bear witness to Connolly's role in helping to dismantle the Italian Mafia in Boston. John Connolly, however, would not take the stand in his own defense. Instead, he would proclaim, through the media, that his cozy relationship with the South Boston gangsters had been sanctioned by his supervisors in the Bureau's war against the Mafia.

Instead of subjecting her client to cross-examination, defense attorney Miner would throw a curve by using a training video showing Connolly as an agent who played by the rules. Prosecutor John Durham objected to airing the tape on grounds the government would have no opportunity to cross-examine a virtual defendant. Durham would have destroyed the once cocksure Connolly, had the G-Man been courageous enough to sit in the witness chair. Many were critical of Connolly's decision to snuggle with his three sons in the gallery rather than take the customary position at the defense table. Some looked upon it as a cowardly act. Judge Tauro ruled in favor of the defense, allowing the Academy training video to be shown to the jury.

Tauro's ruling did more to prop up a stumbling defense than Connolly's lawyer could. The G-Man would be able to pitch his good side without having to face a grilling from prosecutor Durham. The training video, made years earlier, would show Connolly counseling young agents not to be involved in a personal relationship with informants.

"We expect them to be criminals," Connolly instructs in the video. "I don't think we can ever lose sight of who we are and who we're working for." Connolly was able to drive across a point, depicting his understanding of the perils of getting too close to informants. "One of the crucial areas is information that he [an informant] could potentially give you involving himself in a crime," Connolly said on tape. "The guidelines tell us that we have to make a report up on that. That has to be given to the proper authorities." However, that is precisely what Connolly had failed to do, time and again.

"You should be in the driver's seat with these people," Connolly cautioned on the video. "They're either going to rule you, or you're going to rule them; and if they're ruling you, you're wasting your time and the Bureau's time, and it could put you and the Bureau in a very melancholy situation. You're dealing with a criminal here and someday they might make an allegation against you. I always maintain as an agent, we shouldn't try to out-gangster a gangster."

Connolly also warned agents against revealing informant information to other law enforcement officials. "You get a crooked cop, someone then would sell that information to the other wise guys," Connolly said. He also warned young agents not to allow informants to tell them about their crimes. "Don't tell me something you're doing or I'm going to have to act on it," Connolly advised them to caution potential informants. "Other agents can make a case on him," warned Connolly on the tape.

Prosecutors would tell jurors that Connolly had not followed his own advice. Had he done as he instructed the young agents on the training video to do, he would not have been facing racketeering and obstruction of justice charges.

CLOSING ARGUMENTS

On Thursday, May 23, federal prosecutor John Durham would begin closing arguments, calling John Connolly an agent on the take. He painted Connolly as a rogue agent, allegedly receiving bribes in exchange for information that had allowed the gangsters to run wild and avoid prosecution for their criminal behavior. "Mr. Connolly knew what this game was all about," said Durham. "He knew what time it was. He knew what the score was." Durham used Connolly's instructions on the training video as an indication he knew what the Attorney General's guidelines called for when dealing with informants. "John Connolly knew what his obligation was, but he was on somebody else's team," said prosecutor Durham. He would remind jurors of former Agent Connolly's reluctance to report Bulger's and his associates' extortion of the liquor mart belonging to Steve and Julie Rakes, then adding that the unwilling couple had been forced to sell when the gangsters had encouraged their young toddler to place a gun in her mouth. "There is no question that the defendant knew his informants were taking a business from these people and nothing was done. Is there any clearer evidence as to which team John Connolly was on?" Durham asked. "The evidence in this case firmly establishes the defendant was a member of this gang," continued Durham.

Next, the prosecutor would point to Connolly's former secretary, who testified she had seen ten uncashed paychecks totaling approximately $20,000 in the agent's desk drawer. "You ask yourself, what public official, what person you know, is able to not cash their paycheck ten times in a row?" Durham said.

Special Assistant U.S. Attorney John Durham told the jury that Connolly was corrupted from the moment he recruited Bulger as an informant. Durham continued, telling the jury that Connolly had formed a pact and had protected Whitey Bulger as a favor to William Bulger, the then-Senate President. John Durham said Connolly had been compromised and corrupted by accepting at least $5,000 in cash and a two-carat diamond from the gangsters.

The prosecutor also contradicted Connolly's account of Bulger and Flemmi's roles in the legendary bugging of the Mafia headquarters at 98 Prince Street in Boston's North End. Durham argued that Connolly had given his informants star billing in the successful wiretapping only as a means to continue them as Top Echelon Informants. He stated the case against the former agent had nothing to do with the prosecution of the Mafia, and everything to do with an agent who had surrendered his oath for profit. Durham blamed Connolly for leaking sensitive FBI information regarding individuals' cooperation, resulting in their murders. He said that two informants and a witness against the gangsters had been killed on information passed on by John Connolly. In closing, prosecutors told the jurors that their witnesses had to be truthful, or they faced more prison time for lying.

Defense attorney Tracy Miner began her closing statement by referring to John Connolly as a scapegoat for the FBI to cover its own failings in dealing with informants in the past. Miner went on to say, "The government needed a scapegoat for its problems. Who better than the informants' handler, somebody at the bottom of the totem pole? Someone they could label a rogue agent, then say they cleaned house, wash their hands and move on." Miner accused the FBI of making Connolly the victim of a coverup over the deadly alliances created during the government's crusade against the Italian Mafia.

"If there were problems, the Agency should step up to the plate," Miner said. Defense attorney Miner told jurors that the government's case against a decorated agent was based on the testimony of four witnesses, including a corrupt supervisor and a notorious hit man. "You've never seen a bigger group of thieves and liars in your life. They hate Mr. Connolly. They all learned Mr. Connolly was able to convince their friends, Mr. Bulger and Mr. Flemmi, to inform on them," Miner said. "This is payback, pure and simple."

The defense attorney reminded jurors of the inconsistencies in Bulger's lieutenant Kevin Weeks' description of events the day he said Connolly had warned of the pending indictments and advised the gangsters to leave town. Miner painted the government witnesses, mob hit man John Martorano and former Mafia boss Cadillac Frank Salemme, as vicious and remorseless organized crime figures.

"Here, they can't kill Mr. Connolly with a gun, but they can kill him just as easily, just as effectively, by raising their hand and lying," Miner said. "They know it's a slow death. This is payback, pure and simple." Defense attorney Tracy Miner said that Salemme, Martorano, and Weeks had been stunned when information surfaced that their former criminal partner had informed on them by delivering knowledge of their criminal offenses. Miner told the jury that revenge was the paramount factor for their testimony. When addressing charges that Connolly had allowed himself to be corrupted by accepting cash and gifts, Miner said, "Mr. Connolly got the goods; he didn't give up the goods, and all he took in return was a few books as presents and his FBI paychecks."

In closing, defense attorney Miner called the jury's attention to the testimony of former federal prosecutor Edward Harrington, who had stressed the importance of using informants to decimate the Mafia. "Judge

Harrington is a man of experience. He knows what can be black and white on paper can become gray in the field," Miner said. Defense attorney Tracy Miner put on a strong performance, casting doubts upon the government's key witnesses.

U.S. District Court Judge Joseph L. Tauro instructed the jury, then recessed the court. Jury deliberations were set for Friday, May 24, 2002, at nine A.M.

As he left the courtroom, the uncustomary reserved former agent said, "I trust in the jury system, and I leave it in their hands."

–*Chapter 30*–

THE VERDICT

On Friday, May 24, jurors began deliberating the fate of former Agent John Connolly. They promptly requested the transcript of former FBI Clerk John Ford. Ford testified that Connolly had showed him a portion of a phony letter written to U.S. District Judge Mark Wolf in 1997. The letter had been falsely authored by three Boston police officers in order to divert attention away from Bulger and Flemmi. Judge Tauro refused the request, saying he was reluctant to give trial transcripts; however, he did allow Ford's statements to be read to the jurors. Shortly after five P.M., the jury of six men and six women ended their first day of deliberations. They would resume considering the fate of John Connolly on the following Tuesday.

The long Memorial Day weekend would be a time of great joy for most Bostonians. The Red Sox were playing fantastically well, leading their division over the mighty New York Yankees. The two arch-rivals were set to battle each other over that weekend. For the first time in years, the Boston Celtics were deep into the NBA playoffs. They were also scheduled to play that weekend in their quest for a championship. Overall, it would be an exciting and entertaining weekend for most New Englanders. All were still relishing the stunning Superbowl upset victory by the New England Patriots.

Some would tune in to "Nomar" and the Red Sox with passion and great delight. Others would shout for joy as Antonie Walker and Paul Pierce sank long three-point shots. However, there would be no joy in Beanville for the once-mighty Connolly, who would soon strike out.

On Tuesday, May 28, 2002, John Connolly was found guilty of one racketeering charge, two counts of obstruction of justice, and one count of making false statements to the FBI. The once-celebrated G-Man showed little emotion as the verdict was being read. Connolly, who sat with his wife and three sons in the gallery, was acquitted of the remaining obstruction of justice charges. The jury had deliberated for less than two days before reaching its verdict.

The former agent was found guilty of sending a phony letter to Judge Mark Wolf, and urging Steve Flemmi to falsely blame Connolly's supervisor, John Morris, as the source who had warned the gangsters Bulger and Flemmi of impending indictments. He was found guilty of delivering a case of wine containing $1,000 in cash to Supervisor Morris; however, the jurors rejected the other four counts of bribery. Connolly was found innocent of the most serious charges, that he had delivered confidential information to Bulger and Flemmi about three men who were sharing information with the government regarding the gangsters' criminal activities. Jurors didn't buy the government's charge that Connolly was the source of leaks resulting in the slaying of Richard Castucci, Brian Halloran, and John Callahan.

"The verdict speaks loudly to the fact nobody in this country is above the law, an FBI agent or otherwise. The ends do not justify the means," said U.S. Special Federal Prosecutor John Durham.

Connolly was also found innocent of failing to intercede in the extortion of a liquor store belonging to Stephen and Julie Rakes.

"It is always a somber moment when it becomes necessary to prosecute a member of law enforcement who has abused his authority and crossed the line from crime fighter to criminal," U.S. Attorney Michael Sullivan said. "Today's verdict reveals John Connolly for what he became, a Winter Hill Gang operative masquerading as a law enforcement agent."

However, defense attorney Tracy Miner called the jury's verdicts inconsistent. "We are pleased that the jury found that John Connolly was not guilty of the most serious acts alleged in the indictment," said Miner. "None of the acts John Connolly was found guilty of resulted in any physical harm to anyone." Miner's statement was obviously a desperate attempt to put a positive spin on the jury's decision for the purpose of securing a minimum sentence for her client. Although facing a stiff sentence, Connolly was still not out of the woods. Prosecutor Durham's probe was ongoing. Three racketeering and obstruction of justice charges from the superseding indictment against Connolly had been set aside prior to trial, charges that included:

Count 2: alleging Connolly engaged in a racketeering conspiracy with Bulger and Flemmi from September 1975 to September 1998.

Count 3: Connolly was charged in a conspiracy to obstruct justice by leaking secret grand jury information to Bulger, Flemmi, and Cadillac Frank Salemme in 1993 and 1994.

Count 8: Connolly obstructed justice in 1998 by persuading Flemmi to testify falsely that FBI Supervisor John Morris, not Connolly, had tipped the gangster in 1994 to their imminent indictments.

It was possible that prosecutors would consider whether or not to pursue three racketeering and obstruction charges based on Connolly's willingness to cooperate with investigators probing corruption in the Boston Bureau. There was a strong belief that the G-Man/con man could reveal explosive disclosures, some reaching all the way to the top.

When asked if the government was willing to revisit other charges still pending, U.S. Attorney Sullivan said, "I think we'll make a decision on that once we determine exactly what the sentence is imposed by Judge Tauro to see whether or not there's any reason to pursue any additional charges."

Government prosecutors would continue to investigate claims that other agents and supervisors were receiving bribes. "That information will be pursued to determine whether it's appropriate to pursue charges," said prosecutor Sullivan. In particular, Connolly was suspected of interfering with an investigation of a questionable real estate deal involving then-Senate President William Bulger.

Charles Prouty, Special Agent in Charge of the Boston FBI, said, "This conduct is abhorrent to all honest FBI agents. The verdict is exactly what they wanted. We do want to turn the page."

Connolly, who had "no comment," was allowed to remain free on $200,000 unsecured bond until sentencing. The verdict was a bit confusing, and somewhat contradictory.

Connolly did escape the most serious charges, that he leaked the identities of three informants to Bulger and Flemmi, resulting in the murder of all three.

Dennis Halloran, a brother of one murder victim, was furious with the verdict. "It's a joke; it's awful," said Halloran. His brother Brian, along with Michael Donahue, had been slaughtered only a few feet from the courthouse. "You wait and see; they'll walk him out of there with three to five years, tops," Halloran said. "This is crazy. Christ, every cop in the city knew what was going on with Connolly. Personally, I still say he beat the system."

Although the federal sentencing guidelines call for an eight to twenty year prison sentence, the judge does have some discretion when imposing the penalty. Dennis Halloran was so distraught with the results of the trial, it caused him to question what might be next. "Is Judge Joseph Tauro one of Bulger's guys?"

Had the jury convicted Connolly of his alleged role in leaking confidential information resulting in the three murders, it would have bolstered civil lawsuits filed against Connolly and the FBI by the victims' families. However, early on Judge Tauro had barred prosecutors from allowing jurors to hear evidence of the three murders. The reasoning was that since Connolly had been charged solely with obstruction of justice for allegedly leaking information, and not with the actual murders, allowing jurors to hear details of the homicides would be prejudicial. Judge Tauro had ordered prosecutors to trim their case and to make it less difficult for the jury. Yet, in doing so, it is possible the exclusion of the three murders confused rather than simplified the proceedings, thus raising more uncertainty in the jurors' thinking. In truth, the alleged leaks by Connolly resulted in the murders of Richard Castucci, Brian Halloran, and John Callahan. Connolly undeservedly lucked out.

However, the jury did accept Kevin Weeks' testimony that Connolly was the leak who had allowed Bulger to flee. Weeks' credibility was not good news for other FBI agents and a handful of Boston police officers who could be the focus of further investigations.

Jurors did not buy hit man Martorano's claim of Winter Hill gangsters securing a two-carat diamond ring for Connolly's first wife. It is possible they were put off by Martorano's revelations of grotesque murders, displaying no sense of remorse for the twenty hits he had made. In the end, it appeared the jury could not connect all the dots.

Connolly was now branded a convicted mob racketeer who had been corrupted and crossed over the line into criminality rather than an agent who had simply gone off the right path. Not satisfied to be exclusively evil and corrupt, the G-Man was firmly fixed on depraving everyone with whom he came in contact. Those who didn't see things his way and refused to be corrupted would pay dearly. Some would be destroyed career-wise, with the help of his politically-connected friends. Those who posed a threat to his informant pals would suffer murderous consequences. The true facts of his wickedness may never be fully revealed. Yet, it is no secret that Richard Castucci, Brian Halloran, John Callahan, and John McIntyre were slain after word surfaced that they were supplying information to law enforcement. Someone had to have informed the gangsters that these men had been talking; it was not merely by chance they had been slain. Many, including the families of the victims, believed that someone was John Connolly.

Connolly was not a good guy who had simply crossed over the line in his desire to bring down the Boston mob; he was pure evil. His allegiance to his childhood idol had prompted him to warn the ruthless gangster he was about to be indicted. Connolly not only obstructed justice, but allowed Bulger to avoid the possibility of death in the electric chair. He traded his FBI oath for his devotion to Whitey Bulger.

William Bulger, President of the University of Massachusetts, denied ever asking anyone in law enforcement to protect his brother. Connolly, who established his reputation for developing criminals into informants, was himself brought down by three gangster witnesses willing to talk. Connolly could face more charges in the future stemming from new revelations that were brought forth in court. Kevin Weeks alleged that Connolly told the South Boston gangsters that a crew member of the fishing vessel *Valhalla* was cooperating with law enforcement regarding Bulger and Flemmi's drug dealing. Weeks claimed the information from Connolly caused the murder of John McIntyre.

An attorney for the family said Connolly's guilty verdict was a boost for their civil suit against the FBI. Connolly himself could still be liable for the murders. Civil suits filed against agents and the FBI could reach a staggering two billion dollars in damages.

Although convicted of racketeering and obstruction of justice, there are many wrongs Connolly committed in his far-reaching and depraved career, wrongs that inflicted harm and pain on many undeserving victims.

On September 16, 2002, the once cocksure former Agent John Connolly sat humbly in U.S. District Court in Boston, waiting to hear the length of his prison term. The federal courtroom was packed for the sixty-two-year-old flamboyant Connolly's sentencing. He was surrounded by his wife, brother, and other close friends, as well as a handful of retired FBI Agents, all on one side of the standing-room-only courtroom. On the opposite side, resembling a major sporting event, were the opponents comprised of federal prosecutors and investigators who had spent years investigating Connolly and the Bulger gang. Dressed in one of his many costly hand-tailored suits, with matching tie and pocket handkerchief, the once-decorated former agent declined to speak at his sentencing. Connolly, who had been credited with helping cripple the Boston Mafia headed by Larry Zannino, was now facing the similar fate as the gangsters he had successfully pursued. U.S. District Judge Joseph P. Tauro had been besieged with over 200 letters from friends and former agents asking for compassion. However, the letter-writing campaign failed to influence the judge who had a reputation for handing down harsh punishments. John Connolly was sentenced to ten years in prison, the maximum called for under the federal sentencing guidelines. Judge Tauro displayed his outrage for Connolly, who had plotted a scheme to misdirect the court in the late

1990s by way of a false and deceitful letter, and for his role in coaxing Steve
Flemmi to give deceitful testimony. "These were no fraternity house
pranks," said Tauro. "Rather, they attack the very heart of what we attempt
everyday in this building to do, which is administer justice fairly." In addition, Judge Tauro denied a request by Connolly's attorneys to remain free
pending appeal, or permit him to self-surrender at a later date. In most
cases, the court allows the defendant time to get his personal and family
matters in order, usually within sixty days. Then the defendant would surrender to the designated facility. Not so for John Connolly. However, the
judge did agree to recommend that Connolly be permitted to serve his sentence at the Federal Medical Facility at Fort Devens in Ayer,
Massachusetts. Connolly had a form of skin cancer, along with other medical issues. However, gambling mogul Jerry Anguilo was currently serving
his forty-year sentence at the same medical facility, along with several top
New York Mafia leaders. Ordinarily, the Bureau of Prisons takes strict precautions not to incarcerate persons, who have testified against anyone, in
the same institution. Connolly was mainly responsible for destroying the
Anguilos, resulting in lengthy prison sentences for all, including Jerry's
own forty-year term. Why Connolly was sent to the same facility is puz-
zling. The former agent would most certainly not be welcome with open
arms by Jerry Anguilo, or the aging Mafia bosses serving time there.
However, Connolly's incarceration at Fort Devens would be brief, hardly
long enough for the former agent to once again cross swords with his belli-
cose adversary. Connolly would be moved to a new location, the Federal
Medical Facility in Lexington, Kentucky. More ironic, FMC Lexington is
the same institution that another archenemy, Cadillac Frank Salemme,
had once called home. Connolly was a hot potato, causing the Bureau of
Prisons to play a semblance of musical chairs. He would be flown to
Lexington in a Lear Jet, used exclusively for high profile persons, such as
Mafia chieftains or other distinguishing characters. Shortly before touch-
down, the panorama of horse farms with white fences and devil-red trim
dotting the glorious bluegrass landscape, is awe-inspiring. The delightful

vista quickly changes to a 100-year-old, hard-looking brick institution, surrounded by layers upon layers of razor wire. The medical facility is located within the prison, which includes housing for hardened criminals as well as those requiring medical attention. Connolly would be assigned to the Bluegrass Unit, a make up containing small rooms with two bunk beds designed to house four inmates. Being a new inmate, the rogue agent would be forced to take the top bunk. In his first week, he would be required to attend A&O. The administration and orientation sessions are a boring week of meetings, where new inmates are educated to the ways of the institution. Most of the indoctrination is delivered by C.O.s, tobacco-chewing, pot-bellied Correctional Officers with unintelligible diction. Word that a former agent was at the compound quickly circulated through the prison grapevine. This revelation would cause prison officials to move Connolly from the Bluegrass Unit to the S.H.U. (Segregated Housing Unit). Connolly would remain isolated from the general prison population for safety reasons.

On December 2, 2002, University of Massachusetts President William Bulger was issued a subpoena to appear before the House Committee on Government Reform to answer questions about his wanted brother, Whitey. Committee members were hopeful that William Bulger would be cooperative; however, that was not the case. On Friday, December 6, 2002, the arrogant and defiant William Bulger invoked his Fifth Amendment right not to answer questions. When asked by Committee Chairman Dan Burton if he had talked with his brother, Whitey, since 1995, Bulger replied, "The Fifth Amendment's basic functions are to protect innocent men who might be ensnared by ambiguous circumstances," adding, "I find myself in such circumstances." Burton then asked if he planned to respond to all the questions in the same way. "Yes, sir," replied Bulger. Burton was not pleased with the position taken by Bulger. After the hearing, Burton voiced his frustration saying, "I understand that Whitey Bulger is his brother, but he's one of the ten most wanted fugitives in the United States." It is clear: Arrogance is an inherited trait. William Bulger's contempt did not sit well with the Committee.

On the previous day, former federal prosecutor Jeremiah O'Sullivan told the Committee that he knew Whitey Bulger and Steve Flemmi were murderers and FBI informants, but that he failed to indict the pair in a horse fixing case because he theorized he did not have enough evidence to gain conviction. O'Sullivan did admit that John Connolly had interceded on behalf of the two gangsters, but claimed he had already decided against indictment. It was an obvious song and dance routine by the former prosecutor. It's clear that O'Sullivan and Connolly were so hung-up with bringing down the Mob, that they had no concerns in uniting with murderers to achieve their personal objectives.

In early September 2002, Whitey Bulger had been spotted in the Piccadilly section of London by a man who had recognized his face in the movie *Hannibal*. Bulger's profile emerged in a scene in which a detective examines the FBI Web site. The man gave the FBI a new portrait of Bulger. The new look was circulated by the FBI throughout Europe via its Web site. A short time later, FBI officials opened a safety deposit box belonging to the fugitive gangster at the Barclay Bank in London. What made the discovery extraordinary wasn't the $50,000 found in the box, but that the fugitive's brother, William Bulger, was listed as the person to contact. Even more remarkable was the fact that FBI officials had received credible information years earlier that Whitey had a deposit box at the Barclay Bank in London, yet did not take action until years later. Once again, skepticism would surface, questioning the FBI's earnest effort to capture Whitey Bulger. An already perplexed Committee Chairman Dan Burton responded to the bizarre event, saying, "I found it interesting that the FBI, when they went to Piccadilly Circus, they recognized the bank. If they could do that now, I can't figure out why they couldn't do that six years ago. There was either some sloppy work being done, or they didn't want to do it."

Burton called on the Justice Department Task Force to examine the FBI's handling in apprehending Bulger. In particular, Burton was critical of the Boston Bureau. "There's somebody up there who's not being held accountable," he said. "That whole bunch up there in that Boston office during the time that Connolly and Billy Bulger and Whitey Bulger were all in cahoots with one another, all of them ought to be investigated." He was not content with William Bulger's inappropriate demeanor before the Committee. It was evident to many that the former Senate President had avoided any consequences stemming from the investigation of corruption in Boston. Burton and others were not about to give the Machiavellian Bulger a pass. However, in order to secure a case against William Bulger, it would have to come through John Connolly. The now-convicted rogue agent was vital to any success. Throughout his ordeal, Connolly had boasted of his stand-up guy character. He chastised those who had testified against him, calling them liars who committed perjury in order to avoid severe prison sentences. It was easy for Connolly to take that position, at least for now, anyway. He had not yet experienced the dreadful flavor of prison life. His first test would come only after a relatively brief period of incarceration.

In early January 2003, the disgraced agent was transferred from the Federal Medical Facility in Lexington, Kentucky, to the Hamden County Jail in Massachusetts. "He's been released on a federal writ to the custody of the U.S. Marshal's Service," said Traci Billingsley, a Bureau of Prison spokeswoman. "A federal writ is usually used when a federal prisoner is going to testify," she added. The move could possibly indicate an attempt to gain Connolly's cooperation on the continuing corruption probe in Boston. By cooperating, Connolly could have his sentence reduced as a reward for his testimony. If he decided to step up to the plate and "point the finger" at others, he could wind up serving his time at a federal prison camp. A minimum-security "camp" is the least prohibitive in the federal system, with no fence or razor wire. Only non-violent offenders are eligible to serve their time there. A camp also has the benefit of "open movement," versus the restrictive "control movement" used at higher security levels, such as Lexington. With controlled movement, the inmate has only ten minutes between destinations at the facility. Once at that destination, he must remain there until the next movement. The consequence of not adhering to the movement, classified as being out-of-bounds, will result in an immediate lock-up in the "hole," with all privileges suspended.

If Connolly was willing to roll, he would serve his time at a minimum-security institution close to home. Family members would be spared the arduous journey to Kentucky for visitations. Connolly could make the best of a bad situation. All that was required was for him to rat on a handful of remaining targets that had so far escaped the ongoing investigation. Connolly's attorney, Tracy Miner, in an effort to put to rest any speculation or rumors of Connolly's position, stated he was "absolutely not cooperating." However, the firm posture by Miner was considered irrational by those familiar with events as they had occurred. A knowledgeable attorney suggested that "the government doesn't pay to fly you back and forth unless there's the spark of something happening there."

Connolly would be shipped back to the Federal Medical Facility at Lexington, Kentucky, back to an isolated cell in the segregated housing unit. The odds of Connolly holding firm to his bravado as a stand-up guy appeared to be slim. There's no question those likely to be targets of the ongoing probe were extremely concerned. Special Prosecutor John Durham is clearly fervent in gaining Connolly's cooperation on former U.S. Attorney Jeremiah O'Sullivan who had a propensity to protect Whitey Bulger and Steve Flemmi from prosecution. O'Sullivan is also suspected of playing a key role in a controversial real estate deal in which he cleared William Bulger of any skullduggery, thus allowing him to avoid any criminal consequences. John Connolly is once again smack-dab in the middle of it all. Will he remain loyal to his ethnic friends and community is subject to controversy.

Connolly had an opportunity to roll and save himself, yet he continued to remain silent. Connolly's unwavering position, at least for now, closed the door on any further revelations of wrongdoing committed by others in Boston during that atrocious era.

However, just when it looked as though the corruption scandal over the cozy relationship between the FBI's organized crime unit and murderous informants reached its high point, a new wrinkle developed. Whitey Bulger's partner, Steve The Rifleman Flemmi, chose to croon like a "Soprano" in order to save his life. The now frail and ailing sixty-nine-year-old tough guy was scheduled for trial in early October 2003 for the murders of Deborah Hussey and Debra Davis, with whom he had been romantically involved. Flemmi, the gangster, elected to dodge a never-ending procession of witnesses along with mounting evidence depicting the unforgiving and heartless murders of his two former lovers. The ever-calculating Flemmi knew he could not afford to have the gruesome details of the callous murders of the two young beauties become public, particularly the grisly act of extracting the teeth of Deborah Hussey in order to thwart identification.

On October 9, 2003, the pitiless gangster struck a deal in order to escape death by lethal injection in Oklahoma by ratting out retired FBI Agent H. Paul Rico for his alleged role in the 1981 slaying of Roger Wheeler, owner of World Jai Alai in Florida. Flemmi cut a deal with federal prosecutors confessing to ten murders, including the two young women, and racketeering charges, in exchange for life in prison after connecting his one-time FBI handler to the hit. Flemmi would serve his life sentence in a federal prison designed to accommodate others in the Witness Protection Program. Flemmi's life would not be worth a "plug nickel" if incarcerated at any other poky (prison); he wouldn't last twenty-four hours because of other criminals seeking to "whack" the double-crossing rat. Flemmi's decision to swap Rico's life for his own should come as no surprise, even though the G-Man and the gangster had an unusually close alliance. Through the use of treachery and deadly betrayal, Flemmi and Bulger had survived for decades as ruthless criminals.

Once a highly regarded crusader in the FBI, and hailed for his uncanny ability for recruiting Top Echelon Informants, Rico's own pet rat reacted as any cornered varmint would, by turning and taking a giant chomp out of him. Flemmi's admission of Rico's role in the Wheeler murder coincided with an earlier assertion by hit man John Martorano, who claimed that Rico supplied information of Wheeler's daily activities that made the murder easy, a killing ordered by Bulger and Flemmi. Flemmi's portrayal of the Wheeler murder given to authorities prompted Tulsa District Attorney Tim Harris and Homicide Detective Michael Huff to arrest Rico. The seventy-eight-year-old former agent was arrested on October 9, 2003, at his Palm Beach home by Huff, the primary investigator on the Wheeler case. The tenacious homicide detective had dedicated twenty-two years pursuing those responsible for the Wheeler slaying. "Mike was a bulldog" said Robert Fitzpatrick, who served as second in command in the Boston Bureau. "He never let go." Although the now-graying detective had been frustrated by the lack of cooperation from some in the Boston FBI, Huff persevered. "We were chasing leads all over the place," he said. "We very naively thought that as far as the Jai Alai angle, the FBI would bring us into the loop." Huff was directed away from any key evidence during the course of his investigation by those determined to protect Bulger and Flemmi. "When you see somebody who is clearly in your sights, it's very nagging," Huff said. "But in retrospect, the case against Rico is much better with Flemmi." Huff's doggedness, and the threat of death by lethal injection in Oklahoma, caused Flemmi to crack.

As part of his plea agreement, Flemmi will be obligated to cooperate and tell all he knows about the cozy relationship between the G-Men and the gangsters in Beantown. Flemmi's striking resolve to cooperate with prosecutors could cause some sleepless nights for present and past law enforcement officials corrupted by Bulger and Flemmi. Government prosecutors will be all ears when questioning the gangster on what role, if any, former University of Massachusetts President William Bulger played in the gang's unholy alliance with the FBI, and if his testimony before the House Judiciary was candid. When questioned before the committee investigating corruption in the Boston Bureau, William Bulger said he was unaware of any FBI duplicity or of his brother's criminal behavior. Flemmi let it be known to investigators that he did not know where Whitey Bulger was, which is believable since Bulger would never trust his partner with information on his whereabouts. There is no honor among thieves, and most certainly none among informants. Steve The Rifleman Flemmi will die in prison, and former Agent Rico, who was responsible for creating the vicious gangster, is facing a lethal injection if found guilty. Whitey Bulger continues to avoid capture. There are many who very much believe that it is paramount for some in the Bureau to keep Whitey far away from law enforcement scrutiny. His capture may bring even more shocking revelations that could be devastating to an already severely tarnished agency. The FBI created and protected Whitey Bulger and Steve Flemmi for decades on the pretense of its war against the mob. It's difficult to believe that the very same agency that encouraged criminality and looked the other way, is truly fervent in apprehending the fugitive crime boss.

Attorney General Harlan Fiske Stone, who later became Chief Justice of the United States, warned in 1924, when he established the FBI, "There is always the possibility that a secret police may become a menace to free government and free institution because it carries with it the possibility of abuses of power, which are not always quickly apprehended or understood."

EPILOGUE

Attorneys for the victims' families were confident they could connect Connolly to the murders of Richard Castucci, Brian Halloran, John Callahan, and John McIntyre. As had been the case with O.J. Simpson, who was acquitted of criminal charges, standards would not be as high in a civil suit. Far less evidence will be required to link Connolly in the murders.

Some believe John Connolly has information on Whitey Bulger's whereabouts, and whether or not the fugitive is still alive. If not now, perhaps a few years in a federal prison will loosen Connolly's lips. There would be no Steak Mafia or chianti wine as he had often enjoyed at Joe Tecce's North End restaurant. Holidays would be shared with convicted criminals rather than family. Only time will determine if Connolly stands up or takes the easy way out and flips.

During her last days in office, Attorney General Reno drafted new guidelines designed to prevent the warm and snug relationship between informants and their handlers that had contributed to the massive corruption in the Boston Bureau. The sweeping changes signaled an end of the Top Echelon Informant Program. Connolly and Bulger, two South Boston childhood neighbors, had been in the middle of nearly every instance of corruption and evildoing in the Boston FBI.

The new changes require all federal administrations to report unapproved criminal conduct by informants to prosecutors and to alert federal attorneys when an individual is a target of criminal investigations. Agents are also prohibited from socializing and/or exchanging gifts with informants. The checks and balances stemmed from revelations that agents in Boston customarily dined with Bulger and Flemmi and exchanged gifts.

Future informants will be subjected to periodic reviews in order to justify their continued use.

A committee comprised of federal prosecutors along with representatives of the DEA, U.S. Marshal's Service, and other federal agencies worked with U.S. Attorney General Janet Reno to revise the old guidelines. No longer would the informants' handlers be responsible for reporting perplexing or difficult issues; instead, they would be subjected to accountability by prosecutors. Other changes require government agencies to take into account whether an informant poses a danger to the public or to other criminals.

Defense attorneys hailed the new guidelines, which were the consequences of the FBI's relationship with Bulger and Flemmi. One of the most significant changes prohibits agents from sharing information relating to other investigations with their informants, which was obviously a result of a warning Bulger and Flemmi received of the forthcoming indictment that had allowed Bulger to flee. The new rules would also prohibit informants from receiving the identities of others cooperating with law enforcement; this, a reference to the murders of Brian Halloran, Richard Castucci, John McIntyre, and John Callahan.

The new guidelines would exercise control over the FBI's use of violent criminals as informants. The future success of the newly adopted guidelines will rest on decisions made by the Justice Department overseers, and not those of the FBI.

In other developments, Francesco Anguilo, the younger brother of Jerry Anguilo, has resumed living at the 98 Prince Street apartment in Boston's North End. It is the same location where FBI bugs uncovered details resulting in convictions amongst the powerful gambling syndicate. One by one, all the Aguilos would be released from prison; two other brothers had been freed earlier, along with Jerry's son, Jason.

Still in prison, the oldest Anguilo, Jerry, is being held at the Fort Devens Federal Medical Facility in Ayer, Massachusetts. He has filed a motion to have his case reopened. His petition is based on FBI misconduct in its use of Bulger and Flemmi to convince a judge to issue the warrant allowing the bugging of the mob headquarters. Recent revelations of the corruption in the Boston Bureau have led many to believe that Jerry's motion will have positive results. Interestingly enough, while most if not all the Anguilos are free, or soon to be, Connolly, who was responsible for their incarceration, began his own prison term. What goes around comes around.

The families of the victims affected by corruption in the Boston FBI continue their civil suits, despite government efforts to quash them.

The family of Debra Davis, who according to Kevin Weeks was slain by the gangsters, filed a $30 million wrongful death lawsuit against Steve Flemmi and Whitey Bulger.

The Donahue family is prepared to file a $36 million wrongful death suit against the FBI, former Agent John Connolly, former Supervisor John Morris, as well as Lawrence Sarhatt and Robert Fitzpatrick, then Special Agents in Charge of the Boston FBI. The family of John McIntyre claimed damages of $50 million against those who leaked word of his cooperation with authorities.

Stephen and Julie Rakes' civil suit claims nearly $120 million in damages resulting from the FBI's handling of the extortion of their liquor store. Others have also filed, bringing the combined total close to two billion dollars in damages.

On June 7, 2002, Justice Department attorneys filed a motion to have a suit filed by the Roger Wheeler family dismissed, because the lawsuit was filed too late. The Wheeler family is seeking $860 million from the FBI, who they hold responsible for the Roger Wheeler murder. The motion was filed with U.S. District Judge Reginald C. Lindsay, who earlier denied a similar effort to quash the $36 million lawsuit brought by the Donahue family.

Peter Limone and Joseph Salvati, who have suffered a terrible injustice, allegedly at the hands of former Agent Paul Rico and his cohorts, have filed a multimillion-dollar civil suit against those responsible.

Congressional investigators are continuing their probe into the FBI's role in convicting innocent men for the murder of Teddy Deegan and its subsequent cover-up. The committee plans more hearings on the FBI's alliance with criminal informants.

The prosecutor responsible for Limone and Salvati's convictions apologized to the men. A remorseful Jack Zalkind said he would never have prosecuted the case had he known that FBI agents were protecting the actual killers.

In early December 2002, Charles Prouty, who was the supervisor in charge of the 1997 administrative inquiry of corruption and misconduct in the Boston Bureau, was promoted to the #3 job at the FBI. Many called the 1997 investigation a whitewash, and Prouty was criticized by some for going easy on the Bureau.

Kevin Weeks, Whitey Bulger's surrogate son who assisted Bulger and Flemmi in digging the graves of their victims, scoffed at the millions of lawsuits filed by families of those murdered. In particular, Weeks showed little compassion to the mother of Debra Davis, who was strangled and mutilated at the age of twenty-six. Weeks filed bankruptcy and dispensed his portion of the lottery winnings to his ex-wife in an effort to avoid millions in lawsuits filed by the victims' families.

His ex-wife met with HBO officials and agreed to a contract to tell her story. The victims' families are also concerned that Weeks could make serious money peddling his story.

On Friday, January 24, 2003, former mob boss Cadillac Frank Salemme gained a release from prison because of his testimony and assistance. Originally scheduled to remain in prison until June 2005, Judge Mark Wolf cut Salemme's sentence by thirty months.

On March 20, 2003, Richard Schneiderham was found guilty of leaking information that FBI agents, who were looking for Whitey Bulger, were monitoring the home phones of the two fugitive gangster brothers. On June 26, 2003, the retired State Police Lieutenant was sentenced to eighteen months in a federal prison.

On April 11, 2003, John Jackie Bulger pleaded guilty to thwarting efforts in the capture of his fugitive brother, Whitey. The younger Bulger was sentenced to six-months jail time followed by six months of home confinement, along with the loss of his $3,738 a month state pension.

On August 5, 2003, U.S. Rep. R. James Sensenbrenner, Chairman of the House Judiciary Committee, journeyed to Boston for a classified meeting on escalating a Congressional probe of corruption and misconduct in the Boston Bureau.

On August 6, 2003, surrendering to mounting pressure, William Bulger resigned his post as President of the University of Massachusetts. His resignation came months after testifying before a Congressional Committee. The University of Massachusetts President came under fire when questioned about ties to his fugitive gangster brother, Whitey. The renowned dictator of state politics grudgingly gave up a $358,000 annual salary and benefits, along with privileges to a lifetime term as a paid University of Massachusetts professor.

On August 14, 2003, The First Circuit Court of Appeals rejected John Connolly's challenge to his conviction. The three judge panel denied all of the rogue agent's challenges to his conviction, rejecting every argument raised by the former G-Man.

On Friday, January 16, 2004, former Agent H. Paul Rico died in the medical unit at the David L. Moss Criminal Justice Center in Tulsa, Oklahoma, while in custody pending trial. The seventy-eight-year-old ex-G-Man died of natural causes one week after being extradited to Oklahoma to face charges of helping arrange the 1981 murder of Tulsa businessman Roger Wheeler.

In early 2004, John Connolly was released from the SHU (Special Housing Unit) and put into the general population at the Federal Medical Facility in Lexington, Kentucky, where he was assigned the custodial job at the mainline corridor. His clean-up duties there would keep him close to the Correctional Officers so they could keep a watchful eye on the ex-G-Man.

James Whitey Bulger is alleged to have killed nearly two dozen people, most while assigned Top Echelon Informant status. Bulger is currently #2 on the FBI's Ten Most Wanted List. The South Boston gangster is the seventh fugitive in the history of the FBI's Most Wanted Program whose capture carries a reward of at least $1,000,000. The only fugitive on the list whose capture would bring a higher reward is Osama bin Laden to the current $25,000,000.

CHAPTER NOTES

CHAPTER 1

1. Most of the accounts in this chapter come from my own experiences while growing up in the city of Boston; also, from my personal contact with the Anguilos and other associates.

CHAPTER 2

1. "FBI Reportedly Hid Key Evidence"; *The Boston Globe*. Ralph Ranalli; *Boston Globe* Correspondent; 12/21/2000.
2. "Hidden Truth: Hoover's FBI May Have Suppressed Info On Mob Hit"; *The Boston Herald*. Jonathan Wells and Maggie Mulvihill; 12/21/2000.
3. "Real Killer's Lawyer Says Jailed 'Hit Man' Is Innocent"; *The Boston Herald*. Jonathan Wells; 1/3/2001.
4. "Animal, Bear, Lucky To Have FBI As Keepers"; *The Boston Herald*. Howie Carr; 1/3/2001.
5. "Court Frees Limone After 33 Years In Prison"; *The Boston Globe*. Ralph Ranalli, *Globe* Correspondent; 1/6/2001.
6. Judge Mark Wolf's Memorandum and Order; "Good Guy, Bad Guy"; *Boston Magazine*. Sean Flynn.

CHAPTER 3

1. "*Good Guy, Bad Guy*"; *Boston* Magazine. Sean Flynn.
2. Judge Mark Wolf's Memorandum and Order.

CHAPTER 4

1. "Good Guy, Bad Guy"; *Boston Magazine*. Sean Flynn.
2. Judge Mark Wolf's Memorandum and Order.

CHAPTER 5

1. Taken from former Attorney General Edward H. Levi's Memorandum on use of FBI Informants.

CHAPTER 6

1. "Feds Allegedly Helped Hit Man Beat Slay Rap"; *The Boston Herald*. J.M. Lawrence; 7/28/2001.
2. "Globe Spotlight Team, Part 4"; *The Boston Globe*. Shelley Murphy; 7/22/1998.
3. "Arrogant Agent Fails To Silence Haunting Pleas"; *The Boston Herald*. Peter Gelzinis; 1/16/2001.
4. Judge Mark Wolf's Memorandum and Order.
5. "Mounties Join Mob Graveyard Probe"; *The Boston Herald*. Jonathan Wells; 1/18/2001.
6. I received the information on J.R. Russo in this chapter through my direct and personal contact with Russo.

CHAPTER 7

1. Judge Mark Wolf's Memorandum and Order.
2. "Getting Away With Murder"; *Boston Magazine*. Sean Flynn.
3. I received some of the race-fixing information in this chapter directly from those involved while I was living in Las Vegas.

CHAPTER 8

1. "Getting Away With Murder"; *Boston Magazine*. Sean Flynn.
2. Some of the information in this chapter was gleaned from my personal experiences while living in Boston during the given time period.

CHAPTER 9

1. "Stolen Innocence: Bulger Exploited Teenage Schoolgirls"; *The Boston Herald.* Maggie Mulvihill, Jack Sullivan, Jonathan Wells, and Jack Meyers; 4/9/01.

CHAPTER 10

1. Judge Mark Wolf's Memorandum and Order.
2. Some of the information in this chapter came from my close association with the Anguilos and their associates.

CHAPTER 11

1. "Sale of Mob-Linked Store Is Blocked"; *The Boston Herald.* Andrea Estes; 10/19/99.
2. "Whitey Victim Looks To Reclaim Piece Of Her Past"; *The Boston Herald.* Peter Gelzinis; 5/11/00.
3. "Dorchester Body's ID'd As Woman With Ties To Flemmi"; *The Boston Globe.* Shelley Murphy; 6/22/00.
4. "Grave Digger Knows Where The Skeletons Are Buried"; *The Boston Herald.* Peter Gelzinis; 7/13/00.
5. "Gangster Implicates Bulger In Plea Deal"; *The Boston Globe.* Shelley Murphy; 7/13/00.
6. "Weeks Will Sing To Feds about Mob Murders"; *The Boston Herald.* Andrea Estes; 7/13/00.
7. "After Body Found, Mother Tells Of Fear, Prayers"; *The Boston Globe.* John Ellement and Mac Daniel; 10/20/00.
8. "Ex-FBI Agent Set Up Ambush, Hit Man Says"; *The Boston Globe.* Shelley Murphy; 1/12/01.
9. "Murder Charge Sought vs. Rico. Tulsa Cops Accuse Ex-Agent, Mobsters"; *The Boston Herald.* J.M. Lawrence; 1/13/01.
10. "Wheeler Son Fears Tulsa D.A. Will Blink: Want Indictment Of Rico"; *The Boston Herald.* J.M. Lawrence; 1/14/01.

11. "Suit Aims At FBI Agents: Mob Victims' Kin Seek $36M"; *The Boston Herald*. Tom Farmer; 3/9/01.

12. "New Details Emerge As Hit Man Pleads Guilty To Cover-Up Killing"; *The Boston Herald*. J.M. Lawrence; 3/21/01.

13. "Whitey And The FBI"; *The Boston Globe*. Spotlight Team.

14. *Patriot Ledger*, NORTHERN LIGHTS SPECIAL COLLECTION; Quincy, MA.

15. Judge Mark Wolf's Memorandum and Order.

16. "The Hit At Southern Hills"; *Golf Digest*. David Kindred.

17. Some of the information in this chapter was told to me by individuals indirectly involved, but with credible knowledge.

CHAPTER 12

1. Judge Mark Wolf's Memorandum and Order.

2. Talk at Vanessa's was taken from the transcript of Raymond J. Patriarca's bond hearing.

3. I received some of the information in this chapter from J.R. Russo and others associated with him.

CHAPTER 13

1. Judge Mark Wolf's Memorandum and Order.

2. Statement taken from transcripts of Raymond J. Patriarca's bond hearing.

CHAPTER 14

1. Judge Mark Wolf's Memorandum and Order.

2. Information on Chico Krantz's plans to relocate to Las Vegas came from my direct and personal contact with him, and my efforts to assist in acquiring a sports book facility.

CHAPTER 15

1. Judge Mark Wolf's Memorandum and Order.
2. A number of accounts in this chapter are from my personal contacts with several directly involved.

CHAPTER 16

1. _Judge Mark Wolf's Memorandum and Order.
2. "House Leader Seeks Review Of Martorano's Plea Deal"; _Texas News._ A.P.; 10/3/99.
3. "Getting Away With Murder"; _Boston Magazine_. Sean Flynn.
4. "The Club"; _USA Today_. Tony Locy; 7/19/01.

CHAPTER 17

1. Getting Away With Murder"; _Boston Magzine_. Sean Flynn.
2. "The Club"; _USA Today_. Tony Locy; 7/19/01.
3. Judge Wolf's Memorandum and Order.

CHAPTER 18

1. Information received in this chapter came from a confidential source who is a lifelong resident of South Boston.

CHAPTER 19

1. "Ex-FBI Agent Indicted With Two Mob Informers. Racketeering, Conspiracy Alleged"; _SPECIAL to Washington Post_. Pamela Ferdinand; 12/23/99.
2. "Ex-FBI Agent Indicted With Two Mob Informers. Racketeering, Conspiracy Alleged"; _USA Today_. Pamela Ferdinand.
3. "Ex-Agent Lauded For Work With Informants, Judge Told"; _The Boston Globe_. Shelley Murphy; 6/27/00.

CHAPTER 20

1. "Slain Informants' Kin Consider Suit vs. FBI, Seek Files On Mob Tie"; *The Boston Herald*. Andrea Estes; 6/3/00.
2. "Dorchester Body Is ID'd as Woman With Ties to Flemmi"; *The Boston Globe*. Shelley Murphy, Globe Staff; 6/22/00.
3. "Murdered Man's Mom: 'I'm Sick To My Heart'; Haunted By Details Of Slaying"; *The Boston Herald*. Jack Sullivan; 7/13/00.
4. "Missing Woman's Kin Question FBI Role"; *The Boston Globe*. Shelley Murphy and Jack Ellement; 9/20/00.

CHAPTER 21

1. "Sale of Mob-Linked Store Is Blocked"; *The Boston Herald*. Andrea Estes; 10/19/99.
2. "Whitey Victim Looks To Reclaim Piece Of Her Past"; *The Boston Herald*. Peter Gelzinis; 5/11/00.
3. United States Court of Appeals for the First Circuit for the District of Massachusetts. *United States vs. John Bulger*.
4. "Oh, Brother: Jackie Bulger Busted In Whitey Probe"; *The Boston Herald*. J.M. Lawrence. 11/10/01.
5. "Seizure Of Mob Assets Faulted, Victims' Families Seek Redress From Bulger, Flemmi"; *The Boston Globe*. Shelley Murphy; 4/8/01.
6. "Bulger And Flemmi Charged With A String Of Murders"; *The Boston Globe*. Shelley Murphy and Ralph Ranalli; 9/9/00.
7. "Ex-Officer Finds Relief In Bulger Case Indictment"; *The Boston Globe*. Shelley Murphy. 11/12/00.
8. "FBI Linked To Tracking Of Calls By Bulger Kin"; *The Boston Globe*. Shelley Murphy; 11/17/00.
9. "Flemmi's Son Revealed Escape Plan"; *The Boston Globe*. Shelley Murphy; 12/15/00.
10. "Lawyer For John Bulger Rails At Phone Trace"; *The Boston Globe*. Shelley Murphy; 11/18/00.

11. "Trooper Allegedly Tipped Gangsters To FBI Probe"; *The Boston Herald.* Jack Meyers, Maggie Mulvihill, and Jonathan Wells; 4/19/01.

12. "Feds Say Ex-Trooper Tipped Whitey On Police Bug"; *The Boston Herald.* J.M. Lawrence. 9/11/01.

13. A *Boston Globe* editorial; 11/24/00.

14. "Feds Indict Ex-Cop's Son In Bulger Phone Tap Case"; *The Boston Herald.* J.M. Lawrence; 8/28/01.

CHAPTER 22

1. "FBI Ups Reward For Bulger"; *The Boston Globe.* Shelley Murphy; 11/30/00.

2. "Convict May Get Murder Hearing; Judge Mulls Facts In Mafia Slaying"; *The Boston Globe.* Ralph Ranalli, Globe Correspondent; 11/27/00.

3. "Convict's Lawyer Says D.A. Trying To Quash Evidence"; *The Boston Herald.* J.M. Lawrence; 12/12/00.

4. *News Center Channel 5*, Boston, MA. Report by News Center 5's David Boeri.

5. "Papers May Tell of Slay Framing, Judge To Read 1968 Transcript"; *The Boston Globe.* Ralph Ranalli; 12/13/00.

6. "Hidden Truth: Hoover's FBI May Have Suppressed Info On Mob Hit"; *The Boston Herald.* Jonathan Wells and Maggie Mulvihill; 12/21/2000.

7. "Limone Feels Embrace Of His Family, Friends"; *The Boston Herald*; J.M. Lawrence; 1/7/01.

8. "FBI Records of 1968 Mob Murder Case Discovered"; *The Boston Herald.* J.M. Lawrence; 12/13/00.

9. "FBI Hid Key Evidence"; *The Boston Globe.* Ralph Ranalli; 12/21/00.

10. "Convict In 1965 Slaying May Gain Freedom"; *The Boston Globe.* Ralph Ranalli, Globe Correspondent; 1/5/01.

11. "Inmate's Families Did Time Too: Limone Kids Feel Robbed Of Life With Dad"; *The Boston Herald.* J.M. Lawrence; 12/23/00.

12. "Real Killer's Lawyer Says Jailed 'Hit Man' Is Innocent"; *The Boston Herald*. Jonathan Wells; 1/3/01.

13. "Cops Were Suspicious Of Deegan Charges"; *The Boston Herald*. Tom Farmer; 12/22/00.

14. "Judge: Lawyer Can Reveal Hit Man's Confession"; *The Boston Herald*. J.M. Lawrence; 12/23/00.

15. "Lawyer Urges Judge To Free Man Jailed In 1965 Mob Killing"; *The Boston Herald*. J.M. Lawrence; 1/2/01.

16. "Court Frees Limone after 33 Years in Prison"; *The Boston Globe*. Ralph Ranalli, Globe Correspondent; 1/6/01.

17. "Prosecutors Agree To New Trial For Man Convicted Of 1965 Underworld Murder"; *The Boston Herald, Associated Press*. 1/5/01.

18. "Federal Agent's Acts of Treachery Go Way Back"; *The Boston Herald*. Peter Gelzinis; 1/9/01.

19. "Outside At Last, Limone Talks Of Years In Prison, Release"; *The Boston Globe*. Ralph Ranalli, Globe Correspondent; 1/9/01.

20. Some of the information concerning Limone's friendship with Abu Hanifabdal-Khallaq in this chapter was told to me by friends and relatives who had visited Peter during his incarceration.

21. "$375 Million Lawsuit Filed vs. FBI"; *The Boston Herald*. J.M. Lawrence; 7/25/01.

22. "Mob Survivor Can Tell Where True Evil Lies"; *The Boston Herald*. Peter Gelzinis; 1/18/01.

23. "Second Man Exonerated In 1965 Mob Killing"; *The Boston Herald*. J.M. Lawrence; 1/19/01.

24. "FBI Mistake Frees French despite Lawyer's Misgivings"; *The Boston Herald*. J.M. Lawrence; 12/20/01.

CHAPTER 23

1. "Feds Closing In On Former FBI Agent Rico"; *The Boston Herald*. J.M. Lawrence; 1/10/01.

2. "Murder Charge Sought vs. Rico: Tulsa Cops Accuse Ex-Agent, Mobsters"; *The Boston Herald*. J.M. Lawrence; 1/13/01.

3. "Wheeler's Son Fears D.A. Will Blink: Wants Indictment Of Rico"; *The Boston Herald*. J.M. Lawrence; 1/14/01.

4. "Sons Await Charges In 20-Year-Old Slaying Of Tulsa Millionaire"; *The Boston Herald*. Associated Press; 1/22/01.

5. "Feds Close In On Ex-Agent"; *The Boston Herald*. J.M. Lawrence; 2/22/01.

6. "Bulger, Flemmi Face Death Penalty"; *The Boston Globe*. Ralph Ranalli, Globe Correspondent; 3/15/01.

7. "FBI Admits Questioning Bulger Sex Preference"; *The Boston Herald*. J.M. Lawrence; 3/16/01.

CHAPTER 24

1. "Suit Aims At FBI Agent: Mob Victim's Kin Seek $36M"; *The Boston Herald*. Tom Farmer; 3/9/01.

2. "Massachusetts Politicians Back Sweeping Probe of FBI Mob Link"; *The Boston Herald*. J.M. Lawrence; 4/6/01.

3. "Report Finds No Criminal Activity by FBI"; *YAHOO NEWS*; 4/8/01.

4. "Ex-Agent Details Widespread Treachery In Hub Office"; *The Boston Herald*. Jonathan Wells, Jack Meyers, and Maggie Mulvihill; 4/11/01.

5. "Mob Victim's Kin Wants To Talk"; *The Boston Herald*. J.M. Lawrence; 4/23/01.

CHAPTER 25

1. Former Agent H. Paul Rico's statements before a House Committee on Capitol Hill, taken from *C-SPAN*.

2. "Panel Broadens Probe into Use of FBI Informants"; *The Boston Globe*. Ralph Ranalli, Globe Staff; 6/6/01.

3. "Feds Detail Connolly's Alleged Mob Tip-Off"; *The Boston Herald*. Tom Farmer; 5/16/01.

4. "Flemmi Pleads Innocent to Murder, Racketeering Charges"; *ASSO-CIATED PRESS*. 7/17/01.
5. Judge Mark Wolf's Memorandum and Order.
6. "OP-Ed; Flemmi Pleads But It's FBI That's Guilty"; *The Boston Herald*. Rachelle Cohen; 8/22/01.
7. "Items Under Subpoena And Their Significance"; taken from *published Committee records*.

CHAPTER 26
1. "Anguilo Brothers Want Conviction Voided"; *The Boston Herald*; J.M. Lawrence; 9/6/01.
2. "Flemmi's Son Seeks End To Father's Menacing Ways"; *The Boston Herald*. J.M. Lawrence; 4/30/02.

CHAPTER 27
1. "Connolly Pitches His Story To Hollywood"; *The Boston Herald*. Jack Sullivan; 11/19/01.
2. "Congressmen Hit FBI On Mob Trial Tactics"; *The Boston Herald*; J.M. Lawrence; 11/9/01.
3. "Bush Blocks Release Of Papers In Hub FBI Probe"; *The Boston Herald*; J.M. Lawrence and Karen Crummy; 12/14/01.
4. Taken from Burton's talk with Mike Wallace during a *60 Minutes* CBS program interview.
5. "Panel Slams Judge Over Wrongful Mob Conviction"; *The Boston Herald*. J.M. Lawrence; 2/15/01.
6. *USA Today*. 2/28/02.

CHAPTER 28
1. "Flemmi's Son Spills Beans: St. Croix Testifies In Case Against Uncle"; *The Boston Herald*. J.M. Lawrence; 4/24/02.
2. "Son Of Rifleman Claims Dad Confessed To Killing Sis"; *The Boston Herald*. J.M. Lawrence; 4/25/02.

3. "Defense Turns Up Heat On Flemmi's Son In Gun Case"; *The Boston Herald*. J.M. Lawrence; 4/26/02.
4. "Flemmi's Son Seeks End To Father's Menacing Ways"; *The Boston Herald*. J.M. Lawrence; 4/30/02.
5. "Defense Attorney Calls Flemmi's Son Supreme Con Man"; *The Boston Herald*. J.M. Lawrence; 5/1/02.

CHAPTER 29
1. "Former FBI Agent Headed For Trial In May On Racketeering Charges"; *ASSOCIATED PRESS*. 3/5/02.

CHAPTER 30
1. "Former FBI Agent Guilty: Verdict Could Put Connolly In Prison For 8 To 20 Years"; *The Boston Herald*; 5/29/02.
2. "Trial May Spawn Additional Indictments"; *The Boston Herald*. Jonathan Wells; 5/30/02.
3. "In The End, It Didn't Pay To Be A Bulger Pal"; *The Boston Herald*. Peter Gelzinis; 5/29/02.

About the Author

DOMINIC SPINALE

I was inspired to write this book by revelations exposing the macabre side of the FBI, which condoned crimes of drug dealing, extortion, and murder in order to protect their star informants. In particular, I was most troubled by the hypocrisy directed by the G-Men to persons I have known personally. As evidence of FBI abuse surfaced, I would simply shake my head and chuckle. There were times I wanted to scream at the top of my lungs to anyone who would listen. I decided to set the story straight.

I was born and raised in the Italian-American community of Boston where the Anguilos had established their gambling empire. As a teenager, I was a numbers runner for them; later on I would assist in their sports betting enterprise. During the course of my association with the Anguilos and their associates, I became privy to confidential information, some of which is conveyed in this true story.

In the early 1980s, I relocated to Las Vegas, continuing to supply sports betting information and advice to the Anguilo-controlled bookmakers. Thanks to a large cash bankroll supplied by Jerry Anguilo, I enjoyed a successful career as a professional blackjack player, using a very sophisticated card counting method that proved to be very lucrative. I continued to stay in touch with the Anguilos and other associates.

In the mid-1980s, I was intercepted transmitting gaming information across state lines "in aid of racketeering," a Federal violation. I was indicted with Donato Danny Anguilo, along with other Boston bookmakers, on the interstate charge. I pled guilty and received a two-year prison sentence.

During the massive investigation, the FBI informed the Nevada Gaming Control Board of my association with the Anguilos' gambling organization. That revelation prompted the Control Board to place my name in the Nevada Black Book. Being entered into the infamous book prohibits that individual from stepping foot on any Nevada gaming property. Nomination into the Black Book is limited to a select few.

The FBI looked the other way while Whitey Bulger and Steve Flemmi were committing crimes of drug dealing, extortion, and murder in order to bring down Jerry Anguilo's gambling organization. The end certainly did not justify the means.